A Final Verdict

DIVISAT DEL ORBE

Copyright © 2016 Divisat Del Orbe
All rights reserved.

ISBN: 1518820867
ISBN 13: 9781518820861

"The greatest homage we can pay truth is to use it."

— *Ralph Waldo Emerson*

TABLE OF CONTENTS

Prologue	vii
My Journey	1
Make it Happen	9
Self-Righteous	13
Where I Stand With Atheists	16
Where I Stand With "Spiritual" People	17
Where I Stand With "Christians" and Non-Christians	19
The Dilemma	22
Why Bother?	29
A Standard	31
The Biggest of All Questions	37
Encounters	37
Theories	48
Classical Arguments for God	52
The Design Argument	54
Thomas Aquinas	57
Scientific Considerations	60
Arguments Against God	62
Darwinism	62
Evil and Suffering	67
The Subject of Hell	71
Atheist Comments and Responses	76
A Standard II	89
The Necessity of Religion	93
Religion Comments and Responses	100
Word Religion	105
Islam	107
Buddhism	109
Hinduism	111

Why Christianity?	114
World Religion/Christianity Comments and Responses	129
The Christian Fiasco	139
The Investigation Begins	144
Did Christ Establish a Visible Church?	149
The "Wretched" Church	155
Christian Fiasco Comments & Response I	158
The Fiasco Continues	169
Church Hierarchy	169
Scriptural Interpretation	171
Comments and Response II	176
Bible vs. Tradition	180
Fiasco Conclusion	185
Wandering Catholics	187
The Issue of Homosexuality	190
Homosexual Comments and Responses	199
Abortion	223
Abortion Comment and Responses	231
The Christian Challenge	236
My Final Verdict	242
Works Cited And Further Reading	254

PROLOGUE

A lion of truth never assumes anything without validity. Assumptions are quick exits for lazy minds that like to graze out in the fields without bother."

— *Suzy Kassem,*

Life, for as long as I can remember, has made me marvel in the most peculiar ways. Sometimes I stand in awe, amazed at this existence of ours, contemplating its abstract beauty and goodness. In other instances, I find myself in apathy; retreating in solitude, thinking in utter gloom. Whether in joyful bliss or a state of melancholy, I have always had a keen sense of awareness of this sometimes complex phenomenon we call life. I suppose this is why I am referred to as the "analytical type," and I do not deny the description.

Due to this nature of mine, I've often paused to reflect on the dynamics of my surroundings. While lounging in a café sipping caramel Frappuccino, I curiously observed people casually stroll through. Some folks were in deep conversation, smiling with not a care in the world, it appeared, while others marched with a sense of purpose and stern looks on their faces. All of us have a story. As I monitored the traffic, I could not help but wonder about these people: What walks of life brought them to this particular location? What thoughts were being entertained in their minds? Were they full of questions, as I was? At times, this heightened state of consciousness has proven burdensome in my life. I have been accused of suffering from "paralysis of analysis." Maybe the source of my turmoil was analyzing and thinking too much, as some suggest. I have been told numerous times to relax, go with the flow, and let things be. Perhaps I should have taken the advice and simply sat back, at ease, and enjoyed my Frappuccino, but I did not do so—not even close.

This is why throughout the years I have had intense discussions with skeptics, friends, and family members concerning topics that many consider almost taboo in a social gathering. The unspeakable issues I refer to are philosophical, moral, political, and religious in nature. The very topics many avoid addressing are precisely the issues I have struggled with and entertained for the past twenty years. I've often pondered the many whys of life: God, faith, religion, and morality. How does one come to any conclusive grounds on these sensitive topics with so many variant opinions and perspectives?

Debates and divisiveness are widespread. One group or man says one thing while another says differently. At the end of the day, it seems opinions are all we have to hold on to, but one thing I knew, through the laws of logic, is that opposing ideas cannot be true at the same time. Someone is right and someone is sincerely mistaken, and I wanted to know who was which. We all have opinions, but how do we know they are correct? We tend to hold to our opinions as absolutes, as if reality should conform to our ideas. The better approach is for us to attempt to adjust to reality, which carries a stupendous amount more weight than our imagination. We are simply unafraid of our mental confines or capabilities, as if our private thoughts are the end-all. I was not satisfied leaving controversial matters to personal opinions. If all is mere opinion, we could not make any rational or intelligent conclusions about anything. So, is there a method to decipher what is right from what is false? Is truth even knowable? That is part of the heart of this book—to attempt to tackle logically and methodically how to obtain certain truths. There must be a way; if not, truth loses all value.

Now, to make a solid argument for any "truth" one needs a filtering methodology, or at least the best filtering mechanism available. I believe the first stage of this filtration begins by tackling the question of God. I understand there are those who do not have faith or are unsure about a deity, and this is why we will attempt to decipher the most logical conclusion. *If* there is no God, then opinions are all we have outside the material realm. Ideas such as free will, spirituality, morality, conscience, and justice are just figments of our imagination. But if God exists, we must consider some grave implications in terms of standards and revelations, which will take us to another stage in the filtration process. If He exists, we must examine the many groups claiming to be guided by and endowed with the responsibility of His revelations. We must conduct a comparative analysis of various faiths to determine which one is of divine origin and which are invented human alternatives. If God exists and has spoken, is there anyone who can truly claim to be the steward of His revelations? We must study the evidence to gain solid footing and draw better conclusions. Later, after examining these vital areas and having better footing, we will boldly wrestle a couple social issues rampaging through our country.

■ ■ ■

As a result of my experiences, I have compiled my ordeals, not to prove I am right (the reader must ultimately choose his or her own verdict), but because it will prove beneficial to seeking and curious minds. This is a compilation of years of accumulated wisdom and knowledge—a one-source document addressing many principles and godly truths in layman verbiage. I believe that much learning can take place from my experiences, while sparing the reader the many headaches I suffered.

Ultimately, I hope a seed will be planted with these writings. That is my number one objective; to give some food for thought on some of the most crucial questions in life. I want people to think about what it is they do and why. Man's inability to be still and ponder is crippling our society at all levels. Lack of thinking is an epidemic. We have accepted the idea that we must embrace all ideas, never mind their consequences or the tough virtues of thought, righteousness, and responsibility. I wish to challenge this mentality by demonstrating that this world is much greater than our mere sentiments.

Secondly, I want to spark situational awareness. Too many people are being easily swayed by the tolerant wisdom of this generation. Society is sweeping folks off their feet straight into falsehood while crucial questions aren't being asked. Society only deals with opinions, not truth itself. So many people naïvely run like a herd of buffalo right off the end of a cliff, blind to the abyss that lies ahead. We must ask questions and investigate—not just scrape the tip of the iceberg, but dig in deeper. A lot of things look and sound good on the outside, but one can easily be surprised when exploring their inner colors.

This reminds me of a political debate I once had. I asked an acquaintance why she was voting for a particular candidate. Her response was, "Oh, because he sounds smart and is such a great speaker." My eyes widened. Sure, one can vote or pick a candidate for any reason he or she chooses, but there needs to be a little more substance to a candidate than sounding smart and being a great speaker. This alone does not justify putting a candidate in office. But this is what many of us do. We fail to look deeper into matters. So long as it appears good, we give it a thumbs-up, failing to investigate the core, which can be rotten, like a luscious-looking apple with a worm waiting inside.

Thirdly, so many people I know personally are nonchalant about the philosophical domain of life that I suspect many of those I don't know fall into the same category. There seems to be a lack of effort or lack of time for diligent study. Some, honestly, may not have time to investigate while trying to make ends meet. Some are strictly on the money chase or diligently working on their careers. Others could care less, with their "just do whatever floats your boat" mentality. Some are plain lazy, as one friend honestly admitted. Whatever the reasons, I want there to be no excuse for a plea of willful ignorance. By no means do I claim to know it all, but what I do know I intend to relay in a sound and logical manner. For matters I am uncertain about, I will lay out where I searched for answers and why that source has the best credentials.

Although I have been accused of having the reasoning power of a kindergarten child, I assure you that what is found in these pages will not prove an insult to your intelligence. It is important, though, to approach this book with an open mind and a seeking heart. Too often, "truth seekers" awkwardly come to the table with their minds already made up.

Lastly, I dedicate this book to those who refuse to budge out of pride and stubbornness. Most men can't even imagine being wrong, let alone admit it. It is critical to understand that there is nothing wrong with ignorance. Ignorance simply means not knowing; stupidity is not admitting that you are ignorant. Ignorance is destructive only when one chooses to stay ignorant. I will no longer deliberate with individuals who think their opinions or invented truths are what make the world go 'round. Instead, I leave this product, which can either be taken or put aside. This is why it is titled *A Final Verdict*. A decision or verdict must be made, like a jury deliberating after examining the evidence thoroughly. We can't straddle the fence our whole lives. We must eventually take a position. The person who defends everything defends nothing, as the saying goes.

It is a given that some will reject what I have to say; if that's you, know genuinely in your heart that what you are living out is true and not just wishful thinking. Choosing to stay ignorant is inexcusable. Choosing convenience or what makes us feel good over what is right cannot be accepted. *Sincerity is not truth*. Ultimately, we all have to be responsible for what we have done and what we have failed to do, and reap those consequences.

As you read, there will be occasions when your blood temperature will rise. Please do not take these writings personally. We want to dissect theories, not people. It is almost impossible to read such a book and not get some nerves jumping. Disagree with a man about sports, career, or any normal event in life and he will simply laugh or brush it off, but differ with him about philosophical or moral matters and you will find a whole different beast. When our beloved views are confronted, indignation flares up even when the evidence is against us. I urge readers to keep reading even when frustrated so that some other vital information or piece of the puzzle is not missed. One might also feel a tug of potential changes that need to occur. Be sensitive to the inner voice and yield to that divine spark we call the conscience.

Much will be said, but I hope even more will be done than is said. As we embark on this philosophical quest, I hope it brings the wisdom and truth you have been seeking.

MY JOURNEY

"O, God, demand what you will, but supply what you demand."

— *St. Augustine*

When I was younger I assumed my concerns and inquiries about life were widely contemplated. To my dismay, I learned that the general populace gave these subjects little to no thought. I am not referring to "ordinary folks," but professionals I have encountered, such as lawyers, doctors, and engineers, individuals one would consider intellectually oriented or well-rounded. These people had smarts about their particular professions but lacked familiarity with or exposure to the laws of logic, philosophy, and especially, religion. Many did not know how to answer questions in these fields without contradicting or stumbling over themselves. Those who I thought had it "all together" really did not. Such experiences led me to conclude that truly the two most abundant elements in the universe are hydrogen and ignorance, to paraphrase Harlan Ellison.

How people could walk around so nonchalantly, ignoring the countless whys of life, was baffling to me. Did they want to know or did they even care? At times, I found myself a little envious of the indifferent attitudes around me. I was perplexed, with scores of questions lingering in my mind, challenging and dissecting anything coming my way, yet I received the faintest interest from many others when I asked questions about their beliefs. "To each his own" is all a friend told me as he leisurely walked past. I was amazed how satisfied folks were with having no answers. Some strolled as if ignorance were an admirable trait. Why wasn't I built like others, I thought, so I could simply sit back, relax, and enjoy my Frappuccino?

Undeniably, I was an oddball among certain associates. Regardless, I maneuvered accordingly to drag folks into my world, whether cruising in the cockpit of an aircraft or having dinner in the cafeteria. I did what was necessary to immerse conversations in touchy waters. One interesting observation that emerged was that nothing is uglier to a man than reason when it is not on his side. Pride is all some had in their corner. Facts almost seemed irrelevant. Saving face was priority number one, it appeared. When reason was against a person, usually the "What's right for me is not right for you" speech emerged. Interestingly, individuals who took refuge in such statements conveniently did so when the discussion was not going in their favor.

The bottom line is, in my passion, if someone believed something, whether it conflicted with my ideas or not, I questioned it and insisted on knowing why. We all have passions: whether gardening, photography, cars, sports, video games, aviation, or boating. My itch happened to be the seeking of knowledge and truth. I firmly believed a person should know what they do and why. That is the position of any sensible person. The only reason anyone should believe anything in this world is because it is true—that's it! If it's not true, one should not believe it. Such a simple concept, and yet, so many miss it. So simple, but apparently so complex that it is worth repeating: The only reason one should believe anything in this world is because it is true. Truth is discernible, but one must carefully excavate the rubble with our thinking caps on, moving emotions aside.

Today, unfortunately, the genuine pursuit of truth has become a search for personal gratification attached to a sea of sentiment. We cannot cave in to the comfort of our feelings and mere opinions in order to evade the hard virtue of thought.

■ ■ ■

Indeed, at times, tension was in the air during certain deliberations due to passionate opposing viewpoints colliding, as one person did not grasp what the other could not understand. At times, nothing was accomplished, except for a lingering frustration and loss of hope in human thought. I admit I was a fool for allowing certain situations to escalate and made the mistake of entertaining futile conversations. It would have been better to have avoided the dialogue altogether. The years have shown me much and I have matured with them. If I only knew then what I know now, the outcome of many debates would have been much more constructive. "The fact of the matter is nobody cares how much you know, until they know how much you care," as a friend of mine likes to say. At times, I was out to win debates, when the goal of any discussion should not be to proclaim victory, but to make mutual progress. We missed the true purpose of the art of argumentation; that is, the setting forth of logical reasons for one's position for evaluation and possible persuasion of others. I say "we missed" because it was not always a one-way avenue. Both parties should be able to sit down like civilized human beings to discern together.

Ironically, argumentation is a word that evokes unfavorable views, when it used to be a popular field of study. Today, it is associated with conflicts or strife, but that is not its true purpose or end goal, nor is it the object of these writings. Our differences cannot be overcome by ignorance, but by better understanding of those differences. Through the proper use of the art of argumentation, we will justify claims, sow better understanding, and reach conclusions.

I have to mention that despite sour conversations, there were plenty of constructive discussions as well. It was time well spent. I learned from folks and vice versa. Those who entertained taboo topics were curious and inquiring themselves or wanted to dispel some wisdom on the subject. So it was certainly possible to converse about delicate issues with decency, intelligence, and respect. That is all I sincerely wanted. Everything can be discussed; tact is what's golden, not avoidance. Healthy disagreements can be quite good. As Thomas Jefferson wisely stated, "Difference of opinion leads to inquiry, and inquiry to truth."

■ ■ ■

Let me elaborate a little on my background to clarify the origins of some of my turmoil. I am what you call a cradle Catholic. Meaning, I was born and raised Catholic and went through the motions of going to church. I gave God my one hour a week and called it a "good week." I attended church with little knowledge or understanding of my actions. I remember contemplating during mass how Jesus differed from any other spiritual guru. Why so many religions in the world? Do they relate to each other? How can we know what is true? Is right or wrong the same for all people regardless of geography and time? Why doesn't God make Himself more transparent? Why are we here? What is our ultimate destiny? Why so much evil? Many of the questions I had were those of a skeptic, yet I always had a dormant faith within. I had tons of questions about God, but never questioned God or His existence, which is quite different.

While I was an ordinary young man growing up there was something else not very apparent. There was an emptiness within me, resulting in great apathy—a sadness rooted down to my soul. Sometimes a simple melody would instigate a deep emotion within. I often found myself in a complex state of spiritual gloominess, thought, and emotion. It is difficult to put into words. My keen sense of consciousness had me questioning everything I did, including a simple laugh. I contemplated happiness, a state that always proved temporary. All my delights seemed doomed to fade away. No satisfaction was sustainable. Where have the joys of yesterday gone? They have dissipated with all our glory. We are nothing more than fleeting shadows. What society viewed as gratifying in the end made me feel hollow. Where was my so-called inner joy? What is this life ultimately all about? Many can relate to these sorts of questions. We seek certain fulfillments and answers to a multitude of questions. There is a magnetic pull in our hearts to know and seek significance. We yearn to fill the voids of our very being.

My disposition is described accurately by one of the wisest men who ever lived, King Solomon. He was rich in every aspect, and that's what makes his writing so powerful. Solomon writes in Ecclesiastes 2 that he did everything under the sun. He amassed great wealth, and undertook great projects and all the delights of the hearts of men. He denied himself nothing his eyes desired. He concludes by writing, "But when I turned to all the works that my hands had wrought, and to the toil at which I had taken such pains, behold! All was vanity and a chase after wind, with nothing gained under the sun" (Ecclesiastes 2:11, *New American Bible*).

How perfectly I related to his writings. After all I accomplished, I thought, so what? What does it matter in the grand scheme of things? We will find ourselves buried six feet under and pass away into the fading memory of history. We are nothing but dust blowing in the wind. With my nonchalant attitude towards life, I recall flying a jet upside down at twenty thousand feet, looking at Mother Earth, thinking, "Is this it? Is this the allure pilots seek?" I also remember the anticipation of hearing my name called during college graduation, thinking this will be the climax of my life. As I walked on stage to receive my diploma in front of family and friends, I felt a Grand Canyon-like void. Where was this sense of joy I saw in others? My sense of satisfaction was zero. All the anticipatory nice, warm, fuzzy feelings I had prior to being called were sucked out of me as if by a vacuum. All I managed to do was crack a false smile, and I quickly returned to my seat.

No one knew about my inner turmoil. I have always been marvelous at compartmentalizing my feelings, except for the one breakdown I had in my professor's office in college where I expressed my dissatisfaction and inner struggles during what proved to be my worst college semester.

But this was not my turning point, as I slowly recuperated and gained my composure inside that office. A grown man being emotional in front of another was not appealing, especially with someone who appeared indifferent. I took pride in being a "tough guy" from the Bronx. Demonstrating weakness was not something I was going to allow.

As I reflect, I see that, ironically, my internal havoc was most prominent during the most successful points in my life, including graduating college, becoming a commissioned officer in the United States Air Force, and completing pilot training. I tried to fill my emptiness with success, but it proved to be futile. Seeking success and stature did nothing for me internally. Neither came close, so what was I supposed to be seeking?

It took hitting rock bottom to awaken the faith in God that had been dormant inside me. I began going back to church for some sign or guidance. It is amazing how we leave God as our last resort. Only after life has pummeled us to our knees do we seek Him. One particular Sunday an announcement was made that an Alpha course was to begin, with the potential to change lives. I was initially skeptical, since attending any sort of church function was abnormal for me. But I took a leap of faith and attended the course, since nothing else had produced results. All I knew is something had to change, because I simply could not stay on my current course. "If we want something we've never had, we must be willing to try something we've never done," as the director of the course, Gerardo Hernandez, said.

While attending the course, several realizations came to light. It became apparent that my soul-searching was not unique. I met folks from all walks trying to make sense out of life as well. I understood now why God designed us with such a void, so that we might truly seek Him. The void within me was created only for God to fill and nothing else. I did not have a religious or spiritual experience through the course, rather a renewed sense of awareness and understanding. I recognized that our hearts are going to remain restless until they are at rest with God, as St. Augustine said. I wasn't at peace because I had never been at peace with God. I now understood that I came from God and that I must live for Him. I was not made for this world alone. This life is but a minuscule fraction of my being's totality. The void within came from not focusing on the source of happiness—God Himself. To find true happiness one must seek Him and know Him. That is why everything I did or accomplished was a disappointment. People and situations in life are guaranteed to disappoint eventually. The only one who does not disappoint is the Prince of Peace. "He is the way and the truth and the life" (John 14:6). I needed a way! I needed truth! I needed life! I started to see life through unblemished lenses. Now it was worthwhile getting up in the morning with a sense of direction.

As I ventured deeper through the course, I was fed spiritually, but predominantly, it felt like a clogged filter had been removed from my head. Some sort of wisdom and discernment was stirred within me. I had many questions about my faith answered and clarified—it's amazing what a little investigating accomplishes—although it seemed that for every question answered, a new one surfaced. Curiosity to know more consumed me. Uncharacteristically, I started hitting the books on my own time, since the Alpha course was designed for beginners to get their feet wet. The director did not want to overwhelm folks with too much information, but I was ready for it and more.

As I continued to investigate of my own accord, many arenas of the faith became translucent. Even with this newfound learning I was aware this was just the beginning of a journey, and that although there was plenty I did not understand, ultimately, I just needed to cling to the one who understood everything.

■■■

In hindsight, I realize how God had been with me all along, but I was blind to Him, or I chose to ignore Him. I look back now and see the trail of footsteps He had left behind me—it is unbelievable. He put people and circumstances in my life with the hopes that I would respond to Him. I ignored the signs and paid dearly with much heartache. I am thankful He doesn't give up on His stubborn children. We have the propensity to be such fools. Sadly, we love to learn the hard way. Although we must learn from our mistakes, or as people say, "You live and you learn," we unnecessarily take two steps back in order to take three steps forward. It is better to learn from the mistakes of others and save ourselves the turmoil life has to offer. That is true wisdom! As an old proverb says, smarts only helps us make a living; *wisdom* helps us make a life!

Although all of us as individuals must seek, hopefully these writings point you in the right direction. Don't search the whole world when the knowledge of truth may be right before you. Or as a flight attendant would say: Be aware, the nearest exit may be right behind you.

MAKE IT HAPPEN

"The way to be nothing is to do nothing."

— *Nathaniel Howe*

"Whatsoever we beg of God, let us also work for it."

— *Jeremy Taylor*

When entering profound discussions, it is no longer surprising how the same questions and comments surface. It is almost predictable, like clockwork. Some of these popular remarks include: Who is to say what truth is? Doesn't right and wrong depend on the individual? Why is there so much suffering if there is a loving God? How do we even know God exists? With so many religions, is there really one that can claim to be true? Why are there so many Christian denominations? So on and so forth. There are excellent answers to these questions. These same inquiries have been made for hundreds to thousands of years; they are nothing new. Therefore, it is a matter of making time to study and to contemplate these findings. We must investigate and pursue the knowledge.

So many love to question, yet few genuinely seek answers, as if waiting for some spontaneous revelation. It is good to question, but let us complement the questioning with research, because those who truly and sincerely seek will find. For those who knock, the door shall be opened; unfortunately, not everyone knocks and not everyone seeks. At times, Truth is not apparent, since it rarely stands alone. It's usually tangled up with some sort of impurity, but it is discernible indeed. Therefore, we must stand alert, wipe the fog off our glasses to see, and *think* clearly instead of resting on assumptions or credulity. Ego and prejudice must also be tossed aside.

The bottom line is, the average man gives very little thought to what he believes. How much time have you devoted to study? The following are words of wisdom that can be applied in all aspects of life, including the "spiritual" or "philosophical" realm. Although this is not intended to be a self-help book, this small chapter will have such flavor.

■ ■ ■

The evidence of wanting anything in life is the pursuit. Sort of like the movie *The Pursuit of Happyness,* starring Will Smith. It is a story of unflagging persistence to achieve despite all obstacles. No one ever said the road to success was easy. It takes great tenacity to overcome certain hurdles. Even if we've been dealt a "bad hand" in life, what ultimately matters is how we play our cards. Even a bad hand has the potential to win if played wisely.

Unlike the resolve displayed by the character in the movie, we tend to do the exact opposite. We talk tirelessly about our high hopes but employ no action. We even pray to God about our desires, and then sit on the couch waiting for a miracle. That is not how things ordinarily work. Instead, we should diligently work for what we desire. Then, the blessings will follow more abundantly. That goes for anything. In our case now, if it is knowledge you seek ... seek it! Knowledge is acquired. We are not born knowing.

To get out of this stagnant state of mind, one must break the chains of mediocrity. Never settle for "who you are" or what you know, since there is always room for self-improvement and learning. "Settling" is the killer of growth. You may often hear, "Just be yourself." This is some of the worst advice certain people can receive. Of course, one has to be oneself to an extent, but one would not be much of a man if the only person one looked up to was himself.

This "I am, therefore I'll be" mentality is the root of ignorance. To change this mental state requires not only grace, but an acute desire for growth. If we want to see changes in our lives, we have to make some. Einstein defined insanity as a person doing the same thing over and over again, expecting a different result. Our circumstances in life don't simply change by chance, but by choice. We must confront some hard realities on this path of transformation, even if we are moving slowly. Slow progress is better than none, but by all means we must move. As the well-known saying goes, *"A journey of a thousand miles begins with a single step."*

With a desire for growth in mind, to exponentially improve our chances of success it is also imperative to utilize our time wisely. One of the biggest differences between highly successful people and your average Joe is that successful individuals understand there are twenty-four hours in a day. They accomplish a lot more in the same period. They know how to multitask and economize their time to leap ahead of the pack. They understand productivity and the value of time. Meanwhile, the average Joe spends all his free time watching every sporting event, reality show, baby-momma drama movie, and soap on TV … wasting time he'll never get back. We can say that people's success in life is directly related to how they spend their evening.

The point of this small self-help chapter is not just to give some advice on achieving a victorious life, but to relay the understanding that a person who wants to acquire must pursue! To obtain wisdom and knowledge, it takes work on an individual's behalf, like anything else in life. Don't take refuge in staying ignorant or accepting ideas simply out of respect for the one proffering them. Examine claims thoroughly. Be disciplined and set quiet time for contemplation. What philosophical, moral, and/or religious books have you read? Have you taken any courses? Let's not allow the source of our wisdom to simply be a consultation of our personal feelings.

There is a much greater reality outside our own small sphere. Let us attempt to step back to decipher the larger reality or picture.

Seek, and you shall find. Some seek; others do not. Which one do you choose? What have you done in your pursuit of Truth?

SELF-RIGHTEOUS

"It is tact that is golden, not silence."

— *Samuel Butler*

I am flattered and humbled to be viewed by some as a wise individual with strong character. For this reason, I am sought for counsel. One acquaintance remarked that she consults me because "I keep it real and tell it like it is." Her other friends tell her what she wants to hear. Unfortunately, many of us seek comforting advice, instead of true counsel, to avoid swallowing the sometimes harsh pill of reality. We have a tendency to seek support and justification for our doings while risking being misled or prolonging a problem. When one goes to the doctor, an honest prognosis is needed, not anything less, so the concern at hand can be dealt with swiftly before it develops into a menacing affliction.

Anyhow, for every good compliment, there is another who tells me I am stubborn and a closed-minded fool. "It's my way or the highway." This is where I usually say that if one doesn't stand for anything they fall for anything, and lack character. And if some don't like me, it's not necessarily a bad thing; it means I stood for something. You can't satisfy everyone.

All I have attempted to do is maintain fidelity to certain principles, as others who disagree with me do as well, not to elevate myself in vanity to some self-righteous status. We should all be pliable enough to change our position if facts and/or reason dictate otherwise. That is why I dissect ideas in search of inconsistencies, and for that some label me as obstinate. Whatever happened to thought and reflection? Aren't these honorable attributes? It appears thinking is an arduous task most choose to avoid. This is why many people flow down the river of influence without even being conscious of the currents that sway them. *Compliance is the path of least resistance, so people revert to whatever thought-saving route they can find.* Defending complex principles is not easy. This is why many accept simplistic theories which many times have no substance. Others in their avoidance of difficulties sadly accept ideas because some seemingly smart charismatic individual is uttering a few nice-sounding statements. The reality is, there are many great speakers and TV personalities who think quite poorly.

The bottom line is, it is frustrating to see those taking a position, after examining claims, being viewed as narrow-minded for standing their ground. In other words, the man who states that there is a shark in the water, no ifs, ands, or buts, gets crucified. Meanwhile, the one who says it could be a sea lion, marlin, or even a mermaid is the kind of man who is embraced and celebrated. Although they ignore facts and reason, they are considered broad-minded and progressive. *Woe to the man who claims someone is wrong when conflicting ideas exist!*

These so-called tolerant individuals are masters at exploiting the word "intolerant," since the word can have ill connotations attached to anyone labeled as such. Successfully putting someone in the "intolerant" category is half the battle. The reality is that so-called tolerant people can be quite intolerant. At heart, what these "tolerant" folks are saying is that one must agree with their viewpoints and disagree with everything they disagree with; if not, one is closed-minded and "intolerant." These "tolerant" people aren't tolerant at all, since, in their own self-righteousness, they do not admit being intolerant about other's beliefs. If they are so "open-minded," as they claim, why don't they accept those with differing views?

■ ■ ■

Nowadays, one can't tell anybody anything without offending them. We are quite the sensitive generation. Perhaps hypersensitive is more accurate. Silence or turning the other way appears to be the preferred treatment for handling issues. Though proper discretion is necessary, at times, one can use impeccable tact and still offend someone. But in the end, it is better to have said something than to have never said anything at all. Whether or not a message is accepted or rejected, it must be sent. No one should believe in others being quietly left in error. *We must speak if it is our duty to do so.* Constructive criticism is what it boils down to.

Regardless, lectures about how inappropriate it is to "impose" one's ideas on others will always surface. Imposing is almost always wrong, but proposing is not. We know that at the end of the day, people are going to do what they are going to do. We have choices to make, but that does not negate our responsibility to each other. A person has the right to confront anyone if one's disposition is to help. The benefit of getting through to someone far outweighs that of being ignored or rejected. It is not about being judgmental, but about watching out for each other. If someone is not receptive when it is one's duty to intervene, all one can do is let God deal with them. The obligation is done, though one must be open to the possibility of revisiting the issue in the future, should circumstances dictate.

The bottom line is, this work is not about any boasting or self-righteous ego. This is about getting down to the facts of life and the use of reason. Our goal is not to criticize individuals but to analyze theories. If we can't critique concepts, how can one rationalize about anything? With that in mind, let me elaborate where I stand with various groups of people.

Where I Stand With Atheists

"He who knows nothing is confident in everything."

— C.H. Spurgeon

It is riveting how atheists and religious fanatics are so similar concerning their convictions. One can't help but notice the passion nonbelievers display for someone who, to them, does not exist. As atheist Richard Dawkins puts it, "Passion for passion" (19); that's certainly a fair assessment. It is good to have passion for anything we believe or do. Quite honestly, I appreciate an atheist who can stand his ground, rather than simply state "There is no God" and retreat, as if saying so makes it so. That appeals to no one with a spark of intellect or manhood. But, like all tremendous passions and convictions, theirs must be tested.

What fascinates me most about many atheists is their pride and attitude in regards to intellect. Not to say there aren't any such religious folks, but prominently, nonbelievers I have encountered come off as if others are beneath them intellectually. They walk around pretending to comprehend all mysteries and knowledge. But what man can fully grasp the grandeur of Truth? The wisest man in the world, if he is truly wise, will tell you he is a fool. These self-proclaimed thinking people, who claim to be guided by reason, thereby dismissing the idea of God as irrational, leave me dumbfounded at times. What they critique as "irrational" is not at all. The nature of God is not in opposition to our reason; it is above human reason. God is not at our level. Our finite thinking can only bring us so far, and then reasonable faith must take over, not blind faith. Reason, by its own merits, tells us there is something beyond what we see under a microscope.

I struggle with the assertion that it is "thinking" that leads to a lack of faith. As one atheist asked me, "How in the world can people believe such ridiculous bulls***?" Well, I can sympathize, because I wondered the same in this buffet of world religions at one point, but it is imperative to distinguish between belief systems. Each must be judged on its own merits. It is of no use to put all divine ideas on a single platter as if they are all the same—not even close. One concept I hope to impress in these writings is that *the idea that all beliefs are the same quickly ends up with the conclusion that they are equally useless, including atheism.* Belief systems are very distinguishable. Some may be "ridiculous bulls***" while others can be very reasonable indeed. There has been an abundance of material throughout the ages supporting the existence of God, and whether one agrees or disagrees, I don't see how a "thinking person" can refer to these materials as unreasonable or ridiculous. These concepts are quite reasonable — and reason is a close friend of truth.

As I have alluded to, most folks don't consider or take to heart the rationality of their beliefs. Most people are indeed very gullible, as atheists profess. I do commend intellectual atheists on one issue: They insist that people think. A big amen to that! But, there exists a notion of intellectual error and warped reasoning. Intelligence does not necessarily equate to proper reasoning, due to moral cowardice, environmental issues, personal agendas, etc. Whether it is the atheist or the believer who is mistaken, eventually it is up to the reader to determine. I personally contend that atheists/humanists are guilty of what they accuse others of: being unreasonable.

Where I Stand With "Spiritual" People

"The recipe for perpetual ignorance is: be satisfied with your opinions and content with your knowledge."

— Elbert Hubbard

Please be cognizant, "spiritual" folks, of my position. I am referring to the New Age movement, with its relativistic minds who maintain that "right and wrong" is an individual concept and that all beliefs are equally good and all roads lead to the same end goal. I allude to those who strictly believe in universal forces and who meditate to become one with nature or the heavenly realms. The ones who are in a pursuit of happiness in some self-enlightening spiritual phenomenon; those who believe in a higher spiritual being but not necessarily an omnipotent God. I hear so many descriptions from proclaimed spiritual folks that I apologize if I did not reference the term correctly.

To cut to the chase, here is a concept many subjectivists should consider. First, there is a grave difference between what a person does and whether they ought to do it. Though many spiritualists do not hold to any absolutes (objective truth) or "correct path," they claim subjectivism objectively true! The position gets even more difficult when considering the "truth" of subjectivism. That claim (that subjectivism is true) is not true for all, but only for the individual, since it depends on the person. *The subjective mindset doesn't even have ground to stand on when making the argument they defend. They are not claiming to be right or that they know anything, since everything is subjective. All they are doing is sharing their opinion.* Subjectivism, at its core, makes no definite claims and implodes on itself.

Please understand, spiritual friends, this is *not about catering to personal beliefs and feelings.* There are a hundred things a man wishes were true that, unfortunately, are not. It is critical to detach ourselves from emotions. Feelings can't be trusted; they go up and down like a roller coaster. They cannot be the test of truth, especially when others *feel* differently! Therefore, we must concentrate on the evidence. Proofs are superior to feelings, and if something has been proven false, there is no longer room for personal conjecture. For instance, an individual may genuinely believe in Santa Claus, but the fact of the matter is, Santa is not real. I am not claiming I know all truths, but what I know for a fact is that Santa Claus does not fly around the globe with reindeer, distributing gifts. One can understand a person's sincerity about their beliefs, whatever they might be, due to their upbringing, but genuineness is not truth, regardless of how candid it may be. You have heard it said, "But it's all they know." That may be so, but lack of knowledge does not justify personal claims, especially when evidence points in another direction. We cannot commit *intellectual suicide* by accepting what we know to be false in order to appease others. We would put ourselves in a position where we can't even reject the position we cannot accept.

From my observation, it seems some "spiritualists" sacrifice all for the sake of openness and acceptance of all ideas. They suppress reality with a virtual reality to live a life of illusion, but eventually reality must be faced. I am reminded of a friend who tried to dismiss the fact that her husband was cheating on her. As much as she wished the circumstances were different, that was not the case. She insisted on living a virtual reality in which she swore her marriage was ideal. But in order to move forward, she must deal with reality; or rest assured, reality is going to deal with her. The truth indeed shall set one free.

Friedrich Nietzsche once wrote, "A casual stroll through the lunatic asylum shows that faith does not prove anything." I agree. Truth is not dependent on us. It doesn't matter if a person is bad or good, rich or poor, sick or healthy, successful, lonely, homosexual, abused, etc. Truth is stubborn; regardless of what we wish it to be, it remains immutable and applies to all. This is one concept I wish to present to my spiritual friends.

So, while keeping compassion in mind, we must get down to the facts of life. Many, in their effort to appease everyone, have been derailed by failing to keep their eyes on the ball. We must stay focused, and everything will fall into place, including the feelings many "spiritual" folks are pursuing. We must stay the course, because *if we lose Truth, we lose God!*

Where I Stand With "Christians" and Non-Christians

"Do not conform to the ways of this world but be transformed by the renewing of your mind."

— Romans 12:2

Christians uniformly admit to believing in the one to whom all authority has been given, or at least that's what I thought. Being that I am not quite in sync with many "Christians," there exists a disconnect somewhere. Maybe I need to re-examine my faith? Perhaps those I conflict with need to re-analyze what it is they are supposed to believe as Christians? I know this much: If one's Christian faith aligns with today's secular world, then most likely it is not Christianity.

We do not make the rules of the faith, fellow brethren; we only attempt to live by them. If we followed our ideas, it would be our religion, not the religion of Christ. Many "Christians" pick and choose what's convenient about the faith, as if they were on a buffet line, selecting preferable doctrines to their satisfaction. But as faithful followers we should strive for the whole enchilada, not just bits and pieces.

Too many "Christians" also attempt to compile non-Christian ideas, beliefs, feelings, etc., into one entity, and it can't be done. It is like mixing oil and water. If we expect to have purity, impurities must be filtered. Although we must keep the Golden Rule in mind, not everyone can be pleased. As a famous comedian once said, "I don't know what the key to success is, but the key to failure is trying to please everyone."

Please understand where I am coming from, fellow "Christians," with your "live and let live" mentality. I come to "believers" with the notion that God has spoken and set guidelines to be accepted by all. When confronting tough issues from the angle of faith, I'm tackling them with the proverbial phrase, "What would Jesus do?" Not what some government official would do. I refer to genuine Christian teaching for guidance, not Hollywood teaching. A "Christian" should have no objections to this approach, since it is His will be done, not ours. But how and where do we acquire Christian teaching in its purest form? That will be a topic of debate in future chapters. I will expose many believers to an angle worth pondering.

Again, I come to Christians with what should already be ingrained in their minds: that Christ is the King of Kings and Lord of Lords. Too many "Christians" adamantly declare, "Who is to say what is true?" This statement should not be coming out of the mouths of people who call themselves Christian. That statement is only valid if coming from a nonbeliever. "Believers" need to review John 14:6 and Revelation 1:8 to refresh themselves on some Christian fundamentals.

I do not come neutral about the faith to fellow believers. On the contrary, I come with the mentality that God is number one above all, with the greatest *commandment* in mind, not the greatest *suggestion*.

■ ■ ■

In later chapters, we will tackle the delicate subject of world religions. We must ponder core ideas and concepts offered by various faiths to examine where they stand. We must test for legitimacy to radically increase our chances of a sound verdict.

We cannot merely consider personal beliefs alone to validate what we believe. Friends tell me, "You shouldn't claim Christianity to be true." Why? Because if it is True (capital T), all others must be false, even though they may contain elements of truth. We all claim to believe in something, whether it be atheism, Christianity, Taoism, Islam, "spirituality," Hinduism, Satanism, Scientology, etc. We distinguish between ideas to ensure we are not being deceived. If we don't distinguish, we are strolling along this earth blindly on hearsay alone, with no grounds for our actions. Our position would be gullibility at best.

Faith affiliation is more serious than we think because what a person believes is ultimately what they live out, so let us attempt to live a life of truth, not ignorance. That is the goal. Let us step back and examine what exactly it is we are being taught. Hopefully, after study, thought, and grace, the reader can reassess the solidity of his or her position.

THE DILEMMA

"Hear, O wise men, my discourse, and you that have knowledge, hear me! For the ear tests words as the taste does food. Let us discern for ourselves what is right; Let us learn between us what is good."

— *Job 34:2-4*

"The fool takes no delight in understanding, but rather is displaying what he thinks."

— *Proverbs 18:2*

There is a great obstacle that must be addressed before moving forward: the quandary stemming from the multitude of perspectives. Disagreement is the origin of strife amongst men. Much tension and bashing can be found regarding issues considered to be non-negotiable. A definite position must be taken—there is no in-between. Gray areas don't always exist. That is why individuals lean left or right in the religious, moral, and political arenas. What happens when the liberal collides with the conservative on social or human rights issues? Both are pulling in opposite directions. What about religions and churches demeaning each other? Who is right? Is the "spiritualist" or "religious" man correct about the human condition, origin, and destiny of man? Maybe there is no God at all. Perhaps the atheist/humanist is correct. How do we resolve the many issues of our society? Live and let live will not do if you find your country headed in the wrong direction or are being unjustly treated. He who believes things are exactly where they should be in our society is fooling no one but himself.

Anyway, collisions in perspective are inevitable. That is the heart of the dilemma. Thinkers with opposing views have pondered how we should live and function as a society, but have found no clear answers. Some have called for the pursuit of virtue or goodwill in order to establish a utopia, but clearly a conflict arises with describing these terms. It is no wonder we have so much discord in the political realm. Other renowned thinkers believe that the pursuit and indulgence of pleasure is the path to follow, yet, Aristotle counters by basically stating the pursuit of pleasure is a life fit only for cattle. Another will say that good living is that which propels a person to happiness or self-actualization, but then you have those who have reached this plateau on the back of shady business practices, greed, arrogance, and pride, and who are quite content with their acquisitions despite those they have left behind in their wake. Do what you must to arrive where you believe you should be in life regardless of consequences? Really? Some maintain the destruction of a fetus for organs and study are justified acts of virtue, but are they? Another says Capitalism is evil and that Communism is the moral way to govern. So on and so forth. In the rubble of all our varying ideas, there are foundational truths to be extracted and embraced. We must consider then, *Who am I, or anyone else, to say something ought to be so rather than not?* We must establish an authority and credible subject matter expert. It is a great predicament we face.

To solve this problem, we must get critical in thought. It might be necessary to chew the following material a couple of times to fully grasp its implications, but do not get discouraged with philosophical talk, for it will fall into place.

■ ■ ■

I don't believe there to be a more controversial word than "Truth." The mere utterance of the word is enough to stir our spirit. Much contention is found simply defining the word. Truth can be defined as verified facts. One can then argue, what are the facts? We can also say truth is what conforms to reality. What then is reality, with such diversity around the planet? Grasping the magnitude of *Truth* can be a daunting task. Philosophers throughout history have also battled with the word, and some have even thrown in the white towel, concluding there is no truth, or that it can't be known. It is fascinating, though, that a truth claim must be made in order to deny its existence.

Other theorists contend truth is all relative. This conclusion reminds me of a professor who held that no truth is superior to another; therefore, none pulls more weight than the next. In the meantime, she had the audacity to grade our tests and papers! I hope the irony of the scenario is not missed. It is beyond me, the mentality such academics hold. If I say relativism is false, then that idea must be true for me. If anyone corrects my statement, then what is true for me is not true at all, making relativism false. It's that simple.

Throughout history one also stumbles onto scholars who define and redefine an issue in an attempt to reach an answer, preventing one from ever getting anywhere. If we don't know the grandeur of Truth, let's approach the problem with what we do know to be false, so we can at least deal with sound ideas. Greek philosopher Xenophanes suggested that we may not know all the answers, but philosophy/thinking is useful in revealing errors and tells us what is not the case, even if we can't determine what is the case or the entire case (Rooney 84). With that said, we know Truth is narrow by nature, consistent, and not self-contradictory. Anything contrary to what we *do know* is by definition false. These concepts are solid foundations we can at least work upon.

∎ ∎ ∎

It is important to clarify what I mean by "Truth" (capital T), since we have moved from the idea that everyone has the right to an opinion to thinking that every opinion is of equal value. When speaking of Truth, I don't refer to private views, but to universal absolutes that apply to everyone. If it is True for you, it must be True for me or the next person. Subjectivism has its place, but that is not the goal in these writings; it is toward a loftier sphere we are aiming. One can never contend with mere opinions or that which is personal in its proper context.

Indeed, subjectivism is used to define things relative to culture, individualism, or preference. A person may certainly prefer football over baseball. One culture may have more of a taste for a particular attire or food than another. These issues are rightfully subjective, but one can argue subjectivism such as "I don't like broccoli" is not *Truth* (capital T) at all, but a relative preference or a personal viewpoint. What we seek here is not personal or regional, but universal. Meaning that it applies to everyone on the planet. It is critical to understand that we cannot have our own private universal *Truths*. For instance, in the material realm, if exercising and proper nutrition are good for one's health, then it must be *True* for the next person. That gravity acts on anyone who jumps off a building is *True*, regardless of upbringing or race. The same principles apply in the unseen and moral realms. If a person can summon the power of the subconscious mind to better themselves, then we all have access as well. If all men have dignity, then that applies whether you are Caucasian, Indian, African American, etc. We speak of a universal scope only. As Peter Kreeft and Ronald Tacelli wrote, "'I don't want to be selfish' is a subjective truth; 'I ought to be unselfish whether I want to or not' is an objective truth" (*Handbook of Christian Apologetics* 363).

Anytime "*Truth*" is mentioned, we are alluding to consistent or constant universal principles that trump every race, culture, and territory. It corresponds to a reality that exists independently of our personal beliefs. If torturing kids or animals for fun is morally wrong in Australia, it must also be wrong in Madagascar. If it is true that killing a man for his hard-earned property in England is wrong, it must also be wrong in Brazil. If child pornography is wrong in the United States, it must also be wrong in Singapore. If it is with justice that leaders ought to govern in South America, then it ought to be so in the European Union. (Though ideas may differ on what justice is, it still follows that one must attempt to serve justly rather than corruptly. That is the universal law I am trying to bring out). If a thing is *True* in Canada, it must also be *True* in Japan, and vice versa. That is the absolutism we are entertaining. It is constant, and it applies everywhere. We are entertaining blanket statements. Does God exist? The answer is either yes or no, period! Whatever the answer, that Truth applies to every human being on the planet, whether they believe it or not—whether they accept it or not, whether they know it or not, whether they like it or not.

Many hold the idea that "objective" means known by all or accepted by all—it does not. Let us not dismiss the concepts of ignorance, gullibility, and intellectual error. A thing is not so because we believe it to be so, rather it is so because it is so. Our duty lies in finding that which is so. Truth is independent of us. It does not rely on the number of people who believe, nor does it become less true even if the whole world disagrees. It is what it is. A lie is still a lie even if a million people believe it.

To arrive at sensible conclusions, we must be like a detective working a crime scene. One does not need to personally witness a crime to determine the culprit. Through thorough analysis of evidence such as DNA, ballistics, weapons, motives, fingerprints, and witnesses, one can identify the guilty party or at least have worthy reasons, not blind reason, as to who the perpetrator is. If reason can't be used to decipher truth, then we are being intellectually dishonest. Logic and reason stand right behind Truth.

■ ■ ■

Now, with all that said, let me share a conversation I had with my uncle and mother about subjectivism. What they (specifically my uncle) wanted me to understand is that everyone has their own "personal truth," and no matter how much logic you hit someone with, they will not accept it because it is simply not their truth, or what they grew up with, or what they know.

He even said, "One might even be looked upon as crazy or be dismissed altogether for sharing one's idea," but that statement is a speculative conclusion. Assumptions are the mother of all errors. We know prominent figures throughout history have changed the minds of countless people. So it is certainly possible to change a person's mind if the facts are presented carefully and lovingly, whether one is a prominent figure or not. That was one crucial point I was attempting to make throughout the evening, but let us focus on the story my mother was most intrigued by: the man who happily drank his Presidente (the national beer of the Dominican Republic).

Long story short, a parched gentleman puts a coveted bottle of Presidente, imported from the Dominican Republic, in the freezer so he can enjoy it as chilly as possible. He was boasting as to how Presidentes in the U.S. don't have the same quality taste as they do in his native country. He soon departs to tend to some business. Meanwhile, one of my uncles comes onto the scene, notices the beer in the freezer, and inquires about it. He is told it belongs to a gentleman who is momentarily preoccupied and will return. My uncle, seeing the beer is cold enough for his taste, grabs it and switches it with another, less cool, Presidente, but this particular beer was bottled in the U.S. While he enjoys the drink the gentleman eventually returns. With no clue as to what had occurred, he cracks open his now ice-cold beer from the freezer, takes a big sip, and says, "That's what you call a real Presidente."

My uncle giggled while he told the story, but used it as an example to illustrate the nature of truth from one person to another. That man was so convinced that he was drinking his original beer that nothing else mattered. That was his genuine truth, and that is how people hold to their personal views. His point is understandable, but here is where we disconnected. What mattered to my mom and uncle is that the man drinking his Presidente was just as happy as if it were the original Presidente, regardless of whether he was living a lie. But, these writings are *not* about figuring out emotional states or a genuine mentality. We cannot dismiss the fact that we KNOW the gentleman did not consume his original beer. *We cannot accept his genuine sincerity as some real Truth simply because he mistakenly believes so; we know otherwise.* This concept can be applied in the arena of religion and morality as well. Again, *if we do not know Truth, let us at least dismiss what we know is NOT true* so we can deal with more sophisticated claims, like a miner who separates all known impurities from his excavation so that he may deal with more sophisticated precious metals.

To reiterate, we cannot dismiss what we know NOT to be true for the personal satisfaction of others. For example (another topic that surfaced), we know that the Amazonian man who looks at the sky and thinks a 747 aircraft is God is quite mistaken. And no matter how he feels about the aircraft, those who know better KNOW that God is not an airplane flying around transporting people over the vast Amazon. All charity and love goes to such people, because they are simply ignorant. They have not been exposed to the truth, but perhaps one day they will. Again, it is understandable why they believe an aircraft is God, 1000 percent, but we KNOW it is NOT true regardless of the personal bliss a person is feeling. We cannot accept the Amazonian man's "Truth," KNOWING that an airplane is nothing more than a material composition put together by man in order to make a flying machine. To accept the Amazonian man's "truth" as a Truth, when we know it is false, is again to commit intellectual suicide. A Boeing 747 is not God, and since it is not God, that is a universal Truth which applies to all, whether the Amazonian man knows it or not, whether he accepts it or not.

Back to the original example: My uncle knew the beer was switched (a "truth" we know), and at the end of the day the higher reality dominates the lower. The bottom line is, the gentleman did NOT drink what he thought was his original beer, period. That is the truth of the matter, regardless of the beer drinker's sentiments. His good feelings or state of mind have no bearing on the Truth of the matter. Truth does not care about one's personal emotional or mental state. He is SINCERELY mistaken, although 100 percent genuine. The Truth stands as an unmovable pillar, regardless of his ignorant bliss. *We cannot dismiss the notion of deception that happened in this incident, or the hundreds of other reasons that may lead a man astray in other arenas of life.*

Now, whether I have been deceived about my beliefs remains to be seen. They have to be judged on their own merits. That is a topic of discussion presented throughout. This beer story is arbitrary in nature, but this same phenomenon applies to many serious facets of life. Let me make clear, I am not condemning anyone. A person who does not know the facts through no fault of their own cannot be held responsible for what they do not know. We can only be held accountable to the degree of knowledge to which we have been exposed. We who know better will not be held accountable to the same level as the Amazonian man who lacks knowledge. We who know better will be held to a higher standard.

The crucial dilemma we face, then, is determining that which applies to everyone, which can be a prodigious task. At the core of all variant views, there is a common denominator: that the proposition or idea offered *ought* to be so. Like my uncle, who believes others ought to just be, I say one ought to speak should circumstances dictate, or if it is one's duty to do so. If something *ought* to be one way (as my uncle suggests), rather than another, it follows that we are appealing to a law or a standard. What is this standard we appeal to? The implications are mammoth.

We must come as detectives dissecting and searching for clues and reasonableness. Let us refuse to live a lie. If there is no Truth to be had or if it's all arbitrary, nothing is worth dying for, and if nothing is worth dying for, then neither is anything worth living for.

Why Bother?

This "I am, therefore I'll be" attitude cannot suffice. Our mentality should be more inclined toward "I think, therefore I am," as René Descartes famously wrote. That is a more prudent state of mind. Beliefs are not to be left to whatever the mind can imagine.

But why even seek to know? Why rationalize? What if one is not even interested in "knowing," or is indifferent altogether? We should seek because, eventually, reality will find us regardless of our present state, whether we are ready or not. It is better to be prepared than to be caught off guard or deploy a plea of ignorance. Knowing is nobler than ignorance. There is nothing honorable about being oblivious. We were not created to dwell in ignorance. As with all things, we should prepare and stand ready. We don't stay blind to the everyday things of this life, and if we do, the consequences can be dreadful. Ignorance—that is, willful ignorance—is not an excuse. There is an immense difference between sincere ignorance and choosing ignorance to blind ourselves to the responsibilities that emanate from knowing. Those who suspect or know better, and choose the way of ignorance, are fooling no one but themselves. Their mentality is equivalent to an ostrich that buries its head in the ground with the hope that the predator bearing down on it disappears.

A STANDARD

"Art, like morality, consist of drawing the line somewhere."

— G.K Chesterton

"Everything is permissible but not everything is beneficial. Everything is permissible but not everything is constructive."

— 1 Corinthians 10:23

"Perception and experience define personal truth." I agree with that statement, but moving forward we must stay on our toes to distinguish between personal truths (small T) and universal *Truths* (capital T).

Let us more closely examine this issue of personal truth. If individual "perspective" is the final test, as some assert, my question is, which man's perspective is correct, specifically when conflicts arise? Who is right about right and wong? Should we revert to animalistic behavior and let the strongest dictate whose ideas will dominate? Do we become brute animals who take advantage of the weak for our convenience? Is it right for the majority to oppress a minority simply because they carry more weight? Is a popular vote really the determining factor for what makes something right? Some say yes and other say no, but that depends, of course, on the results of the vote. For instance, the majority of Californians voted that marriage should be between a man and woman (Proposition 8). Those who disagreed continued to fight the results, claiming their "rights" were still being violated. If Prop 8 had been in their favor, they would have been clinging to it in support, I would imagine. The point is that popular vote did not settle the matter; gay marriage continues to be an issue of controversy. So whether the issue is decided by a majority or not, popularity has no bearing on the question of right or wrong. If the idea of Truth and right/wrong boil down to popularity, as many in this Hollywood generation believe, the statement "The majority of people participated in that wicked deed" would not make any sense. We should not allow wicked behavior, precisely because it is corrupt and immoral. The bottom line is, the general acceptance of an idea is not an assurance of its truth.

A humanist suggested that the U.S. Supreme Court ultimately determines what is right. Really? Since when has authorship of Morality (capital M) been given to these nine judges, and by whom? This is the same court that once ruled a black man is three-fifths of a human being. The black community had quite a different perspective from that of the Supreme Court, even when it was enforcing its absurd conclusions. Our Rights (capital R) are of a higher domain and do not rest upon some appointed judges. Can we honestly say that an issue such as abortion was wrong one day (prior to *Roe v. Wade,* which legalized abortions) and suddenly made right the next, simply because these pure, moral, sinless judges or "authors of morality" have spoken? It is critical to understand that there is an immense difference between what is legal and what is right.

Others go beyond courts and voting processes to decipher truth and morality. It is a process that just grows from society as it develops, whether one is conscious of this phenomenon or not. The question then becomes, which society? Could it have been Romans as they were spreading their empire around the world claiming there is none like Caesar? Did we have no right to condemn and go to war with the Nazis or the Japanese? What if the Nazis had won the war; would that have made their societal views correct? Is it proper to watch others get innocently slaughtered so as to avoid infringing on someone else's perceptions in order to maintain tolerance?

Again, society in general is not concerned with real truths, but with opinions. So we can purge society or others' cultures as the determining factor of universal standards, particularly when other societies view otherwise, such as the Islamic State group known as ISIL.

This all suggests an established guideline. *To be a civilized human race is to live by virtue of standards,* or else unparalleled lawlessness would be the result. There is no question that different societies have different interpretations of things such as morality. But in every society there are behaviors that are not permissible, and since not everything is permissible, a Standard (capital S) must exist. To illustrate this point we can see how people who practice different morality still share a mutual morality. For example, pro-life and pro-choice activists agree murder is wrong, but they disagree on whether abortion is murder. So we can see an absolute, universal Morality to be true: that one ought not to commit murder. One can see absolutism surface from subjectivists who claim they are being treated unfairly or protest in order to receive certain rights. Why are they fighting especially if all is subjective? If there is no absolute, than those statements are outright worthless and make no sense since they are appealing to a standard.

Right and wrong cannot be manmade creations; they must be from a higher domain. If it were up to the individual, then nothing would be wrong, since anything goes. One would essentially be free of any guilt. Personal actions would boil down to whatever anyone liked, with no responsibility or consequences attached; but there is a reality outside of us, since we know that we err, evident by the outlandish conclusions men of every generation have jumped to.

The one who can never be wrong is he who resides in his own personal domain, like a novelist who can never be mistaken about anything in his stories—but they can certainly be wrong about biology and physics. That is because there is something outside of ourselves. In the same way, concepts such as morality and Truth are not something we make up as we do a story. They are independent of us. It is something outside our story or our mind, not inside.

The chief argument subjectivists petition is that of being open-minded and accepting of others. While being accepting of the *person,* we cannot tolerate all perspectives and conducts simply because people like them as evident in the chaotic six o'clock evening news. Our appetites cannot be the compass of rectitude. Besides, as mentioned, relativism is a self-defeating position, since "tolerant" people do not tolerate those whose views are different. The majority of subjective minds can't even state why anyone should be tolerant in the first place. The reality that we should tolerate people, even when we disagree, derives from the *absolute* moral rule that we should always treat others with fairness and dignity. Quite frankly, without universal moral standards there can be no real goodness.

■ ■ ■

So what is this fixed point of reference or standard moral code we unconsciously appeal to every time we defend our position? Folks do not realize the implications of their statements when they claim something *ought* to be a certain way. Ought supposes a law. A law assumes its authority from a lawgiver. In other words, pleading to a standard forces us to revert to an author of all standards. Why? Because universal laws have more authority than any individual. Commands only have as much authority as the one giving them. If I desired to raise taxes, no one would have to pay them, because I simply do not have the power to implement such a law. On the other hand, if government officials decided to raise taxes it would be quite a different proposition, since they have the authority to do so. In the same way, an individual cannot make a *universal* standard, due to a lack of authority.

The bottom line is, if there are no standards, anything goes. Selling pornography to kids, for instance, would not be wrong; it would just be something someone deems necessary to make a little side money. Ultimately, to say a thing ought to be because "I think so" or "I say so" forces a person to admit he or she is the definitive authority. That just cannot be accepted. One can only ask, who made them the authority? Plain and simple, universal laws, Standards, Truth, and Morality must have been commanded by someone who has authority over all. This is one critical concept I have come to learn over the years: *No one can prove a thing ought to be or not (universally) unless they possess the highest authority on their side. No one can substantiate convincingly that what they think to be right is right, unless they refer to the author of all right; that is, God Himself.* This is a pivotal point that must be embedded in the reader's mind. "This ought to be because *God* said so" has far greater implications than "Because I said so." To obtain definite grounding, we must admit we are seeking something greater than ourselves, something that transcends all cultures, societies, races, and individualism.

■ ■ ■

The concept that we live by virtue of standards is essential to grasp because it takes center stage in future chapters. There must be an authoritative source. I haven't come across any job, project, or endeavor in life where there wasn't something or someone declaring expectations. Standards are not merely a necessity of life; they are life! They are implemented for our well-being in all aspects of our lives. Even a simple game would not be enjoyable if there were no rules.

In this age of "tolerance" we want everything to be permissible, until, of course, something occurs that is not to our liking. Now we cry out for justice, but where is the "live and let live" mentality? "Live and let live, so long as others think like us" seems to be the proposition. We can't even cry foul without violating the principles we defend. "Live and let live" does not work how people imagine, since what we do, whether right or wrong, affects all of us. *There is a transcendent power in behavior.* We are all intertwined to an extent. Parents, for instance, eventually place their kids under the influence of public schools. Any good parent would wish that their child be exposed to right teachings, examples, and conducts wherever they go, not just in the school to which they send their kids. That is why it is imperative that we as a society push right principles, because it touches all of us in one form or another, whether at the movies or watching TV in the comfort of one's home.

A coworker of mine suggested that the remedy for this entire dilemma is the application of common sense to our behavior and being "good" to others (the Golden Rule). But whose "common sense" and standard of goodness should we use? The predator online, with his devious intentions, who is mostly good? If not, why not? The Golden Rule sounds nice on paper but in practice it falls short. Truly, common sense is not very common. And why ought we do good in the first place? Atheists say we are nothing but matter. Why should mere "matter" be concerned with the responsibility or welfare of others? Why should we do good regardless of how others treat us? To do good for the sake of doing good takes us back to the author of all good: God.

We should consider then, *is there a God who has set universal Standards?* That is at least valid for the atheists or agnostics, who maintain that morality, right and wrong, is an evolutionary/cognitive phenomenon derived from societies that ultimately determine these factors. Contrarily, I hold that the source of our Morality, Standards, right and wrong, has its origin elsewhere—that is, God. He must have something to say about Justice, moral codes, and conduct. If not, no atheist can reasonably claim that the genocide of a race is wrong, when it is purely the byproduct or function of animalistic actions. In other words, when animals kill there is nothing wrong with such behavior. If we are nothing more than animals or matter, why should such behavior be wrong in us? Or does the cry of injustice admit something beyond all of us?

THE BIGGEST OF ALL QUESTIONS

"There are only three kinds of persons; those who serve God, having found Him; others who are occupied in seeking Him, not having found Him; while the remainder live without seeking Him and without having found Him."

— *Blaise Pascal*

"Your wisdom and knowledge mislead you when you say to yourself, 'I am, and there is none besides me.'"

— *Isaiah 47:10*

The key ingredient to any good discussion is good sense, so before venturing further, it is imperative to first address those who deny the existence of God. We should move forward with a seeking attitude as we lay the framework that leads to a deity and, in turn, a Standard. We must contemplate some foundational truths for the rest of this work to fall into place.

Encounters

I had not come across so many nonbelievers and those of uncertain faith as I did when I instructed student military pilots. At first I thought they were just young and not quite to that soul-searching stage of life, but after conversing with a few young officers they appeared fixed in their positions. A couple of them even quoted popular atheists such as Richard Dawkins and Christopher Hitchens. This only made me more eager to engage in discussion with these young aviators, though some appeared unenthusiastic. "God talk" came across as an inconvenient matter, but a good handful of agnostics did engage in conversation.

In supporting their agnostic views, several students spoke of tragedies both personal and worldwide. "How can there be an almighty God who allows atrocities, earthquakes, tsunamis, cancer?" I told them that if God were not almighty in the first place there would be no natural disasters or humans to have cancer. There would be no us to dispute Him, either. Death will come to us various ways. Such events happen in the natural order, and God does not have to interfere with them because we are amazed or affected by them. Mother Nature is alive, breathing, and dynamic, not stagnant. To say "I don't comprehend all of God's ways; therefore, I don't believe" is not a rational position, just like a lack of understanding on a subject matter in school does not prove falsity, but rather our inability to comprehend. To this, one student countered zealously and asked for concrete proof of God: "Show me any solid evidence." Well, I always like to return a question with a question. I asked him to prove to me that there is no God. Many assume the burden of proof falls only on the believer, but this same rule must apply to the idea of disbelief.

For whatever reason, people think evidence of God must be visible or tangible, like when a detective tries to determine the weapon used in a crime and finds a 9mm handgun under a couch. Evidence is not just found in the material realm. We are not brute animals, but glorified beings endowed with intellect and reason who can appreciate intellectual evidence. How do we prove or measure the beauty of a song or a portrait? We don't use a yardstick. A joke, for example, is not put in a test tube that measures its funniness. The evidence is in the human mind, not in our senses. Dinesh D'Souza, in his book *What's So Great About Christianity*, could not have said it any better: "Non-believers want evidence of God from a domain where the normal rules of evidence do not apply" (194).

God is not physical, but spiritual, and He will not be contained in a test tube. We believe in immaterial things such as love and thought with no qualms, yet this is the kind of realm one must venture into when dealing with spiritual matters.

After sharing these basic points with agnostic students, what followed was a good exchange of ideas. I encouraged them to investigate further, to widen their spectrum so as to make sound conclusions. Some were open to the idea, which implied some sort of investigative mode. If they genuinely pursue, they will find answers. Quite frankly, other students did not show the slightest interest. It makes sense why Pascal would say that there are two types of men, those afraid of losing God and those that are afraid they might find Him.

■ ■ ■

"If one draw near to God with praise and prayer even half a cubit foot, God will go twenty leagues to meet him."

— Sir Edwin Arnold

It is ironic how many enlightening moments happen after the fact. What hit me after one discussion was a memory of playing basketball with some fellow who was vigorously telling me to prove to him that I could do a particular dunk. "Show me," he said, with a snobby, insistent attitude. Finally, I said, "I don't have to show you anything." I became reluctant. I knew I could do the dunk. If he had come to me with a different attitude, I would have been delighted to show him my "Airness." The problem was his approach.

A similar incident occurred with another individual, who questioned the fact that I had flown in support of Operation Iraqi Freedom and Enduring Freedom. "You ain't no pilot," he said. "Show me! Prove it to me!" I recall telling him I don't have to prove anything, but, on the other hand, I would be delighted to if approached correctly. In the same way, why does God have to prove Himself to someone who comes to Him defiantly, with disbelief and attitude? God is God. We should come before Him with proper protocol. Usually, the ones who find God are those who humbly seek Him. We can say the distance between us and God is directly proportional to the size of our ego, pride, and attitude. He is the great "I Am," not us.

But creation itself is plenty evidence of His existence, with the complex beauty of nature, the oceans, trees, mountains, animals, and the celestial bodies above. The world is full of wondrous miracles. "Nature is the living, visible garment of God," as Johann Wolfgang Von Goethe put it. For those concerned about evidence, God would be delighted to show them the proof they seek, provided they come with a genuine and contrite heart. Deuteronomy 4:29 reads "You shall seek the Lord, your God; and you shall indeed find him when you search after him with your whole heart and your whole soul." It says "with your whole heart and your whole soul," but most of us generally walk around half-hearted about everything we do.

■ ■ ■

> *"Some people, in order to discover God, read books. But there is a great book: the very appearance of created things. Look above you! Look below you! Read it. God, whom you want discovered, never wrote that book in ink. Instead, He set before your eyes the things that He made. Can you ask for a louder voice than that?"*
>
> — St. Augustine

I had some great conversations with agnostic students, but the ones who captivated me most were the adamant atheists. They adamantly believed in *no* God, but their reasons did not leave me in awe. One mentioned that he did not believe because "religions only lead to war." A second argued that we can only believe in what we can "quantify." One particular student got deep and said he doesn't believe "just because … it's how I feel," as I stared with a blank look, awaiting further elaboration. It's interesting how men strive to convince themselves that there is no God. They fight their inner inclination to believe. We don't grow into the idea of God; rather, we attempt to grow out of it. Belief in a higher power is as instinctive as a baby who knows that food must be put in its mouth for nourishment.

I essentially told my students that I thought quite differently on the matter. After sharing some broad ideas about God, I noticed atheist students, who stood firm in their position, suddenly began to waver. They became more subjective when the questions and concepts being presented appeared reasonable. When one has little maneuvering room on the hot seat, relativism always seemed to be the scapegoat.

Quite honestly, the hardcore nonbelievers I encountered were not particularly the sharpest knives in the drawer. They sounded like clueless religious folks, so this prompted me to pick up several books to get a better grasp of the atheistic perspective. This is where I became acquainted with the renowned atheists of the times. I must say, I was captivated with what these "intellectuals" had to say; shrewd comments indeed. They reminded me of some of the difficult questions I had about God, such as the difficulties of evil, the human condition and His revelation; yet, my faith has always remained steady.

I admit there were thought-provoking points brought to light. It became apparent that shaky believers can easily be swayed by these clever atheists, especially those who think faith is an emotion or feeling. Believers need to understand that faith is not an emotion. Faith is an intellectual confession or a recognition that although we have not seen something ourselves, we can accept it based on reason and/or the authority of the one saying so. We can't rely on emotions alone, which send all sorts of mixed signals. It's good to have emotional faith, but it must be accompanied by intellectual faith. Many believers don't know their faith as they should, let alone stand their ground with a savvy atheist. Doubt can easily be instilled in someone who has little intellectual grounding in their faith. With "smart talk" and "wit," atheists capitalize on the ignorance of believers, catching them off guard. The beauty of it all is, believers could make atheists backpedal just as quickly, if only they would just educate themselves a bit.

■ ■ ■

"The purpose of life is a life of purpose."

— Robert Byrne

I used to ponder about how the most militant atheist battled the same voids I contended. It is impressive how, in the infinity of reality, a nonbeliever goes to his grave with faith in himself. What an extravagant proposition. I am reminded of French- Algerian writer and philosopher Albert Camus, who claimed human existence is absurd and that we try to make sense of a senseless world. We spend our whole lives achieving nothing. The inevitable question to ask in this pointlessness of existence is why should I not commit suicide? (Rooney 78) Even with this gloomy, although reasonable assessment, many nonbelievers cope well with their accolades hanging on their walls, money, fame, and success. Regardless, achievements or not, it seems those who have no faith "man up" and accept their fate. Others, I'm sure, don't manage so well. I find it hard to believe that an atheist can honestly tell me they are truly happy knowing life is ultimately meaningless. We are creatures of meaning, yet, in the end, nothing matters. To have a destiny to rot into the ground is a notion my very being repels. Purpose is the essence of every human being.

A gentleman who declared that our destiny is simply to be six feet under suggested that this is why "We must live good lives and accomplish as much as possible. We only get one shot, and we had better make it count, so that when we get old we can look back and feel good about our run." One has to wonder why. First, we are not guaranteed to get old. Tomorrow is promised to no one. And why should we take the difficult path of virtue and hard work to accomplish as much as possible, when doing wrong often seems to be the easier and the more attractive approach? If life is ultimately meaningless, why even bother with life's challenges? In the end, accomplishments mean nothing if we are ultimately only matter. If death has no meaning, then life can't possibly have any meaning.

Do some of these nonbelievers ever consider the possibility of being wrong? Personally, I never considered being wrong about God's existence, until I was blindsided with the question during an evening of social gathering with friends in North Carolina. What if believers are wrong about their faith? That is a perfectly legitimate question. Intellectually we must be open to the possibility of error. The person who asked me this question never realized my sudden urge to excuse myself to the restroom in an attempt to avoid a question I had never considered. What if I am wrong about my faith? Then it quietly hit me! The atheist can't boast, even if they are right. The man of faith can hardly feel a fool. If the believer is wrong, we'll meet six feet under and that will be the end of that. At least I attempted to live that "good" life, with plenty of "accomplishments." Shortly after this incident, I came across philosopher/mathematician Blaise Pascal's Wager, which states, "Let us weigh the gain and the loss in wagering that God is. Let us estimate these two chances. If you gain, you gain all; if you lose, you lose nothing. Wager, then, without hesitation that He is."

My friend appeared satisfied with the answer I gave him, but a "funny character" in the room sarcastically remarked that he'll believe when a voice comes down from Heaven, or God himself appears to him personally. One has to wonder why he was so special that God should pay him a personal visit. There needs to be proper protocol before the presence of a king or president. How much more would the presence of God require? That's all I had in the tank that evening for discussion, but I would remain restless with some comments made during that gathering. Why doesn't God make Himself more obvious in order to settle these matters, to quiet people like the "funny character" demanding His presence? That was one of my biggest concerns about the question of God, but understanding would come later. Although there are plenty of external signs given in creation alone, God does not suffocate us with overwhelming evidence so as not to coerce our decision to choose Him freely. He maintains a balance between those who want to accept and those who want to reject Him. That is what free will is all about. If God imposes belief in Him, He takes away freedom; our choice would not be truly free. Relationships are never forced; they are an invitation. *The bottom line is, faith is what pleases God and is the vehicle He has chosen for those who desire to know Him.*

So to the likes of the "funny character" I would say that there is an issue of coercion in his demand for God's presence. God appearing to someone would probably be a startling, fearful experience, and that's not how He operates. Faith is what pleases God. He works in subtle ways. He will not be found in chaos (1 Kings 19:12). Psalm 46:10 reads, "Be still and know that I am God," but most of us can't be still for ten seconds.

■ ■ ■

"We don't know one millionth of one percent about anything."

— Thomas Edison

My conversing would continue intensely with atheists. As mentioned, a common denominator I found with these engagements was that many nonbelievers held some sort of intellectually superior attitude. They came across as if their thinking allowed them to be more cognizant of reality, exempting them from some fairy tale existence. At least this was my impression. They deduced that the average believer, due to a lack of thinking or inability to reason, fails to understand that there is no God. There is no doubt that a lack of thinking persists amongst believers. Some of the things they say are outright painful, but the typical atheist falls right next to them as well. With their own gullibility and less-than-stellar thinking, they cling to every word these "learned" evangelical atheists utter, as if IQ is the test that dislodges the existence of God. Quite frankly, for every "intellectual" who does not believe in God there are plenty of others who do believe. I bring up this IQ issue because much effort is made by atheists to recruit historical intellectuals to add credibility to their position. That certainly is better than citing a bunch of average Joes, but for every "intelligent" assertion they come up with, equally or more intelligent men disagree or refute. All I'll say is, if teams consisting of great intellectual believers and great intellectual skeptics were assembled to debate the matter of God, it would hardly be a fair fight for the atheists.

But what are most of these intellectual atheists known for besides their wit? Their occupations vary, including playwrights, poets, politicians, businessman, actors, and comedians. Most of these men have abandoned the "philosophical" or "religious" domain of knowledge to become experts in their given fields. Any humble scholar with expertise will admit that he knows only a few things about which he considers himself an expert. Many atheists *(not all, of course)* talk about fields of study that they really don't know much about, i.e., religion and God. These individuals have stated their opinions on these topics never having been appropriately educated in matters of theology and philosophy. Their views are tagged with exaggerated value because of their reputations in their given field of expertise by the average man, as if expertise in one area qualifies them as experts in other subjects. All I see are individuals mistrusting their knowledge and reasoning capacity, talking about what they know little about, but using their reputation in their given field to come across as though they do.

The influence of these men can be illustrated by my brother's friend, who lost his faith because Bill Maher does not believe in God. I thought that Bill Maher was a comedian/actor, not an authority in matters of philosophy and theology, though he certainly has the right to share his opinion. I investigated further and found that Maher made a documentary, and curiosity propelled me to watch. It was agonizing, watching him feed on the ignorance of folks throughout the film, but he did not dare sit down and talk with any reputable theologians. That would not have been too helpful for his documentary. If one wants to look good, it makes sense to play with weak players. My brother's friend drank the Kool-Aid; since Bill Maher, the comedian/talk show host, believes in no God, therefore, there is no God. That's quite the mentality that this young man took. I suppose he thinks Mr. Maher is the standard that proves all other men irrational. Hopefully, he will look into the matter more closely and see what real professionals or experts have to say about folks such as Bill Maher and their "witty" comments, so that he can make better decisions and not just hear one-sided arguments.

Regardless of intelligence, there are many nonbelievers who aren't very bright and don't believe in God. "Smarts" is not the only reason for rejecting God. There is something else in the equation.

∎ ∎ ∎

"Our headstrong passions shut the door of our souls against God."

— Confucius

"If you do understand, then it is not God."

— St. Augustine

I recollect asking one nonbeliever to pretend and just assume God did exist for a moment. If He did, would we be able to fathom His infinite mind, as the finite humans that we are? "Probably not," he said. "Then, could it be possible that this is the existence we are living?" I asked. "No. Because God does not exist," he remarked. What an interesting assessment. His reasoning is like saying that since there is no empirical evidence of alien life, therefore aliens do not exist; but is that really reasonable? No one can say with certainty that nowhere else in this vast universe does some form of life exist. Can we at least entertain the *possibility* without physical evidence? I believe we can, even though we have no physical evidence. Why? Because of *reason*. Reason tells us that in the infinite cosmos there might just be a planet that can sustain some sort of life. Reason also tells us God's existence is possible as well, though we have no physical evidence of Him.

After some consideration, my atheist colleague commented, "If God did exist, He would have given me understanding." The question to consider now is, why would God make you His equal for the sake of your understanding? Instead, He asks that we trust Him, as in a father/son relationship. Though the son lacks understanding concerning the ways of the father, those ways will become clear to the son in the future. The believer will also receive enlightenment in due time, but we cannot demand it now since it is from a state essentially future.

The frustration that comes with a lack of comprehension is understandable, but it simply does not disprove God. What it proves is the obvious limitations of the finite human mind. There are indeed mysteries beyond us, but we should not expect anything else. Man's intelligence is not the end-all. If God were at our level, he would be no God at all!

It is extraordinary how often this matter of God usually boils down to the individual. Undeniably, it seems every time I talk with an atheist it is all about number one: "Me" or "I." "I" did this, "I" did that, "I" accomplished all "I" have, etc. They certainly did all those things—with the brains God gave them in the first place. The issue with many of us is that we want to be our own god. The average atheist departs from faith in God not because of any real intellectual inquiry or because they are in search of loftier ideals, but rather, they find it less bothersome and restraining. We want to give full vent to our appetites. We want to be Master of the Universe and refuse to accept the responsibility that comes with faith.

The bottom line is, the believer ultimately places his trust in God; but is our believing some kind of psychological apparatus we've made up in order to fend off the reality of death? Can science account for the cosmos and all that is? "Religious fools," as one atheist put it, dismiss lack of understanding as God. But, could sciences be the means God uses to make the universe possible in the first place? Are we only to believe what is fully understood or visible? These are some of the questions we will explore further, keeping in mind that we are only scratching the surface. This was never meant to be an all-inclusive, exhaustive document. If so, it would have been tens of thousands of pages long. Heaps of books have been written on the subject, but I will highlight major points to ponder in hopes of stimulating further pursuit and thought.

Theories

"If I tell you about earthly things and you do not believe, how will you believe if I tell you about heavenly things."

— John 3:12

Besides the reasoning already stated, I want to share arguments that have lured me to believing in the existence of a deity. These may be simple concepts that to the "intellectual" may seem unsophisticated and subjective, but nevertheless, these are ideas I have held for as long as I can remember.

■ ■ ■

Though I was not the most attentive to divine or religious matters growing up, I have always had the compulsion to believe. God simply made sense. Maybe some things are not as complicated as we suspect. A little common sense may be all the common sense we need. Why some lacked faith was a mystery to me. Was it the sheer conditioning of my environment, as some suggest, being that I grew up in a believing home? I don't deny environmental factors, but my destiny does not solely derive from my environment. If so I could have easily taken the wrong route, having been raised in a single-family home in the Bronx. The point is that one can certainly break free from their environmental cocoon, evident by the numerous believing friends of mine who departed their Christian faith.

Anyhow, growing up I had a concealed faith; I did pick up a few ideas attending catechism class and church. We spoke of laws; does not a law suppose a lawgiver? Laws don't appear out of thin air. Legislation assumes a legislator, right? Concepts such as injustice spoke volumes. It demanded there be a God. Most recently, I am reminded of the movie *12 Years a Slave*, where one slave (Solomon Northup) is forced by his master to beat a fellow slave. When he refuses to oblige, the slave master takes it upon himself to beat the woman. All Solomon can do is look on in despair and say, "Thou devil! Sooner or later, somewhere in the course of eternal justice thou shalt answer for this sin." It is a powerful scene. That is why accountability, Heaven, Hell, and personal judgment make good sense. Our inferior sense of justice points us to an absolute justice; that, of course, being God. *If we are just matter subject to corruption, as atheists claim, then all moral principles lose their strength.* But that cannot be, when we have a genuine sense of right and wrong, evident by our conscience that rings at us when we do what we shouldn't. Morality is real and rooted in something other than us. All these ideas made God a common-sense issue to me. I'm reminded of my Earth science teacher, who mentioned the possibility that the universe may have come from nothing. Now we have nothing working upon nothing to become something! It is no wonder I believed in God.

In my simplicity, I questioned whether we could be the highest level of intelligence in this unfathomable reality of ours. If that is the case, this majestic universe has very little to offer. It is a *difficult* idea to accept. In my "common sense" I thought about how opposites must also exist. If there are those who believe in God, there must be those who do not. Faith must contest with doubt or unbelief for faith to exist at all. How can one know winning if there is no losing, or know light without darkness? Since there is truth, there must also be that which is false. If the visible, so also the invisible. If there is mortality, the notion of immortality must be entertained. At least this was my outlook from an opposite angle spectrum. If there were no atheists God would not exist, but since atheists exist, therefore there is a God.

I also reflected on many movies and books inspired by spiritual phenomena, paranormal activities, witchcraft, haunted houses, and evidence of the supernatural. Can all these accounts be false? Can they all be made up or psychologically induced? Maybe, but it only takes one account to be true. Growing up, I thought all these were solid considerations, but I would eventually learn it was looked upon as foolishness.

■ ■ ■

In what I call the "Who are you?" theory, I just look at the credibility of the person making the claim. In other words, the one who makes a colossal assertion had better be a proper and dependable authority on the subject. We all have our opinions on any given matter, but I recognize there are those with much greater aptitude on the subject of God than myself and many self-appointed experts.

Logically, and normally speaking, a person who wants to be wealthy should avoid the advice of someone who finds himself in grave debt making $20,000 a year; he has no credibility on the subject of economics and affluence. Relatively speaking, this is exactly the type of trust we give to others in various arenas of our lives, in very grave areas. Wouldn't it be more prudent to turn to a billionaire investor such as Warren Buffett for guidance on attaining wealth? He is not on the same level as Joe making $20,000 a year; his advice carries much more weight. Buffett can back up his advice with his mammoth fortune. As a matter of fact, when he speaks, Wall Street listens.

Every now and then, when I hear someone utter "There is no God," I think, who the heck is this, making such an extravagant assertion? Not knowing much else, I knew Christ was a most prominent and authoritative figure in history, and He says there is a God. Like Buffett on finances, so was Christ on divine matters, many times over. When He speaks of God and morality, it would be wise to listen. Not knowing much else, in my simplicity, I take Christ's words over those of some Joe who finds the idea of God irksome to his lifestyle.

■ ■ ■

As far as pure reasoning is concerned, a concept I came across years ago explained how objective truth speaks volumes for itself. It described how eternal truths such as ten plus ten making twenty can't be shredded and destroyed like a piece of paper. It is beyond the sensual realm. St. Augustine explained that our minds could discover eternal truths, but such truths cannot reside in our finite mind, since our minds disintegrate. Therefore, there must be an eternal mind where such truths reside. This mind is also known as God. *(Handbook of Christian Apologetics* 67)

My last proposal stems from the emptiness and longing from within, which I have already expounded on. Something inside yearned for its rightful place. Atheists would attribute my condition to some mental condition. C.S. Lewis describes my disposition in his book *Mere Christianity* more accurately by writing that for every appetite there is something that satisfies that particular desire. Desires are not in vain. If one is thirsty, there is water to quench that thirst. Likewise, sexual desires are fulfilled through sex. When a baby is hungry, food can satisfy that desire. Work or hobbies can subdue boredom. So on and so forth, but what satisfies an empty heart? Not success, possessions, or adventures. Men have experimented with this since the beginning of time and the results are the same. These will keep one happy at a superficial level for a finite time. No matter what success or ventures, there is always that lingering question in the back of our minds: Is this it? All the world has to offer eventually leaves us barren and unfulfilled. No earthly or temporal good can satisfy our ultimate desires. As water satisfies thirst, the soul cannot be denied its rightful object, that being God. He is the longing our soul seeks.

These are concepts I held growing up, in spite of how simple they may appear. Let us examine what thinkers throughout the ages had to say. Let's step it up, with some *classical arguments for the existence God, while remaining within the scope of this book.*

CLASSICAL ARGUMENTS FOR GOD

"The Universe flashed into being, and we cannot find out what caused that to happen."

— *Astrophysicist Robert Jastrow*

"All I have seen teaches me to trust the Creator for all I have not seen."

— *Ralph Waldo Emerson*

Many scholars study *causes* in reality but do not ponder the *ultimate cause* of reality. It is important to reflect on the difference. In doing so, the limits of science become evident. Dinesh D'Souza illustrates this point through an example of boiling water. A scientist will talk in terms of movement of molecules, heat, and temperature to explain why water boils, but the deeper reality, which science can't touch, is the *purpose* of the boiling water. The deeper reality or purpose being that someone just wants a cup of hot tea. In other words, science can study causes in the universe, but it is not able to answer the ultimate *whys* of our existence, such as why the universe began at all (D'Souza 163). To emphasize this key point, we can once again look at a crime scene. Science can deduce who committed the crime, but it can't explain the motive. Scientific knowledge, in other words, is not the only kind of knowledge, but merely a piece of the puzzle, as D'Souza suggests.

We have a misconception that nothing is real beyond what we can perceive. We tend to put too much reliance on our fallible senses to determine "reality." If we can't feel it, touch it, smell it, hear it, or see it, then it should not be given serious consideration. The great thinker Immanuel Kant had much to say concerning the assumptions we make about reality. In his book *Critique of Pure Reason,* he writes, "Just in the same way did Plato, abandoning the world of sense because of the narrow limits it sets to the understanding, venture up on the wings of ideas beyond it, into the void space of pure intellect" (6). Kant reasoned that there is reality we experience, and then there is reality itself. We only experience particles of true reality. The whole of reality is obscured by our sensory limitations (D'Souza 170). We falsely assume that what we observe is true reality but, really, it is much greater than what we can even imagine. D'Souza uses Plato's observation of people living in caves, experiencing only shadows on the wall their entire lives. To them those shadows are reality, but those shadows are actually images of a greater reality. We cannot truly say that what we perceive now, with our finite senses, is the totality of reality. We, to an extent, are like those individuals looking at shadows.

We must also consider the link between our perception and reality itself. To illustrate how "actual reality" eludes us, take, for instance, the electromagnetic waves Earth gives off; we can't sense them, but we know they exist. What about eagles, with their superior visual acuity? Certainly they have a better visual perspective than we do. A smell that is evident to a dog goes easily unnoticed by us. Our limitations deceive us as far as the bigger picture is concerned, just as when we used our senses to determine the Earth was flat. We only capture the immediate things we experience, but there is much going on in reality itself that we are unable to process. It is like an ant walking on a large portrait, not seeing the whole picture on which it marches (D'Souza 172; 177).

In the same fashion, deeper reality goes undetected (even with our technology), so we must dwell in the realm of pure reason, as Kant suggested. The material world we know is only a piece of the puzzle. Reasoning points us to a higher level of reality, but only to a certain extent, then faith must pick up. It is like trying to see around an obstruction and jumping on a footstool to have a better view of what lies ahead, but not getting a complete or clear view. Although reason points us to God, it does not declare it knows all about Him; but it at least allows us to take a confident step of faith toward Him.

Reason extends its dominion beyond the limits of our experience. Reality is so much greater than what we see under a microscope. "We don't know one millionth of one percent about anything," as Thomas Edison said. A more humble position is warranted. Faith makes sense; that is, reasonable faith. Science makes good sense too, since it is the vehicle dispensed by the creator to sustain this intricate universe. Faith and science, rightly understood, go hand in hand.

The Design Argument

"The world we inhabit must have had an origin; that origin must have consisted in a cause; that cause must have been intelligent; that intelligence must have been supreme; and that supreme, which always was and is supreme, we know by the name of God."

— Unknown

"Nature is the living, visible garment of God."

— Johann Wolfgang von Goethe

As surely as it takes intelligence to understand our surroundings, there must be intelligence behind those surroundings. Blind matter is not endowed with knowledge that it should produce intelligence. Too much credit is given to chance, when the imprint of intelligence can be found anywhere from the microscopic level to the infinity of space. That is why the evidence of design makes a powerful case for a deity. It is like archeologists finding ancient tools and artifacts and rightfully concluding intelligence behind the discovery, rather than concluding, "It just happened." There is a twofold question that must be entertained by archeologists: What happened, and who made it happen? Mere chance cannot solicit such credit. The same can be said for the universe as a whole, which resembles a fine-tuned apparatus. Universal laws are in a stupendous balance, allowing self-governance. Every force in the universe comes together, like an orchestra with needle-point perfection.

Take the DNA codes in our cells, for example. All they do is give every cell in our body instructions on how they should function, much like a computer program. It is purely written information. Now, when we come across written information, we can, hopefully, agree that there is intelligence behind the data. All instructions have an intent or purpose. One has to ask how this data or "software" ended up in each human cell. Natural and biological causes lack any suitable explanation. Maybe there is a designer behind the scenes acting as a computer programmer. This helps explain why reality is structured one way instead of another.

How some scientists can look further into the universe and deeper into the molecular world and not stand in awe of the grand design is baffling. The laws of physics and chemistry were not made by scientists, but discovered by them. This is why God and science cannot contradict each other. Science only attempts to study how He created. Science is God's handiwork. Some scientists today have lost God in the wonders of creation. Their sole focus is on the created, ignoring the creator. Pearl S. Buck said it best: "I am so absorbed in the wonder of earth and the life upon it that I cannot think of heaven and angels." Or Ruth Hurmence Green, who states, "The natural is so awesome that we need not go beyond it."

■ ■ ■

Atheists claim that nature produces the appearance of design; it is simply a blind, automatic process of nature. We use reason to determine that design demands a designer, but when it comes to design attributes in nature and ideas beyond the human scope, is it all a spontaneous process? Apparently, the human mind is the highest form of intelligence capable of the notion of design. Are we to conclude that the principles and reason we use every day are limited to our domain? If they are true principles, they carry tremendous force, and we know it is a fact that design, not random chance, causes meaningful and coherent patterns such as bridges, books, and computers. Surely we cannot inhabit this small space of order in the universe and be surrounded by chaos.

Many skeptics take refuge in the belief that in the future, scientists will have better explanations for the world we live in, and what we don't know now, we will eventually know. There is no doubt we know more now than we did two hundred years ago. Two hundred years in the future we will know much more, also. Regardless, we will never have *full understanding*. As Bernard Shaw wrote, "Science never solves a problem without creating ten more." Discoveries will only lead to new ventures. Questions will lead to more questions and a new arena of complexities and studies. All of them will give rise to the grand question: Why? Reality is so great that even our imagination falls short. We can only capture small particles. Yet, some hold fast to the "scientific method," as if it were the only way to prove something. A method that, by the way, can't even prove that it is the only way to know truth.

Reasonable faith makes sense, and I commend and embrace science, as many men of faith do. It is doing great work for mankind, while destroying superstition and false religions.

Thomas Aquinas

"I will destroy the wisdom of the wise, and the learning of the learned I will set aside. Where is the wise one? Where is the scribe? Where is the debater of this age? Has not God made the wisdom of this world foolish?"

— 1 Corinthians 1:19-20

Thomas Aquinas was a renowned theologian in the Catholic Church in the thirteenth century who argued for God's existence through reason alone. We will be addressing three of his arguments.

The first is known as *Motion*. This means moving from being purely potential to being actual. For example, a bridge designed by an architect is only potential until it moves into actuality, i.e., once the bridge is constructed. The bridge was potential (or possible) in the architect's mind, then became actual when constructed—but not by itself. The architect was the "mover," that is, the one who moved the potential bridge to become an actual bridge. If there were no construction, the bridge would be potential forever. Only something already actual can move something into potential, and then into being actual.

Aquinas reasoned that the universe before creation was potential until something or someone moved it from its potential state. In other words, it went from being a potential universe to an actual universe. Now, since everything has a beginning, everything was potential at one point. Only something always *actual* could be considered a supreme being. Now if God had a maker, then that means there was a point where there was no God. So what would have moved Him from a potential to an actual God? Aquinas concludes there must have been something that always existed, the prime mover (God), who moves everything from being possible to being actual.

The second method used by Aquinas is called *Causality*. This has to do with the principle of cause and effect, where a succeeding stage is caused by a preceding stage, like a domino effect. All phases are dependent, and no stage can explain itself independent from another. This is nothing but putting one and one together. Every effect has a cause, otherwise it would not exist. You and I, for instance, are effects, and our parents are the cause. Using this logic, we can backtrack in time to find the first cause, or the cause that gave cause to all causes. It had no cause, since it has always existed. The reason for all purposes or causes, the prime mover or supreme being, is God. The universe could not have been its own cause. It could no more come together, with all its varying laws, than a football stadium or a perfectly working aircraft. Therefore, there must be an uncaused cause that toppled the first domino and began the chain reaction.

A colleague of mine brought up the point that quantum physics debunks causality. In order to remain within the scope of this book, all I will say is if cause and effect do not exist, then everything breaks down. These writings would be no different than gibberish such as [ap#$so9dJU&^%$feou. In other words, there would be no meaning or knowledge. The very existence of theories supposes causality. Without causality, we would not even be. What must be understood is that all causes are not necessary. My colleague narrowed his arguments of cause and effect to unnecessary causes only, and concluded that since some causes are not required, then none are. To add some light to a confusing topic, take for example Thomas Edison, who invented the lightbulb. Long after his death, electricity is still powering lightbulbs. He is not a necessary cause; electricity is. We can also take ourselves as an example. As much as some of us boast of our importance at work, the fact is, if we were to die today, someone would replace us tomorrow. We are not necessary for the survival of our company or employer.

Anyway, in our conversation my colleague also mentioned that if God created the universe, then who created God? Why does causation have to stop with God? Why can't it go forever? First, the evidence does not show the universe to be infinitely old (Big Bang). Aquinas answered this question by thinking of God as the author of a novel. The events in the book happen in a logical order. Something that occurs in the beginning is the cause of something that happens in the middle or the end. But the author is the cause of the story on a remarkably higher level. The rules of causation that apply within the novel do not apply to its author. If some unanticipated character appears in the middle of the story, it is logical to ask, where did this character come from? But it is not logical to ask where the author came from. He is outside of the narrative, and the fact that he created something in his story cannot be grasped fully by the character in the story. God is outside of nature looking at his creation. We are in space and time as part of the story. That is why God is known as eternal. He is outside of time; we are in the realm of time. Being that He is outside of space and time, it makes sense that He would transcend the laws of cause and effect.

Lastly, we have what is called the argument of *Gradation*. There is a natural law of hierarchy in the universe that we use to rank things from least to greatest. Relationships of degree require a reference to the *"utmost."* For example, a thing is said to be colder only because it resembles closer that which is the utmost coldest. The max in any given is considered to be the *cause* of the standard. Aquinas reasoned that there must be something that is the cause of our nature, virtues, and every other noble ideal. That being responsible is the one we refer to as God. He is the utmost, or standard, by which we measure holiness, love, power, goodness, etc. To put this into perspective, consider when a person calls another person "good." To whom are they comparing them? A neighbor? A family member? A saint? There is only one who is good and who can be considered to be the utmost. God.

There are many more details and volumes of work by great thinkers that we are not going to cover. We are just touching the tip of the iceberg here. Even so, it leaves me dumbfounded how atheists dismiss these thinkers as "ridiculous." They are far from ridiculous. Instead, they should make us think about the powerful claims of reality.

Scientific Considerations

"For the scientist who has lived by his faith in the power of reason, the story ends like a bad dream. He has scaled the mountains of ignorance; he is about to conquer the highest peak; as he pulls himself over the final rock, he is greeted by a band of theologians who have been sitting there for centuries."

— Robert Jastrow

Until now we have only been employing reason to make a case for a deity. Let us depart from this topic via a couple of scientific considerations. While skeptics may claim there is no scientific evidence of God, let's see what the laws of thermodynamics have to say.

The first law of thermodynamics states that while energy can convert into matter, and matter into energy, there can never be an increase or a decrease in the combined amount of both. So, however much energy and matter is now combined in the universe, there can never have been any more or any less. The total amount remains constant. All it can do is transform from matter to energy or energy to matter. So if thermodynamics states that one can never have an increase or decrease of matter and energy, where did it come from in the first place? It cannot have created itself, since something does not come from nothing. The question then becomes, how did we get all the matter and energy in the universe if there is no God? Especially when we know that the universe is not infinitely old but had a finite beginning. The bottom line is, all the matter and energy we have cannot come into existence on its own, yet here we see everything around us. Why do we have something rather than nothing at all? Personally, it is difficult to accept that the universe created itself with no outside stimulus. Maybe a necessary and eternal Being does exist.

The second law of thermodynamics has much to say about the age of the universe. Its theological implications are evident. While the first law states that quantity remains the same, the second law says the quality of matter/energy deteriorates gradually over time. This is because energy is used for assembly and restoration. In this process, energy diminishes. This is the reason why our bodies eventually break down (entropy). Aging is what the second law of thermodynamics boils down to. In space, things are also getting old. So the universe is constantly losing energy and never gaining, much like a cup of hot tea slowly losing heat. That being the case, one can conclude that the universe is not infinitely old, which raises many questions for the skeptic. If the universe were infinitely old, certainly enough time would have passed to dissipate its finite amount of energy. The bottom line is, per the second law of thermodynamics the universe had a finite beginning—its youngest possible state. Like a wound clock, the universe is winding down. The question is, who wound the clock?

Some atheists say the universe and its contents are eternal in some sort of repetitive cycle. It boils down to two choices: having an eternal universe recycling itself, or an eternal God. Even accepting the atheist's argument of matter being eternal, we know there was a time when there was no life on Earth; therefore, there was a time when life began. We now run into another massive wall in attempting to explain how life began on Earth in the first place, let alone how the universe was created.

As stated, there is too much to be said on these issues. A plethora of material can be found on these subjects. Therefore, it is imperative to continue one's pursuit. Let us proceed to some of the most popular arguments against a deity.

ARGUMENTS AGAINST GOD

"Question with boldness even the existence of a god; because, if there be one, he must more approve of the homage of reason, than that of blindfolded fear."

— *Thomas Jefferson*

"The most formidable weapon against errors of every kind is Reason. I have never used any other, and I trust I never shall."

— *Thomas Paine*

Darwinism

One of the most popular arguments embraced by atheists is Darwin's theory of evolution and its idea of "survival of the fittest." The theory contends to explain the state of man today. We evolve and survive through what is called natural selection: Nature favors species that overcome and adapt to their environment, resulting in their survival. We have heard it said that only the strong survive. Those strong individuals will pass their survival genes on to their descendants, and so on down the line, while the weak, or those who fail to adapt, die off. That is the theory in a nutshell.

On the surface the theory makes sense, but it is not without its critics. One of them is Dr. Michael Behe, who argues against Darwinism in his book *Darwin's Black Box*. Behe essentially explains how the organic world is so complex at the level of molecular biology that unguided evolution cannot be responsible for it. Opponents decry his book as being nothing more than yet another argument for intelligent design. Some accuse Dr. Behe (a Christian) of misrepresenting the facts, of approaching the work as a creationist rather than with a scientific (i.e., neutral) mind. Though some may disagree with Dr. Behe's assessments, he certainly raises powerful ideas worthy of consideration.

It must be understood that there is no conflict between evolution and faith. The creation story in the Book of Genesis was written thousands of years before the age of scientific thinking. *It was intended to convey religious truth, not give scientific details about the world.* The primary theme in the Book of Genesis is that God is the creator and source of all life. Now, I do not deny evolution, to an extent. Evolution could explain why some insects become immune to certain types of pesticide, or why we humans no longer need an appendix, for example. But the believer's position on evolution is that God created all *and is also responsible for the evolution we know through His creative acts* (D'Souza 153).

It is a mistake to compare us blindly to animals as if we were on the same level due solely to our ability to adapt. We may share commonalities with animals, but there are grave differences. We are not mere animals; we are glorified animals endowed with indestructible souls, intellect, and free will. We are made in the image of God, not King Kong. Our similarities are due to the harmony and unity of life, being that we come from the one great designer. To quote theologian Leslie Rumble, "We cannot argue that because a superior principle [i.e., humans] is capable of lower operations [i.e., animals], an inferior principle is capable of higher operations. Nor can we say that an inferior principle could be endowed with higher powers, when those higher powers belong to a completely different order of being" (3:12).

It is also worth noting that Darwin's theory of evolution is exactly that, a theory. In his writings, Darwin put forth many ideas on how one species may have led to another, but he offered no evidence regarding what is known as "transitional forms." In other words, if we are half monkey, we should find some evidence of a half-human/half-monkey creature. This should also apply to all other animals. Darwin writes, in *On the Origin of Species*, "Why, if species have descended from other species by fine gradations, do we not everywhere see innumerable transitional forms? ... As by this theory innumerable transitional forms must have existed, why do we not find them embedded in countless numbers in the crust of the earth?" What fossil evidence suggests is that species appear distinct and unchanged, not transitional. A great read on this subject is Ray Comfort's *How to Know God Exists*.

Besides the lack of transitional evidence, Darwinians run into a wall in explaining where life began in the first place. Darwin didn't even try to explain the origin of life itself. He assumed the first living organism and tried to explain how one thing leads to another. Again, one can't argue that Darwinism isn't true to a certain extent, but where did life come from? That is the burning question! In order for there to be biological evolution there must be life in the first place. Did non-living or lifeless matter contemplate itself into spontaneously becoming this complex matter we are today, as some suggest?

Many experiments have been done in an attempt to prove that life can begin on its own. One of the more popular theories worthy of noting involves a fallen comet. This idea challenges whether life began on Earth at all, proposing that it came here from a distant world via comet or asteroid. If life came to Earth the way a bee spreads pollen, this still fails to account for the beginning of life itself, wherever it sprouted. Another theory, known as the RNA world hypothesis, explains how RNA guided the primitive stages of life, but it doesn't explain how RNA came to exist in the first place. A third idea, known as the Random Chance Theory, states that the universe is infinitely old, and because of this was supplied enough time and the proper conditions for the building blocks of life to form. Mainstream science rejected this idea through radiation testing that concluded the universe is not infinitely old, but only about 14.5 billion years old, while Earth is about five billion years old. (If the universe is infinitely old, as some believe, one has to wonder how today can even exist, since it would take an infinite amount of time for it to come about.) Even with a known beginning, in regards to random chance Dr. Behe states that the probability of creating just one protein molecule (a building block of life) by chance would be the same as a blindfolded man finding one marked grain of sand in the Sahara, and then doing it twice more. Along the same lines, Frederick Hoyle said that the chances of life emerging on its own are about as likely as a tornado going through a junkyard and assembling a fully operational Boeing 747. It is safe to say that the probability of life emerging on its own is zero (Strobel 142).

Other theories suggest that life emerged from clay or from vents in the oceans. I have not come across any scientist holding fast to any of these theories. Life, to even be possible, is a miracle in itself. If anything were different, we would not exist. Some atheists contend that however astronomical the chances of us being here, those were the circumstances. If it were another set of conditions, then something else would have existed. Quite often, nonbelievers explain issues away or place them in the "got lucky" basket. They demand concrete evidence of God, but their own theories are only speculation. On the surface, their hypotheses have a certain allure, but when examined more closely, their arguments fall to pieces.

∎∎∎

> *"Only a rookie who knows nothing about science would say science takes away from faith. If you really study science, it will bring you closer to God."*
>
> — James Tour

In tackling evolution, Dinesh D'Souza makes a noteworthy point. He considers the question of why humans would evolve in such a fashion as to believe in things that don't exist, such as God. What evolutionary advantage is offered by a belief in God, since such belief requires sacrifice, time, money, and self-giving (D'Souza 14)? "The greatest among you shall be the servant of all," Christ said. This goes completely against survival of the fittest, which is all about watching out for number one. There is no evolutionary advantage or survival edge for the believer, since nature would not favor such a gene. So why does the overwhelming majority believe in a higher power? Why are we such spirituality-seeking creatures? We can go to the farthest corner of the earth and find people in isolation worshipping a higher power. Why?

D'Souza cites atheist Richard Dawkins who speculates that "The idea of immortality survives and spreads because it caters to wishful thinking" (14). He then counters by stating that it doesn't make evolutionary sense for minds to develop comforting beliefs that are ultimately false. For instance, how would it benefit someone to believe in Santa Claus to make himself feel good about the holidays, knowing that he doesn't exist? Steven Pinker writes, "A freezing person finds no comfort in believing he is warm." Wishful thinking does not alter the reality of the matter; it goes out the window when one's limbs don't function due to extreme frostbite. In the same way, it would make no evolutionary sense for a person to believe he was created by a God who has plans for him, versus being purely a biological entity (D'Souza 14-15). And if a mind harbors some (untrue) belief for its own benefit, couldn't we say the same for atheism?

What we must ask is why nature would breed people who seek no higher purpose in life. The grave is our final resting place according to atheists. It is natural for those who have a sense of purpose to live longer and happier lives than those who don't. In this respect, it seems Darwinism does not help atheism.

Evil and Suffering

"If God would concede me His omnipotence for 24 hours, you would see how many changes I would make in the world. But if He gave me His wisdom too, I would leave things as they are"

— J.M.L. Monsabre

"God whispers to us in our pleasures, speaks in our conscience, but shouts in our pains."

— C.S. Lewis

One of the toughest conflicts people of faith confront and nonbelievers tenaciously hold on to is reconciling a benevolent God with the suffering and evils of this world. What becomes of the idea of a loving and omnipotent God in the face of so many atrocities? It is an age-old question. Well, if the horrors of this world disprove God, using this logic, we can also say that since much good exists, therefore God exists—but it's not that simple.

There is no denying the reality of suffering and evil. At times it can be difficult to associate this world with a caring God. But the fact that we are outraged at the horrible things that occur connects us to a standard of goodness by which we judge the defectiveness of this world. The only way we know of evil is through the lack of goodness to be found. We use a standard of goodness to measure what ought to be. This points us to an objective moral law which can only have its origin in the being we know as God. So in a sense, the problems of the world can be used as an argument for God, since justice says that *this life cannot be all*.

To be direct and to the point, I acknowledge that evil presents a great obstacle to faith, but to me it is simple. Evil is the result of having the freedom of choice. That is the best way to summarize this predicament. Our free will gives us maneuvering room to make decisions, whether good or bad, therefore, the possibility of evil arises. Sirach 15:14-17 states, "When God, in the beginning, created man, he made him subject to his own free choice. If you choose, you can keep the commandments ... Before men are life and death, whichever he chooses shall be given to him." God has made us masters of our own destiny. We have been endowed with free will, and due to our poor choices, evil and suffering exist. If men are free to choose good, they must also be able to choose evil. Creating a world where there is free will and no possibility of sin repels logic. If force is used to prevent evil, one takes away freedom. To avoid evil, God must take away our freedom, which would make us something other than human. Without free will, we would be no different than a machine, and a machine cannot love. Love is the very purposes of our being.

As for death and suffering, we must comprehend they are a part of life and the natural order. They will come to us in numerous ways, but this world is not all there is. Besides, much of the suffering we incur is due to our own negligence. We drink and smoke, and then complain that we must undergo a painful surgical procedure. It's puzzling also why atheists complain about the "horrors" of this world. It there is no God, war and suffering are purely a result of biological or evolutionary function. There should be nothing wrong with these things; it's just nature taking its course.

■ ■ ■

Evil and suffering are hard to bear for nonbelievers and believers alike, but faith in God was never intended to annihilate these hardships. Rather, faith gives a person hope and joy in the midst of misery. We can also legitimately rationalize some of the difficulties with this issue by observing those who go without proper provisions. The world produces enough to provide for everyone. An argument against God would be valid if He failed to provide for our basic needs such as food, water, and shelter, but He has given this world for us to govern. Man is to blame for the mishandling and injustices of this world. This is where much rectification is needed ... in us. One can only imagine a world where men genuinely looked out for each other's welfare, where selfishness, greed, and other vices were put aside. What else is God to do? If He were to interfere with every diabolical deed of men, this would be something other than Earth. Rectification will come in due course.

Even with the reality of evil and suffering, God takes that which is not so good and turns it into something good. Atrocities and disparities have the potential for a greater good, but not everyone capitalizes on those potentials. Not all of us learn from the dramas of life. As we face trials and tribulations, we sometimes can't imagine any good emerging. We can all relate to going through some ordeal and becoming better, stronger, and wiser. Gold is refined in fire. Diamonds are made under pressure. We learn through hardships. "Prosperity is a great teacher; adversity a greater," as William Hazlitt said. The greatest believers throughout history will confirm that what doesn't break us makes us stronger. By overcoming and enduring obstacles, we develop moral character, perseverance, and hope. As a result of being tested, we will have a testimony to share with others, and will be witnesses to the strength God has given us in order to overcome challenges.

Sometimes, as harsh as it may sound, it is best for a person to suffer for their own good, as any parent or teacher will attest. "You live and you learn," as a friend likes to say. In the midst of affliction, we learn lessons that can't be learned anywhere else. We can't put everyone else's burdens on our shoulders, as much as we would like to. The fact is, a proper amount of affliction can be healthy. Whether working hard in the gym to make the football team or taking extra classes while working forty-hour weeks to become more competitive in the job market, affliction serves a purpose. Even catastrophic events in life help us maintain perspective and help us grow interiorly or mentally.

The miseries of this world have also served to lead countless people to God. Those who obtain all the pleasures of this world *might* be hindered in their salvation. Suffering teaches us to not set our hopes or ambitions in this world only, as if this world were all there is. If suffering leads to the salvation of souls, then it is worthwhile. Life is not just about comfort. This life involves training and preparation for eternity. But don't believe for a second that those who inflict suffering are getting away with their deeds. If justice does not catch up in this life, death cannot be escaped. There will come a day when God will bring every deed into account, whether good or evil. Justice delayed is not justice denied.

■ ■ ■

For those who persist in questioning what God ought to be doing, remember that if we were God, we would be doing the same thing as Him. We look at the matter from a human perspective only. As J.M.L. Monsabre wrote, "If God would concede me His omnipotence for twenty-four hours, you would see how many changes I would make in the world. But if He gave me His wisdom too, I would leave things as they are" (Lutzer 193).Whatever our ideas, they are certainly wrong if they conflict with God's. Instead of questioning Him on how things should be, as if we were almighty, let us do something about the problems we encounter. We find ourselves in circumstances or environments that require attention so that we may do something about it. We are the instruments or tools He uses to do good. So in the same way that we ask, "Why doesn't God do anything?" He will also be inquiring of us why we didn't do something. Because that's why He put us in the situation.

What's interesting is that most people around the world have it much harder than we do in the United States, and yet, they endure because of their faith. We take our comforts for granted. Even with our many consolations, we must remember that we as Christians are followers of a crucified master and should not be surprised if we are called to walk a similar path. We all have crosses to carry. If suffering was true for Christ, then it is true for us. The disciple is not above his master. We often cry out, "Why, God, why me?" If we can ask this question, we should also be able to ask, "Why not me?"

In the end, when we are in His presence the suffering we have endured will not matter. Everything will be made right. "Trust in the Lord with all your heart and lean not on your own understanding" (Proverbs 3:5-6). Some of these answers may not satisfy certain readers who question God. Perhaps we will never grasp the problem of evil and suffering in our earthly state. Here is what the Lord had to say to Job about his difficulties: "Brace yourself like a man; I will question you, and you shall answer me. Where were you when I laid the earth's foundation? Tell me, if you understand. Who marked off its dimensions? Surely you know! Who stretched a measuring line across it? On what were its footing set, or who laid its cornerstone. Have you ever given orders to the morning, or shown the dawn its place? Have you journeyed to the springs of the sea or walked in the recesses of the deep? Have you comprehended the vast expanses of the earth? Tell me, if you know all this" (Job 38:3-6,12,16,18, *New International Version*).

The Subject of Hell

"Hell is God's great compliment to the reality of human freedom and the dignity of human choice."

— G.K. Chesterton

"There are only two kinds of people, in the end: those who say to God, 'Thy will be done,' and those to whom God says, in the end, 'Thy will be done.'"

— C.S. Lewis

Some years ago I was in Daytona Beach visiting old college friends, some of whom I had not seen in almost a decade. I had dinner and reminisced about the "good old days" with a good buddy of mine and his family. In one of our prolonged conversations, the subject of God and religion came up. I was surprised to hear the disparity we had in our shared Christian faith, specifically when they expressed a belief that there is no such thing as Hell. I was under the impression Hell was a fundamental teaching of Christianity and that Christ spoke about the subject. The non-existence of Hell was a familiar argument, one expected from spiritualists and atheists, but coming from fellow believers it was quite a surprise. What was I missing? The problem of Christian denominations was the culprit. This is a topic we will later tackle in detail. But, since many believers and non-believers raise this subject of Hell, it is worth highlighting in this section.

■ ■ ■

The theological debate on Hell must be examined more closely, since the topic raises many issues. If God is love, why would He send people to Hell for eternity? Can God and Hell co-exist? For one to say God is love, yet Hell exists, sounds almost contradictory. But those who only think of God as being soft-hearted, lenient, or compassionate have only a partial understanding of His character. God is loving and merciful, but He is holy, just, and detests sin. People want to think about the more soothing virtues of love and tenderness, while forgetting the tough virtues of holiness, righteousness, and justice (Strobel 242).

Nonetheless, we are confronted with difficult and legitimate questions. Why do finite sins in a life that is as fleeting as the wind warrant infinite punishment? It doesn't sound fair-minded, but then, we often commit the error of substituting our definition of fair when discussing the infinite wisdom and justice of God. Philosopher J.P. Moreland explains that the degree to which a person warrants punishment is not a function of the length of time it took to commit a crime (Strobel 252). He gives the example of someone pulling a trigger in an act of murder. It may take only one second to do, but the consequence can be life in prison. On the other hand, stealing somebody's seventy-two-inch plasma TV may take much longer, including the time it takes to scheme and plot. If caught, one will end up getting fined and maybe doing time behind bars. But the degree of someone's just punishment is not a function of how long it took to commit a crime, but rather, it is a function of how atrocious the deed itself was, Moreland explains.

We can agree that stealing a TV is not as bad as killing someone; hence, the difference in punishment. That brings up a crucial point in this particular discussion: What is the most heinous act a person can commit, the one that warrants the highest penalty? I agree with apologist and author Ravi Zacharias on this topic. It is not murder, rape, or animal torture. It is not stealing from the poor or hungry, human trafficking, or dealing drugs. The most heinous act a person can commit is to mock and reject the one who created him. Why? Because the individual who rapes, steals, or kills can still recover from those deeds. There is redemption for that person as long as he still breathes. God's forgiveness is greater than any sin! But what redemption is there for someone who disowns and rejects God? There is none (Strobel 222). Scripture tells us, "If a man sins against another man, one can intercede for him with the Lord; but if a man sins against the Lord, who will intercede for him" (1 Samuel 2:25) The greatest law states: "You shall Love the Lord, your God, with all your heart, with all your being, with all your strength and with all your mind" (Luke 10:27). It makes sense that the ultimate sin is to discard God and all He has done for us. In the physical world, homicide is usually the most heinous crime, calling for the ultimate sentence, life in prison, and in some states even death. Similarly, in the spiritual realm there is an ultimate sanction, that is, separation from God for eternity. Hell.

We must take into account who we are offending. In other words, the degree of authority and dignity we insult must be considered. A young man, for instance, faces consequences for wronging his brother or cousin, but harsher ones for defying his parents. The severity of his actions would be even greater if he defied a police officer, judge, military leader, or government official. He would be penalized even more significantly if he tried to harm a president, prime minister, emperor, or king. The higher up the chain an offense occurs, the greater the transgression. *The penalty for our actions is directly proportional to the office, dignity, and authority we are offending.* God is infinitely Holy, and those who sin against immeasurable dignity and authority incur an infinite penalty. Sin must be punished; if it is not, the holiness and righteousness of God means nothing. From our perspective, it may seem harsh. Our rebellion against God may not seem so serious, but from the standpoint of a loving and just God, who gave us life and so much more, our rebellion is a very serious matter.

For those condemned to Hell, many wonder, why does God not offer a second chance? That question assumes God did not do His part for that person's salvation while they lived. He does everything needed for a person to respond to Him. No one will be standing before Him claiming, "If only I had a little more time," or "If only my circumstances were different." He grants the necessary time and circumstances. And whatever our circumstances, we can be sure the perfect judge of all will do what is just.

It must be mentioned that God laments the necessity of Hell and the wickedness of men's choices. "The Lord was grieved ... and His heart was filled with pain," as we read in Genesis 6:6. He doesn't get some sort of malicious satisfaction. Unfortunately, we are a good creation gone astray. Ultimately, whatever we choose He will respect. We have a tendency to treat God like we do a schoolteacher. We say, "Mr. Anderson gave me an F," instead of saying, "I earned an F." We never account for our lack of effort or study, but start the blame game. In the same manner, we accuse God of sending people to Hell, but we choose to go to Hell through our own choices. God simply honors our decision. That is what free will is all about. If we are truly meant to be free, but God does not honor our choices, the universe would be off balance.

The bottom line is, He does not force anyone to do anything. If He did, He would be dehumanizing us. When God allows people to say *no* to Him, He actually respects them, as Moreland states (Strobel 254). Hell is really the final "handing over" of what we want.

■ ■ ■

It would take too long to go into detail, but one more popular concern that frequently arises must be mentioned. Why did God create people He knew would go to Hell? Does He not know the future? To try to answer this question, we must take the example of a married couple. Would a couple avoid having children because of the possibility that one of their children might become rebellious during their delicate teenage years? Knowledge of future action does not mean the parent is responsible for the child's misconduct when it occurs, or that their knowledge made the teenager act. It does not make sense to avoid having children simply because they might turn out bad. What about those who would have been good? The atheist would say, "But God knows for a fact who will be bad. Why allow them to be born?" If God arranged it so that only good people were born, then that would be a world without humans again. Free will must contain the possibility of rejecting Him. What would the skeptic have God do? Remove free will so that no one can be blamed for their actions and we'd be no different than machines? If only those who go to Heaven are born, then how are we truly free, if God is in the background manipulating the cards?

One of the greatest tricks the devil ever pulled was making people believe they have all the time in the world to make changes. The reality is, tomorrow is promised to no one. Each passing day should serve as a reminder that we will eventually face our mortality and that we should take inventory of ourselves. Hell is real. God does not like it and neither do we, but He simply cannot allow everyone into Heaven regardless of their moral state. If so, a murdering rapist would have a ticket in. Such abomination cannot be associated with God's holiness. The truth is, Hell will forever be a place that respects human choice.

ATHEIST COMMENTS AND RESPONSES

"Have you come to believe because you have seen me? Blessed are those who have not seen and have believed."

-John 20:29

What follows are some discussions I have come across with atheists via online discussion boards and face-to-face encounters. It's impressive how people can be so far apart on a given subject. One seeks common ground but finds very little, if any. It seems the only commonality is trying to change each other's minds. I suppose that is the goal of debating. Though being far apart, it follows that one is correct, the other incorrect. The question of God's existence is either yes or no, with no in-between.

Here are some sample dialogues:

Comment: For whatever reason you falsely believe one can't judge anything without a transcendent moral standard, but we can by using empathy based on the principle of reciprocity. In other words, treat others how you want to be treated. It's really simple with no need for a fictitious absolute moral standard. In fact, so many examples can be made to counter moral absolutism as to reduce it to absurdity.

Response: Empathy. Is that the source and standard of morals for an atheist? Where is the empathy of an atheist when he kills, steals, cheats, etc.? Why do you call these actions wrong when other atheists don't subscribe to your standard of "empathy"? Why do they commit these acts when they do not want them reciprocated on them? What if they enjoy hurting others—are they justified in their conduct? Empathy or not, one can dislike a person due to prejudice, cultural reasons, political position, etc., but we are still called to treat others with dignity and respect regardless of whether we have a single drop of empathy for them. Why must we treat others with decency regardless of whether we like them is what you must ponder. Or are you making the case that we must stoop to the level of ignorant behavior of others because we have no empathy for them? No, we are called to rise above ignorant behavior. The compassion you speak of just means behavior you personally don't like.

But please tell me whose standard of empathy we are using to call an action empathetic. Yours? Why yours and not some other atheist who is unsympathetic to the suffering of children in Africa or the poor around the world? What about the millionaire atheist donating $50 to a humanitarian cause—shall we use his standard of empathy? Or is he cheap according to you?

The fact is, atheism ultimately means no soul, no human rights, no human dignity, no meaning in life, no objective morality, no free will, no moral obligation or accountability, etc. This universe is nothing more than an accident that produces humans only for seeking pleasure, selfishness, and survival. In the end, nothing needed for meaningful morality is grounded in atheism, yet I have seen you talk about how others ought to behave!

Comment: I bet you feel bad when you are cruel to others. Likewise, I wager you feel good when you do something decent. Since we've evolved in a social setting, we have foster what we call morality in response to the need to interact cooperatively with other members within a group.

Response: One cannot grind this to what feels good or what feels bad. That is entirely subjective and does not explain why we must do right regardless of how we feel. But to answer your question, sometimes it feels good to do the wrong thing, and by the same token, sometimes it doesn't feel so good to do the right thing. Yet, we are still called to do what is right. Your concept of feelings implodes on itself.

Comment: As atheists, my colleagues and I have no wish to hurt anyone. We do not need archaic writings telling us murder, stealing, adultery, and so forth is wrong.
Response: And what about those who wish to harm others for their benefit? Let's not be that naïve. First of all, morality does not come from any religion itself or "archaic writings." Morality transcends the material realm. Again, why is it that you try to act in a manner which would be considered "good?" How do you have the audacity to judge adultery wrong when others think quite differently about sleeping around? What you must contemplate is where your moral standard comes from that allows you to criticize others' behavior as wrong. What you find is that it will point you to the author of all right. If morality were a matter of opinion, you would have no basis for calling adultery, lying, murder, or stealing for economic gain wrong.

One has to wonder why it even matters whether atheists follow a moral code, whatever it may be. What does it matter in the end if an atheist acts one way rather than another, given the meaningless of life? Why put morality first and self-centeredness second?

Comment: Do yourself a favor and free yourself from the burden of religious restrictions. You'll thank me for it in the future.
Response: I understand the way of the atheist is generally to give vent to whatever he wishes, but what I want to know specifically is, what restrictions do you wish for me to get rid of? What am I supposed to free myself from? Am I not supposed to free myself from the grips of vice? From following my own appetites and bulldozing those who stand in my way? Should I not be reminded to stay away from depravities such as lying,

pride, greed, lust, and stealing? From treating all with dignity and respect even though I may not always want to? This and a hundred other things is what my faith inspires and teaches me to do, and it continues to pound on me because of my concupiscence or my tendency to go astray. It teaches me to die to myself when I want to do the exact opposite of what I ought to do. I am constantly reminded of my failings in order to keep myself in check and become a better man.

What else am I supposed to free myself from? Tell me. A God who loves me despite all of my imperfections? A God who is mindful of me and wants the best for me? A God who wants a relationship with me? A Master who says, "Come and learn from Me," and who wants me to live an abundant life? What am I to free myself from? What restrictions? From His laws and decrees that are in place to protect me and for my benefit? From giving money to do charitable works around the globe? I take it, then, that I should turn towards the way of the atheist ... but for what purpose and what meaning, when atheism ultimately means no purpose and no meaning? I don't get this "free yourself from religion" theme song from seculars. On the contrary, we should be fleeing towards Him. May I suggest freeing *yourself* from this MTV/Hollywood culture and its lack of thinking, its "I don't have time to pick up a book" and "Everything I read on the internet is true," its worship of Miley Cyrus, Kim Kardashian, Thug Life, and Twitter; its belief that government is god or some politician is savior, this money-chasing "I do whatever I want, it's all about me, myself and I" generation? That is what you should free yourself from.

Comment: I have had so many bad experiences with religious people, and those experiences are enough to prove that God and religion is a farce.
Response: I put atheists in three categories. There are those who are only concerned about the affairs of this world, and their arguments really have no backbone. They simply want to indulge in whatever they wish, on demand. We know it is very attractive at the flesh level, so they simply dismiss whatever calls them to restraint.

Secondly, you have the category of atheists who have had bad experiences, through no fault of their own, in a religious institution and/or a church, or with other religious people. They have been wrongly mistreated or shunned by their so-called believing parents, friends or family members, and they are rightfully upset. Although this is very unfortunate and saddening, and hopefully one day things can be rectified or they can come to an understanding of the inevitable distortions of men, it still remains that ill experiences have no bearing on the fact that God is. I myself have had horrendous encounters with believers, and I can sympathize with and understand where such people are coming from, but God is not to blame. Due to these unpleasant experiences, people hold grudges and become indignant towards this heavenly figure who is all-loving and caring. In their mind, God is responsible, or they conclude He is not real. Then they begin to entertain all sorts of false ideas about God, and spread them; thereby, dismissing faith altogether.

Lastly, you have the intellectually weak atheist, whose argument basically is that because there are false religions, they are all false. Or because men have committed heinous acts in the name of religion, all religion is wicked. Regardless of the travesties of men, God still is, and His existence is not determined by our conduct, good or bad. God is, whether we break His commandments or follow them. He is, regardless of the failures of people of faith. He IS, regardless of all the falsehood that has been spread in His name.

Comment: "It is the greatest happiness of the greatest number that is the measure of right and wrong," as philosopher Jeremy Bentham stated, not some invented God.
Response: That would hardly do to those left outside the circle of happiness. Philosophers have attempted to rationalize right and wrong, and even quantified pain and pleasure through some algorithm, to no avail. Philosopher Henry Sidgwick attempted to keep the notion of God out of morality, only to admit that the problem remains unsolvable without involving God. In *The Methods of Ethics* he writes, "...the prolonged effort of the human intellect to frame a perfect ideal of rational conduct is seen to have been foredoomed to inevitable failure" (Rooney154).

Comment: We are nothing but matter.
Response: What we are is composition of both matter and soul. Our skin and bones cannot think and love, for example. Renowned theologian Father Leslie Rumble explains: "The soul is the difference between a corpse and a living being. A dead body cannot move, eat, think, express itself, enjoy or be miserable. It can but fall to pieces and go back to dust. There is something that stops your body from doing that now. It is your soul. For every activity, you must find a principle of operation behind it. The principle in a man which thinks and loves, and is happy or miserable, is a very real thing. It is not nothing that very body animates. Nor is it a chemical formula. No doctor, examining a corpse, can tell you what chemical is missing that it should not live. If there be nothing else save chemical substances, let doctors and scientists gather together the requisite chemicals and say, 'Live!' They can affect nothing like this. There is something that chemistry cannot reach; it is the soul or spirit" (1:7).

Comment: What do people even mean by the term "God?"
Response: I can only quote Father Carty, who was asked the same question and answered so eloquently. "God is a spiritual, substantial, personal being, infinite in intelligence, in will, and in all perfections, absolutely simple or lacking composition, immutable, happy in Himself and by Himself, and infinitely superior to all that is or can be conceived apart from Himself. He is incomprehensible in His infinite perfection by all lesser intelligences, although knowable as to the fact of His existence as Living Creator and Lord of Heaven and earth, almighty, eternal, immense, and distinct from all that He has created" *(*1: 2*)*. That is what is meant by God.

Comment: Have you heard of the God paradox which states God is not omnipotent because it is contradictory? If not, consider this: Can God create a rock so big that he cannot lift it? Or "If God is all powerful, could God create a being more powerful than himself?" If He can't do these things He is not all powerful; if he is not all powerful, he is not God.
Response: I have heard of the paradox, but it seems you have not heard some of the replies by theists. God is capable of anything that is not a

self-contradiction. The "paradox" is as nonsensical as saying since God created the universe, He is not all powerful, because He cannot make Himself *not* be the creator of the universe at the same time! Just because one can put a sentence together does not mean it makes any sense. All powerful includes wisdom as well. God cannot do something infinitely imprudent, since it is against His nature. Again, the erroneous logic is like saying that God is not all powerful since He cannot sin like men. I would venture to say that there are things an omnipotent being can't do, like make Himself stupid.

Comment: The inconsistent revelations of the Christian Bible, the Muslim Koran, the Hindu Vedas, the Book of Mormon, etc., prove that this God of truth does not exist. Science can at least agree. There is no African science or European science, etc. There is just science.

Response: There is no doubt there are contradictions between religions. They are not the same, as evidenced by their teachings, so contradictions are no surprise and are expected. The only common attribute these scriptures contain is that there is a God of some sort. What we must do is separate and judge each religion by its own merits, but it does not follow that because there are erroneous beliefs there is no right religion. If various companies are producing a bootleg version of a Rolex watch, it doesn't mean a genuine Rolex is not in the midst.

But even in sciences we can see geographic differences in "revelations." What is possible and knowable in most advanced countries in the world may not be knowable to those living in the Amazon or third world countries because of lack knowledge. A particular Truth (capital T, whether religious or not) being known in one area does not automatically equate to it being known in all areas (although that capital-T Truth does apply regardless of ignorance and sincerity). The same principles apply in the spiritual realm, which is more difficult to ascertain, since it is not material.

Now different religions and cultures will not agree because one must allow room for the distortions of men, sincere although ignorant disposition of men, perversions, free will, etc. Human reason and emotions are not frozen. Man's inner being is much more complex than observing the scientific fact that the sun rises in the east and sets in the west. We are dealing with two realms of reality: the physical (science) and the metaphysical (immaterial) domains. They are two different beasts. Through science, we invented the atomic bomb, but it cannot answer the question of how it should be used. Inventing a bomb is fixed. How to use it is not. There is an immense difference.

By the way, would you really say that all scientists agree on all scientific matters? Are there really no disagreements in the scientific community?

Comment: A topic worth mentioning regarding the many religions in the world deals with Pascal's Wager. Philosopher Denis Diderot refutes Pascal's claim by stating there are actually many wagers to be made. Pascal only dealt with the Christian God, but there are countless other gods to choose from. Pascal would live according to his Catholic God, but die and be damned for not believing in Zeus, Krishna, Allah, the Moon God, Thor, or the Spaghetti Monster.

Response: Pascal's Wager remains intact, for his position is that it is more reasonable to believe than to not. Believing puts odds on one's side. If one had to pick their destiny from a deck of cards, for example, the nonbeliever's chance of winning would be zero, since he selects none. In the meantime, at least Pascal chose the Christian God, putting himself in a position of advantage. Select a card as Pascal did. You refuse even to pick one, guaranteeing that you lose. Even if the nonbeliever were right in refusing to select, he could hardly rejoice or boast about his decision rotting in the ground.

In addition, Pascal was a brilliant man and I "wager" that he did his homework; thereby, dismissing the god of thunder Thor, Zeus, the Spaghetti Monster, and so forth, stacking chances further in his favor. He knew there were countless gods fabricated by the imaginations of men. But for an opinion or idea to have any backbone or substance behind it, it must have good reasons. Pascal, I'm sure, as a man of reason, found there were no good reasons for believing in Thor or any moon god, while there are many Good reasons for believing in the Christian God. Pascal is right. We stand to gain everything or lose nothing. Wager that God does exist. Stack the odds on your side.

Comment: I agree with Stephen H. Roberts' popular quotation: "I contend that we are both atheists. I just believe in one fewer god than you do. When you understand why you dismiss all the other possible gods, you will understand why I dismiss yours."

Response: I contend we are not both atheists. I understand the reasonableness of rejecting moon gods, volcano gods, etc., but I also know quite well why many dismiss the idea of a true God. If you focused and studied the rational foundation of faith, you would dismiss atheism.

Comment: One has to wonder why an omnipotent being created the universe. Was He bored or in need of attention?

Response: Since He is omnipotent He acts as He wishes, not as we would presume. He is a God of creation and activity. There is nothing God lacks to complete His perfection. He does not need our attention, love, or worship. God is not dependent on us, but the opposite. He is the creator and giver of all, which proves His unlimited abundance, not His lack. No one has ever given Him anything. His nature is love and love gives freely. What do we have to offer Him? Nothing but toe jam, boogers, and ear wax, as my old pastor Father Bob used to say.

Comment: If absolute power corrupts absolutely, where does that leave God?

Response: Right where He is. You can't compare the author of all morality to our morality—there is no parallel. Besides, I disagree with the statement. It is the *ambition or pursuit* of absolute power that corrupts. The one who has absolute power has no need for corruption since he possesses absolute power.

Comment: David Hume tears up the design argument popularly used by theists. He states there are analogies that harm the believers' cases. We have a lot of experience with a wide range of things, which gives us a basis of who makes what. For example, we know craftsmen make tools because we have observed them designing and building them on many occasions. However, we don't know what usually makes a universe. We simply have no experience with this kind of thing. We can't be too sure that whatever was responsible for making the universe is going to be much like the designers we are familiar with.

Response: You are a big fan of Hume and quote him often. Let me quote Immanuel Kant, who writes, "... where experience affords us neither instruction nor guidance, lie the investigations of reason" (4). No one can prove without a shadow of a doubt whether God exists or not, so what we have to do is examine the evidence to determine the most logical explanation. If I encounter an intricate mosaic on the beach, with no one working on it, I cannot prove someone made it, just as someone else cannot show it was made by the wind, waves, and sand cooperating with one another, so we have to determine what reason tells us is the most plausible explanation. You may say we know for certain it is humans who create such things on the beach, but the point is, the mosaic represents meaning and design that cannot be brushed away. We also see coherence and design in nature, not chaos. Again, we have intelligence and intelligence is required to discern intelligence. An animal can look at the same mosaic on the beach and not appreciate the creativity. As Kant said, "For reason is the faculty which furnishes us with the principles of knowledge" (15). Now the universe shows evidence of design at all levels; do you really think the principles of creation and design are isolated to human beings alone? No one can give tangible proof God exists like the computer in front of you, but based on the avalanche of evidence, at least for me, it takes a lot more faith *not* to believe in God than to do so.

Comment: Hume also remarks regarding the countless tragedies and imperfections in nature such as diseases, famines, plagues, floods, etc. If God is a divine watchmaker, the world looks more like a cheap watch rather than a quality watch. In other words, it does not seem we can conclude the creator is almighty and perfect, because the world is anything but perfect. Hume suggests that perhaps our universe was created by a junior deity who is just learning the ropes of universe creation and did not get things quite right this time around.

Response: If God were anything but perfect there wouldn't be anyone to dispute His perfection. Whoever said we had the right to be designed or born without diseases, famines, and plagues? Injustice is the depriving of an innate right. If He chose to leave us in misery and sadness, He would be doing us no injustice, because all that we are belongs to Him. The son of a world-class athlete can't complain to his father for not being born with great physical abilities. In the same way, we can't complain to God that we can't breathe underwater or have wings to fly. We are what we are. We may regret having "poor design," but we cannot say it is unfair or that it is due to a fallible designer. *We were designed impeccably in the sense that we are all God intended us to be.* Or do you complain because you aren't His equal?

Even given Hume's analogy, what he calls poor design is nevertheless a design demanding a designer. Besides, men consist of both body and soul, and the soul is of superior "design." This world is not all there is—Heaven is where the ideal design dwells and where our rightful place lies.

Comment: I sometimes believe the improbable just happens! It just happens that we were what happened.
Response: Throwing the universe in the "it just happened" category is like finding hundreds of rocks scattered in one location formulating a fine quote, and merely stating, "Sometimes the improbable happens." It is true that sometimes the unlikely happens, such as getting hit by a softball while walking down the sidewalk after leaving work. But, if it continues every day, one can no longer say "The improbable just happens." The point is there are too many improbable events taking place for this universe to exist. Paul Davies has concluded that the chance of the appropriate conditions for the formation of stars is one followed by at least a thousand billion billion zeroes—but I know you would say "Sometimes things just happen."

Consider the rate of expansion of the universe immediately after the Big Bang. The famous physicist Stephen Hawking concludes that if the rate of the universe's expansion one second after the Big Bang had been smaller by even one part in a hundred thousand million million, the universe would have collapsed into a fireball—but "sometimes things just happen" (Strobel 77).

Astronomer Fred Hoyle calculated that the odds of the random formation of a single enzyme from amino acids are 10^{20}. But that is only the beginning: "The trouble is that there are about two thousand enzymes, and the chance of obtaining them all in a random trial is only one part in $(10^{20})^{20,000} = 10^{40,000}$, an outrageously small probability that could not be faced even if the whole universe consisted of organic soup." And of course, the formation of enzymes is but one step in the formation of life. According to Hoyle, "Nothing has been said of the origin of DNA itself, nothing of DNA transcription to RNA, nothing of the origin of the program whereby cells organize themselves, nothing of mitosis and meiosis. These issues are too complex to set numbers to." In the end, he concludes that the chance of life originating by random ordering of organic molecules is essentially zero.

But why continue? All this fine tuning is distributed across enormous ranges and found in just the right proportions around the universe. I suppose things do happen, but if you think it is reasonable to dispense this one in the "Things just happen" bin, I disagree.

Comment: If creation needs a creator, who created your creator?
Response: The universe must have been created by an uncreated being; if not, the problem goes on forever. The chain of cause and effect must begin somewhere. We can argue about an uncreated God, but we can't argue about who created Him. If He was created, He would be a creature and not God. God has always existed. We are within space and time—He is not. He is eternal (Rumble and Carty 1: 3).

Comment: It is said God is all powerful, all knowing, and all loving. All three attributes must be true at the same time, but what we see is contradiction with the conditions of this world. If He is all loving, and He knows about all the woes and suffering (all knowing) and has the ability to do something (all powerful) and does not do it, then all three attributes can't be true.
Response: The conditions of this world do not violate any of God's attributes. Him being all powerful is why we even exist. Being all knowing, He is aware of the risk free will entails and has carried out a rescue plan. Being all loving, he has prepared a better place other than this world for our indestructible souls. This world is not all there is.

Comment: I would think it is logical for you to kill yourself, if you think you are going to paradise hereafter.
Response: God doesn't call us into this world so we can snuff ourselves out. There will be plenty of time for the grave when it comes upon us; all in due time. We're on training grounds in this life. We are being refined for greater things to come. Suicide means we have thrown in the white towel and given up. Jeremiah 29:11 tells us that God knows well the plans He has for us; plans for us to prosper and not for harm; plans to give hope and a future. Killing ourselves was never part of our destiny. We have much to do in this world and blessings to bestow. Blessings only we can make happen. Each person has a mission which was not intended for anyone else. Besides, we are also called to enjoy life. Suicide is a more logical proposition to the nonbeliever who believes the grave is his final resting place and chooses to deal with the burdens of life.

At this point it feels like we are beating a dead horse, and although there is much more to share, let us keep trucking forward under the implications that it is most reasonable that there is a God. Now, if there is a God, the implications are grave indeed.

A STANDARD II

"I, the Lord, your God, teach you what is for your good, and lead you on the way you should go. If you would hearken to my commandments, your prosperity would be like a river, and your vindication like the waves of the sea."

— Isaiah 48:17-18

"Why do you call me 'Lord, Lord,' but not do what I command?"

— Luke 6:46

Earlier we made the case that we live by standards. As surely as God has implemented law and order in the universe, He must have done the same for the creatures created in His image. We require established guidelines to function or pandemonium will be the end result. That is why societies have prisons, to quarantine those who have breached these standards. But the dilemma is, whose standards or guidelines should prevail? Keeping in mind that we want to tackle what is right, not just what is legal. Again, all cultures have standards that should *NOT* be breached, pushing us to an objective reference. In dealing with objective matters, one must ask which individual's idea should prevail? Which society's? To reiterate, no one can definitively demonstrate that what they think is right or wrong *is* right or wrong, unless they refer to the author of all right—God.

Hopefully, the previous chapters have established a solid and reasonable case for God. If there is a supreme deity, we must switch our focus onto what He has to say about standards in the realm of truth, morals, and faith. He is the only benchmark by which to measure these volatile issues against the multitude of perspectives that preside.

Since God is the measuring stick, this implies that He is not a democracy where we vote for what we want or lobby in order to sway Him. We don't pick and choose what we like as if we were grocery shopping. God is God. When the creator speaks, the created must simply accept his provisions. Whether we choose to act or take heed of those provisions is another story.

There appears to be a lack of reverence concerning the dignity of which we speak. This stupendous being we refer to as God is all powerful and infinitely superior to all that is or can be conceived. He is the Alpha and the Omega, the one and only, Lord and creator of all. The implications of this being are so titanic that words can't do justice. Yet, we speak of Him so nonchalantly or apathetically. We need to step back and reflect on what this all means.

These standards we continue to allude to are set not to hurt us, but rather for our own good and protection. Many consider rules to be a confinement to our liberty, but this is because these people lack a relationship with the lawgiver. "Rules without relationships breed rebellion," as Gerardo Hernandez, director of Body of Christ Ministry, likes to say. When parents, for instance, enforce rules in their household, they hopefully don't discipline their children blindly. A nurturing parent teaches their children why there are rules and consequences. Lack of a relationship in conjunction with discipline breeds animosity. The same goes with God. Many revolt against Him thinking He is only about rules when, above all else, God seeks a relationship with us and looks out for our well-being.

There are good reasons for His laws, in the same way that the state requires us to wear seat belts and not drink while driving. The state law is the state law; it is not a suggestion. In the same way, God has also given commandments, not suggestions. We can certainly go against the law of the land; remember, "At the end of the day a person is going to do whatever they are going to do." But we must understand, consequences are part of defying rules. How can the government impose laws if there are no penalties? It would be a mockery, a joke, not a law. Similarly, how can God have commandments and not follow through with His justice? He is a God of love (which is the only way many choose to view him), but He is also a God of justice. Love and justice demand accountability. Many assume that when it comes to us knowingly breaking His laws, "He'll just understand."

■ ■ ■

If there is an absolute supreme being, the burning question becomes, through whom has He revealed himself, if at all? How do we discover His true wishes when so many claim to know them but have such different ideas? To tackle these questions and more, we must turn to religion.

Many might be sneering at this point. "Religion is a personal thing"; "The truth of religion depends where a person was born or what they believe"; and so on and so forth. We have briefly covered some of these arguments, and we will tend to them in further detail later, but to help us solve this dilemma of religious Truth, let us at least look at what Truth is not— that is, error. For example, when it thunders, it is not because God is angry, as some believe. We also know that cutting one's body and bleeding half to death does not rid one of their mother's genes and appease God, as I saw on a program on the Discovery Channel. We also know that crushing the bones of a mentally handicapped person after his death does not get rid of the family "curse," as some believe in when I visited West Africa. Through this process of elimination, we can at least discard many inaccurate religious beliefs, despite the believers' sincerity, and concentrate on the world's most popular faiths. By disposing of what we know to be false, we can focus on more sophisticated claims. We must deal with reasonableness alone.

At one point, when I was more naïve, I thought the teachings of all religions summed the totality of God's revelation, but the reality is quite different. Contradictions and absurd notions are all I confronted. All these conflicting ideas could not have been revealed by God, who is Truth. Truth cannot contradict itself. It is consistent. With this said, let us venture into the world of religion to see if we can get nearer to God's revelations.

THE NECESSITY OF RELIGION

"The nature of man bears unequivocal testimony to the necessity of religion."

— *A.A Livermore*

"Western civilization is for the first time in its history in danger of dying. The reason is spiritual. It is losing its life, its soul; that soul was the Christian Faith. The infection killing it is not multiculturalism, that is, other faiths, but the monoculturalism of secularism."

—*Peter Kreeft*

"Religion" is a word that can have various implications, positive or negative, depending on how it's used. In its most common context it describes a group of people with a set of common beliefs. But, one has to wonder, when does a belief become a religion? When it has ten adherents? Five hundred? A thousand? People point fingers and label others as "religious," not even aware that they are quite religious themselves. I dare say we are all religious with our established beliefs since the number of believers that makes a "religion" is irrelevant.

To determine if religion is necessary at all, we must begin by asking why it exists in the first place. Many answers have been proposed: religion exists because we are social creatures, for example, or because people have been indoctrinated by their parents or born into a certain environment. Or maybe because it gives a sense of belonging, builds communities, and, for those seeking purpose, answers the unknowable.

"That is the reality" as far as the origins of religion, an atheist will claim—not that there is a God. I agree with some of these assessments. They possess particles of truth, and particles of truth can be dangerous when removed from the whole. These may very well be contributing factors in the genesis of religion, but they also demonstrate the facts of the human condition—we are what we are. We cannot disregard or exploit our human nature in order to dismiss faith altogether as some fantasy. There is a reason why we crave something more than materialism or individualism, something that drives us to the higher realm of religious spirituality and faith. That reason is that we are not composed of just a material body, but mind and spirit as well. There is an interrelation and an attempt to align and intertwine body, mind and spirit. It is this effort that has produced religions.

■ ■ ■

The fact is, religion is in our midst so let us examine more closely the nonbeliever's theories on the rise of religion. The most popular idea is the indoctrination of children by parents. Children have religion "shoved down their throats." In other words, they have no choice. At least, that is the way seculars describe it. I describe it as parents doing their duty as parents and raising their children according to what they believe is true to the best of their abilities, instead of taking their cues from Hollywood, the media or knucklehead friends. They raise their kids the same way seculars instill their own values and beliefs in their own children. Children need guidance and direction. I am supposed to mold my children, passing down knowledge and wisdom to arm them for the world they are going to face. As a man of faith, I certainly don't believe atheism is the prudent way to go. Seculars claim to be parenting properly because they raise their children using their own beliefs (atheism), but believers are unreasonable parents for teaching them Christianity. What a fantastic conclusion. What are Christians supposed to teach their kids? Paganism? Scientology? The way of the Jedi? Nothing at all? "Raising children to believe in fantasies is detrimental and should be stopped at once," one atheist uttered. In my view, what should be stopped is how atheists raise their kids to believe God does not exist. That's all it is, faith—not certainty—that He does not exist. Personally, I will continue to do my duty as a parent and teach my kids what I believe to be true and right, and when they are older they will certainly have the choice to opt out, if they wish.

Fear and conformity is another popular motivation the nonbeliever uses for crediting the ascension of religious faith. In other words, the fear of God's wrath and the wrath of one's religious peers. Speaking for Christianity, I am awestruck by how nonbelievers have made themselves the judge of others' beliefs. Believers do not fear God; they love God and want to serve Him. That is reality. As Aristotle said, "Wicked men obey from fear; good men, from love." And no, I am not afraid to question my faith. I have questioned it to pieces, as innumerable others have, and have been met by my peers not with fear or admonition, but rather admiration.

So, on it goes. Some claim religion is about stealing money from people. No...It is not. Though I don't deny abuses, abuses are the exception, not the rule. Others claim religion is used to control people. No...It is not. The Christian faith holds no one against their will—one can leave whenever one wishes. That is reality. It is said that some men created religion to answer what they could not understand, or to explain natural phenomenon. That is accurate, to an extent. What it proves is that men have erred since the beginning of time and continue to err today—but their premise is correct: God is the creator of all. Man has not only evolved in the realm of material knowledge, but also in metaphysics, philosophy and theology. Still, the modern believer understands there are mysteries and miracles beyond human comprehension, regardless of the terms scientists slap on them.

Others say religion is the result of weak minds, fit for those who refuse to take responsibility for their actions, but instead blame some deity for their misfortune. So many false ideas are unfortunately entertained about religion as if true. I acknowledge there are always exceptions—I am a realist—but the misconceptions prevail greatly. It is easy for folks to disparage religious beliefs. Atheism, on the surface, has an immediate appeal for the non-thinker. But here is the reality of the matter. Religious activity is not for the weak-minded. The way I see it, religion has risen not primarily because of community or tradition, but because humans are curious, conscious and intelligent beings who have the audacity to question why they exist. That is an angle the nonbeliever will never admit to, that there is an element of thinking in religious faith. I am religious for the main reason that nonbelievers claim to be atheist—logic and reason.

We can probably all agree that manual labor can be strenuous and difficult. Working with your mind is even more difficult. Thinking is challenging, but nothing in my life has proven more difficult than obtaining religious spirituality and its works; the mastering of self and the focusing of the mind above the sensuous. It is great to understand the laws of our solar systems and other natural phenomena, but greater still is knowing the laws governing the mind and the will, and subduing them. I have complete admiration for a laundry list of mystic saints who have achieved the conquering of the inner self. How difficult it is to reach their level of spirituality stemming from their religious activities. Most seculars don't dare set foot on such a strenuous path. The religious person is in a daily battle between the sensual and spiritual. So, no, religious spirituality and its activities are not for the weak-minded. Rather, it is for the disciplined and strong-minded who have undertaken the most difficult exercise the mind can experience as they attempt to go beyond their finite senses and reasoning to tap into God's infinite power through prayer and meditation. Religious thought has stimulated the mind to its utmost state, and that is one reason why it is necessary to pursue it and study it. The nonbeliever instead prefers to limit man to the material world, society, and the here and now.

Throughout history, religion has been one of the most compelling powers in advancing the human race and achieving incredible feats. I don't deny that there have been irreligious men and women with admirable traits who did good work, but the ones who have gone above and beyond, the ones who have electrified humanity, have been men and women with spiritual or religious backgrounds. Their lives have inspired the masses for the common good, and their influence is rooted in their religion. They have tapped into the ocean of power available to the spiritual man of faith in order to accomplish great and virtuous deeds. They have shown exemplary character and brought hope and peace to the downcast, while relieving a great deal of pain and anguish. All of this good can be credited to genuine religion.

Lastly, religion and its activities have proven to build not just a community amongst believers, but a bond. This bond is stronger than one's origin, race and even family. Genuine religion is color blind, geographically blind, and gender blind. Again, as a realist, I acknowledge there are various sets of beliefs that run contrary, but again, they are the exception, not the rule. And what I mean by genuine religion will become clearer in further chapters. It remains that the force of religion has inspired men to stand side by side and carry each other's burdens more consistently than any other cause. Religion, I would also argue, has kept the human race moving forward. It provides hope and a future, whereas in a secular society, the inclination is to serve oneself. The strength of society has come from genuine religious people, and the day genuine religion begins to lose ground, society as a whole will begin to deteriorate. Perhaps the U.S. can stand as a present-day example.

People without religious spirituality will say we need to be more practical by capturing the present and taking care of our world, instead of diverting our energies into spiritual fantasies. I agree that we must take care of our present world and the material, for we are living in the flesh as well. Again, we are body, mind and spirit. But if too much focus on the spiritual degrades our worldly present, we can also say that too much worldliness affects our religious spirituality and the hereafter. Man must balance himself, for he is not just a material being. We should never regard the material as our final destiny.

The bottom line is, genuine religion has done tremendous work for humankind; therefore, it is essential, and ought to be embraced. Most religions have great aspects, but it is the false and bad aspects that nonbelievers focus on. Well, if the bad is what they want to focus on, there is plenty of bad in the nonreligious world to choose from to easily counter their arguments.

■ ■ ■

Now it stands, if there is a God, then religion becomes a necessity in our lives, since religion and its activities is the manner by which we give to God the honor, gratitude, praise, and relationship He desires of us. All this we owe to Him, not simply in the way we wish, but in the way He prescribes. We can't declare, "I believe in God," then ignore His definite claims.

I know many aren't concerned about religious duties and may even sneer at the very word. By not having religion, many believe they are not missing out on anything, but what they don't know is they miss much more than they think, like U.S. government officials who ignore the country's mounting debt.

This logic that religion is only for "religious people" is erroneous. The word "religion" is not just a set of beliefs, but also means relationship. People are religious about money, pleasure, power, titles. There is no such thing as a nonreligious person. We are all religious by nature. The only difference is, there are false gods. We are all called to a relationship with our creator, not just people who feel "religious."

Religion is not only necessary for the relationship God seeks; it is the very essence of obedience. The first law God gave us was one of obedience. We turned from Him due to disobedience; if we retrace our steps, obedience will take us back to our rightful place with Him, as theologian Leslie Rumble wrote (2:310). Obedience is the clear-cut evidence of our love for God.

Organized religion is also necessary to protect the genuine teachings of the faith and to prevent the infiltration of errors. This is a topic that will surface later and needs to be covered in more detail, specifically when discussing Christianity.

Many are the reasons and even excuses why a man disregards his religious obligations. Besides indifference, one of the prime reasons is that people choose to worship God in their own way. One can do so to an extent, of course, but one has to wonder how they know that what they are doing is pleasing to Him. Personal worship, to some folks, means opening scripture semiannually. To others, saying "I believe," or attending one or two yearly services, such as Christmas or Easter, suffices. The point is, the one who is to be venerated has the right to claim how He should be worshipped. God is no fool and did not leave instructions on a whim.

The bottom line is, when dealing with the question of God we must explore world religions, since they deal directly with a supreme deity, and with sets of beliefs, morality, and ethics that should be followed. We must first distinguish between views. We cannot for a second maintain that hundreds of contradictory religions around the world are correct or that they pull equal weight. *If we do, we will quickly end up concluding that all are equally useless.*

RELIGION COMMENTS AND RESPONSES

As we venture into the realm of religion, here are more sample discussions I find most applicable.

Comment: Just face the fact religion is a failure, and unnecessary! Look at the atrocities it has left in its wake while doing little for the hunger and pain around the world.
Response: I cannot "face" that, since it is not a fact. Again, speaking for Christianity alone, it has not failed. Rather, men have failed to live up to Christian ideals. Let all men dare to live up to the teachings of the faith, and if the world is not a better place, by all means blame Christianity. But, until then, we know the world has benefited greatly because of Christianity. The troubles of pain and hunger you speak of would be exponentially higher if it weren't for the faithful Christians doing countless works of charity around the globe. Go into the many slums of the world and what you will find is devoted men and women working for love of God. There are very few nonbelievers, if any, working in the slums of Calcutta, India. I am willing to bet that if we had a thousand God-fearing Christians versus a thousand nonbelievers that the most good and positive impact on the world would easily come from the believing side. By the way, keep in

mind, the ultimate purpose of Christianity is not to rid the world of hunger and pain, but to save souls.

You also need to review your history concerning atrocities. I can easily make the case of godless devastation being much more profound. Men have torn each other to pieces throughout history concerning matters having nothing to do with religion. Countless have lost their lives or committed atrocities in their pursuit of money, power, pleasure, resources, etc., *NOT* because they were spreading their Christian faith. The likes of Stalin, Mao, Kim Jong-il, Nicolae Ceausescu, Pol Pot, Lenin, Brezhnev, and so forth make religious extremists look pretty good. *These men truly confirm that if God is not, everything is permissible.* Do you seriously think a world without religion will be this utopia you envision? You are thinking of a fairy tale world. If it isn't religion, which often times it isn't, you'll have atrocities for all sorts of worldly and material gains.

Comment: Thanks to the breaking from the shackles of religion in the last five hundred years, men have been able to advance in the field of science and reason. Just take, for example, the persecution of Galileo.

Response: I don't deny inappropriate handling of cases throughout history. The fragile human element is always involved, but in no way has the Christian religion interfered with reason or the pursuit of knowledge. In physical science the invention of many instruments are credited to men of faith, past and present. For example, the invention of the printing press by a Catholic (Johannes Gutenberg) contributed to the more rapid dissemination of information and promoted study and progress. But in the last five hundred years, as you mentioned, more advances have been made due to normal development of human thought. Knowledge building upon itself in a snowball effect. A multitude of Christian scientists are credited for great works of science, including Newton, Ampere, Galvani, Laplace, Magellan, Lapparent, and hundreds of others. Their religious beliefs did not halt their scientific thought, and in many cases these men were inspired by their faith. Science and faith are in harmony.

Comment: I believe there is a God, but I will follow my way to Him, not whatever man-made religions have to say.
Response: No one wants you to follow a man-made religion. Test the Christian claims before dismissing them based on preconceive ideas. You ignore the ways God is calling you to follow Him. He has constructed a road to Himself, so there is no need for us to carve our own. And can you tell me how your way is not man-made, since you are following your personal notions?

Comment: I have no time for religious nonsense.
Response: So the truth comes out. You do not understand the purpose of religion; therefore it is useless, but it's as necessary an activity as exercising. As mentioned, religion and its activities is the bond that unites us to God. As eating and resting are required for the body, religion is the necessity of the soul.

Comment: According to Seneca the Younger, "Religion is regarded by the common people as true, by the wise as false, and by the rulers as useful."
Response: Let's put this quote to the test. Many common people don't believe in religion. Many great thinkers and wise men both past and present believe it is true. Many atheist rulers such as Lenin, Mao, and Pol Pot had no use for it. It appears Seneca's statement cannot hold.

Comment: With all the diversity in the world we can pretty much say religion boils down to opinion.
Response: Until a matter is proven, it is very much a matter of opinion, but God has revealed Himself definitively, making the question at hand no longer an issue of opinions. It is now a matter of using our brains to figure out how He has revealed Himself.

Comment: What I don't like about religious people is they always seem to be pointing at the specks of dust in the eyes of others, yet never notice or tend to the logs in their own eyes. Maybe if the religious learned to stop throwing stones from their glass houses, there wouldn't be so much animosity.

Response: What makes you think that all men with a log in their eyes are not tending to it? Some do, some don't. But I do understand your point, and it must be taken into account. A person who walks uprightly is certainly much more credible than one who does not. Even so, here is a point consider, don't all of us have logs in our eyes? That being the case, that log does not deprive us of our duties of telling our wives, kids, friends, and neighbors that they are in error should they find themselves in it. The person may lack some credibility, of course, but it is better than keeping one's mouth shut. *The message must be carefully delivered.* That is the key. The man who is or was a drug dealer certainly has the duty to dissuade young kids from dealing drugs or behaving violently in the streets.

But tell me, when the nonreligious fail to live up to proper conduct, are they deprived of their duty of doing what is right when it's within their power do to so, in order avoid being called a hypocrite?

Comment: You have a way with words. Stop rationalizing things away. The hypocrisy of religious people is sickening...Period. It is precisely why less people attend any form of Church services every year.

Response: I would not call it the precise reason but certainly a factor. Many discredit or avoid attending services because of the failures of the religious, but that makes as much sense as not going to the gym because people there are out of shape. The hypocritical man who goes to church is at least in the right place to stimulate change. Credit is due to him for trying to fulfill the most important obligation of all, which is acknowledging God. Rendering to God is above rendering to man. Not that we should ignore what is due to our fellow man, but genuine love for God automatically overflows to our fellow man. I would confidently bet that the man who puts God first in his life is the man who is less likely to be hypocritical. No one justifies the failures of a religious person, but their faith *might* save them despite their faults. A person's declared "goodness" or righteousness based on their own personal standards will not suffice, *knowing* that there is more required. Besides, there are plenty of hypocrites who don't bother with religion. What do we make of them? If misconduct negates religion, does the hypocrisy of the nonreligious prove the necessity of religion? I don't hear the yell of hypocrisy when seculars fail, but the same rules must apply to them. Instead, the rule nonbelievers apply to themselves, if a secular fails, is that it is the individual at fault, not their secular or humanistic ideas. But, if a Christian fails, they don't see it as the individual's fault, but Christianity is to blame. It is a double standard that makes no sense.

Comment: It is not rational to accept religious dogmas that can't be questioned, fool.
Response: Who says religious dogmas are not questionable? I question them all the time. Every rational man should know what he does and why. Of course, to you, I am a fool simply because I do not come to your conclusions.

Comment: I believe in God but feel religion is nothing but a big scam.
Response: If feelings are the basis of your argument, let me just say I feel quite differently. I agree with you that there are scams out there, and there will always be scams; hence the notion of false religion. But, to maintain your position, you must prove Christianity and Christ a scam, and you will never be able to do so.

Comment: The goal of religion is to strip people of freedom while sinning jerkwads on top of the chain do as they wish.
Response: There are "jerkwads," but rest assured that minority will have to give an account of their misconduct. Also, you speak of freedom, when there is no such thing as absolute freedom. It boils down to being subject to virtues; if not, one is subject to vices. True religion keeps one away from the snares of vices (Rumble and Carty 1:15).

We are venturing into sensitive territory, but let us attempt to keep an objective frame of mind as we continue into the realm of world religion.

WORD RELIGION

"People with no ear for music say that it all sounds the same, but lovers of Bach, Handel, Beethoven, and Brahms know better. So, too, people who lack spiritual concern or factual knowledge or both tell us that world religions are really all the same, and are as good as another, so that it does not matter which is yours."

— J.I. Packer

A popular idea rampaging through society is the concept that all paths lead to the same destination, like the well-known illustration presenting many trails leading to the same mountain peak. Although this image is embraced by many, keep in mind that one can't get to Florida by traveling west from New York. And if there are roads that lead to a destination, it follows that there must be roads leading away. We can't simply assume everyone is heading in the right direction; therefore, a proper evaluation of outlooks must be undertaken before deciding which road to travel. Are we going on the prescribed highway or are we making circles on a roundabout? Could we be heading in the wrong direction altogether? Using this mountain peak and road analogy, we can also say some roads lead to dead ends. Some mountainsides are not even suitable for paving. We might be off the prepared surface altogether, carving through the woods with a machete. Even if we find ourselves on a paved road, we are not guaranteed to reach the final destination.

I strain in vain to understand this "All roads lead to the same destination" idea. Acceptance of such an idea forces truth to lose all value. *The road of thievery and vice cannot lead to the same destination as the road of hard work and virtue.* In the same way, anyone who is knowledgeable about world religion knows each system has its own set of "road signs" pointing to distinct locations.

There is no denying that religions have similarities by virtue of being religions, just as entirely different people have similarities by virtue of being humans. But both people and religions can differ significantly at their core. There is an unbridgeable chasm. *It is just impossible and contradictory to believe that opposing ideas can both be right. They can all be false, but they can't all be true.* The proper illustration for one who seeks religious truth is more like a maze; only one path makes it out. This coincides with the nature of truth—that is, it is narrow—while other ideas and concepts meet dead ends, though some go farther in the "maze" than others due to substance or particles of truth.

Some may believe that a comparative analysis of major world religions would fuel religious hatred and intolerance, but that is the wrong perspective. Religious tolerance cannot be built on ignorance, but on understanding of commonalities and differences. The information that follows highlights some basic teachings and differences of major world religions. There are many good books that go into specifics, such as *The Compact Guide To World Religions* by Dean C. Halverson, but specifics are not the intention here. Although religions such as Confucianism, Taoism, Judaism, etc., are well known, they are *not* covered here. We will only be using the religions with the highest number of adherents to accomplish the purpose of pointing out how much discrepancy is found between one religion to another. At the same time, it will be emphasized and become evident that all these roads do not lead to the same destination. Hopefully, this material will clarify some teachings so that better understanding and "verdicts" can be made in this supermarket of world religions.

Islam

Let's begin with the second-largest religion in the world, Islam. The term "Islam" means submission to the will of God, and those who follow Islam are referred to as Muslims. They believe in one God (monotheistic), known in Arabic as Allah. This religion began in Arabia and was revealed by Muhammad (570—632 AD). He was a trader who later became a religious, political, and military leader. He is regarded as the last messenger, or prophet, of God by Islam. Muslims teach that in 610 AD Muhammad began receiving revelations from the angel Gabriel. The content of these revelations, the Koran, was memorized and recorded by his companions. During this time, Muhammed preached to the people of Mecca, imploring them to abandon polytheism (many gods). As he preached against paganism, persecution of his movement began to mount. Through multiple battles, Muhammad would eventually establish his political and religious authority.

Here are some notable teachings of the Islamic faith and how they compare to the largest religion in the world, Christianity:

Muslims reject the Christian concept of the Trinity. They believe God is a singular entity, while Christianity professes a complex unity of three beings but one essence. The Koran teaches, in Surah 5:73, "They do blaspheme who say: Allah is one of three in a Trinity: there is no god except God. If they desist not from their word (of blasphemy), verily a grievous penalty will befall the blasphemers among them."

Islam teaches that God has no son: "Allah forbids that He should have a son" (Surah 4:171). "He begets not, nor is he begotten, and there is none like unto him." (Surah 112:3). Christianity clearly teaches that Jesus is the son of God. In Hebrews 5:5 we read, "You are my son. This day have I begotten you." Christ claimed to be the son of God, according to Luke 22:70 and John 10:36. "The high priest said to him, 'I charge you under oath by the living God: Tell us if you are the Christ, the Son of God.' 'Yes, it is as you say,' Jesus replied" (Matthew 26:63). Even demons confessed Jesus to be the son of God: "And demons also came out from many, shouting, 'You are the Son of God'" (Luke 4:41).

Right off the bat it should become clear these "road signs" are not cooperating. They are pointing in different directions. Christ cannot be both part of a Trinity and not. Nor can he be the son of God and not.

■ ■ ■

Muslims believe Muhammad was the greatest of all prophets, but they do not believe he was divine. Christ, they also hold, was *not* divine, but just a prophet, like all others. "The Messiah, Jesus the son of Mary, was no more than Allah's apostle" (Surah 4:171). Christianity teaches the contrary. Scripture credits Christ as much more than a mere prophet. He was "the very nature of God" (Philippians 2:6). He was attributed names such as "Alpha and Omega" (Revelation 1:8) and "Immanuel," meaning, God With Us (Isaiah 7:14; Matthew 1:23). His apostle referred to Him as "My Lord and my God" (John 20:28). He Himself claimed to be God when he said "Amen, amen, I say to you, before Abraham came to be, I AM" (John 8:58). Worth reviewing on this matter of divinity is John 4:26, 10:30, and 14:9. Christ also claimed the power and authority to forgive sin, which only God can do (Matthew 9:6; Mark 2:7).

All the attributes of God, such as omniscience, are present in Him (John 4:25; Matthew 12:25; Luke 5:22; John 2:24). He is omnipotent (Matthew 28:18; John 3:31; 1 Peter 3:22) as well as omnipresent (Matthew 18:20; 28:20; Ephesians 1:23). Scripture claims that Christ is eternal. He pre-existed the creation of the world and was present with the Father from the beginning of time (Genesis 1:26; Isaiah 48:12, 16; John 1:1-3, 10; 1 Corinthians 8:6; Ephesians 3:9; Philippians 2:5; Colossians 1:15-19). There is no other major religion that claims its founder to be divine. This is one of the core beliefs of Christianity. But, again, take notice of the opposing and contradictory teachings. Jesus Christ can't be God to one person and not to another. The question to ponder is, is He God or not? The answer applies to all.

■ ■ ■

Another crucial doctrine Islam denies is the crucifixion of Christ. In Surah 4:157-158, we read, "They declared: 'We have put to death the Messiah Jesus the son of Mary the apostle of Allah.' They did not kill him, nor did they crucify him, but they thought they did. ...They have no knowledge thereof but the pursuit of conjecture; they slew him not for certain, but God took him up to Himself." Muslim tradition teaches that Judas was the one crucified instead. They believe it disrespectful to have such an honored prophet crucified (Halverson 108).

The doctrine of the resurrection is probably the most fundamental teaching of Christianity. Without the crucifixion, there is no Christian faith. Paul writes in 1 Corinthians 15:14, "And if Christ has not been raised, our preaching is useless, and so is our faith." Scripture supplies enough proof that Christ was bodily resurrected after his passion (Matthew 28:6). He appeared first to Mary Magdalene (John 20:14-18), followed by the other women (Matthew 28:9). He followed suit by appearing to Peter (Luke 24:34) and to Cleopas and the other disciples on the way to Emmaus (Luke 24:15). In a closed room, he appeared to his disciples (John 20:19-20). One cannot omit the famous interaction with the doubting apostle Thomas (John 20:27). There are other incidents, including five hundred brethren He appeared to at once (1 Corinthians 15:6). The questions we must consider are, did Christ rise from the dead and was He the son of God? The critical point is, again, it can't be both.

This small synopsis of the two most followed religions in the world has hopefully illustrated the drastic differences found between major beliefs. We can't blind ourselves to the facts of many prevalent contradictions. Let us continue with other popular religions.

Buddhism

Buddhism has approximately four hundred million followers worldwide. It is most dominant throughout China, Japan, and Southeast Asia. It was founded by Siddhartha Gautama (563—463 BC) in approximately the sixth century BC. He was a prince who lived an affluent and sheltered life until taking a journey during which he experienced poverty and sickness.

He was stunned and troubled at all of the suffering around him. This incident caused Gautama to leave his home and family in search of answers. He committed himself to seeking the source of suffering and finding a way to eliminate it. He sought enlightenment through self-discipline, self-mortification, and simplicity, but to no avail. With much resolve, Gautama sat beneath a tree and vowed to be still until attaining what he sought. After a period of time, he arose as the Buddha—the "enlightened one." He would then spend the rest of his life teaching others the path to liberation from suffering, while founding a community of monks.

Buddhist beliefs differ across sects and schools, but all pay tribute to the figure of the Buddha and the goal of ending suffering by eliminating desires that stem from one's pursuit of things that do not give lasting happiness. Buddhism has no God in a monotheistic sense of the word, nor does it believe in an indestructible soul. It teaches that there is no ultimate reality and that nothing is permanent. There is no self. The Buddha also taught that humans are in a continuous cycle of rebirth, life, and death. Each rebirth may be into an improved, a worse, or a similar life, depending upon the merits of the person's previous life. The goal is to end this vicious cycle, which derives from an individual's cravings. As one successfully purifies oneself and eliminates all attachments, yearnings, and desires, the effects of karma will have nothing to attach themselves to, releasing the individual from the realm of the "illusionary self" and reaching the state of Nirvana. Nirvana is a state of bliss derived from the liberation from the cycle of death and rebirth; therefore, the end of suffering is attained, which is the ultimate goal of Buddhism. Once this is achieved, the mind experiences complete freedom, liberation, and non-attachment. To achieve this end, Buddhists follow strict religious and meditation methods.

The variances in doctrine between Buddhism, Islam, and Christianity show explicit differences. Since the foundation of the Christian faith, it has taught that everyone has one life to live (Hebrews 9:27). After death, the personal self (not the illusionary self) will face Judgment and give an account for what it has done or failed to do, in the hopes of attaining eternal happiness with God in Heaven.

The idea of a savior born of a virgin, crucified, resurrected, and ascending to Heaven is completely foreign to Buddhism. They do *not* acknowledge the need for a personal savior whose crucifixion enabled salvation through atonement of sin, nor do they accept that a person lives on, unchanged, after death for all eternity. Their meditation also concentrates solely on discipline, not on praying to or having a relationship with an almighty God.

Christianity's views on suffering are quite different. It teaches that the problem of suffering is not in desiring what is temporary, but rather that suffering is the consequence of sins that have alienated us from God. Buddhism teaches getting rid of desires, while Christianity teaches having the right desires. The differences in this small synopsis are evident. While Islam points north, Buddhism points west, and Christianity east. We cannot admit for a second that they are all leading us to the same location.

Hinduism

Hinduism is one of the oldest world religions. With no specific founder, today Hinduism is described as the product of religious development in India spanning thousands of years. It is one of the most diverse and complex belief systems, and has literally tens of thousands of gods.

With approximately one billion Hindus worldwide, it is the third-largest religion, after Christianity and Islam. The oldest and main sacred texts of Hinduism can be found in the Vedas. These writings give religious leaders instructions on performing rituals and contain hymns, prayers, philosophies, and poems from which Hindus derive their beliefs. It also contains stories that blend myth, theology, and history in order to achieve a story-like feel.

It is challenging to summarize Hinduism, since the various Hindu schools contain a vast assortment of beliefs. Their faith does not constitute a unified set of philosophies or practices, unlike Westerners, who have creeds or formulated belief statements. One can pretty much believe what they want to about God and the path to "liberation" and still be considered a Hindu. As the famous Hindu saying goes: "Truth is one;

sages call it by different names." With so many gods, Hindu beliefs can be monotheistic, pantheistic, or theistic. Given all its diversity, the fundamental belief that differentiates a Hindu from a non-Hindu appears to be the reverence expressed in the Vedas.

Mainly, Hinduism views mankind as divine because Brahma (the Hindu god of creation) is everything. Therefore, everything is considered divine. Behind all the individualism stands one reality: The self is one with Brahma. All of reality outside of Brahma is seen as mere illusion. So in essence we are in a stage of ignorance, not realizing we are divine ourselves, since we are part of Brahma.

The objective of a Hindu is to eventually become one with Brahma, and in doing so one ceases to exist in an illusory form of individual self. This spiritual state is known as "Moksha" (liberation). Until Moksha is achieved, a Hindu believes, one will repeatedly be reincarnated in order that they may work toward the self-realization that only Brahma exists, and nothing else. They will meditate and grow in knowledge to achieve this end, or dedicate themselves to various Hindu gods through religious ceremonies and rites. The bottom line is, we have forgotten we are an extension of Brahma and have attached ourselves to the wants of our separate selves, or the things of this world, and suffer the consequences of these actions. We, in this life, are reaping the consequences of our previous life. So if a person is poor, sick, or in whatever negative circumstances, they are deserving of that condition due to their past life.

It is readily seen that Hinduism at its core is in opposition to Christianity on almost every count. Their "salvation" is based on personal efforts through the cleansing of bad karma, selfless actions, meditation, and devotion. There is no concept of forgiveness of personal sin in Hinduism. Hindus hold that we are divine, or gods ourselves, looking for union with the divine universe. The Christian perspective says our goal is to have an everlasting *relationship* with God, but we are *not* part of God, nor are we gods. We are separate, distinct individuals made in His image and likeness. Brahma is also considered to be an impersonal god; meaning that he is not interested in a relationship with us. Christianity teaches that

God loves us and is seeking us out. He created us so that we may live in relationship with him.

Though Hindu teaching has value as far as the sacredness of life, good conduct, and the laws of cause and effect (karma), at the core of Islam, Buddhism, Christianity, and Hinduism there are differences we cannot ignore. They are quite unique. Just looking at basics, Hinduism says there are countless gods and goddesses, while Buddhism says there is no god. Islam says God does not consist of a trinity, and so on and so forth. These contradictions continue between any other religions. Judaism, for example, rejects Christ as savior, while Christianity revolves around the person of Christ. There are religions that even worship Satan, yet we're supposed to accept that all roads lead to the same location? A sincere man looking for religious truth does not concentrate on similarities but focuses on core and irreconcilable differences. To say all these beliefs are working toward the same end goal, the Buddhist would have to admit there is an omnipotent god, the Hindu would have to give up his thousands of gods, and the Muslim would have to abandon the idea that there is only one god. To say that traveling north is the same as going south cannot be accepted. That we are in a *journey,* as many like to state, is a given, and by virtue of being "travelers," we have commonalities. As in journeying or navigating, when hitting forks in the road, we must make sure we are selecting the right avenues in order to prevent getting lost or drawn off course.

WHY CHRISTIANITY?

"Christianity is a statement which if false is of no importance, and, if true, of infinite importance. The one thing it cannot be is moderately important."

— C.S. Lewis

"Moses could mediate on the law; Mohammed could brandish a sword; Buddha could give personal counsel; Confucius could offer wise sayings; but none of these men was qualified to offer an atonement for the sins of the world."

— R.C. Sproul

We all know the passions and convictions many religious believers hold. Many maintain that they're right about their faith without giving it a second thought. Being wrong is something they can't imagine. I am reminded of my own inability to consider being wrong about the existence of God. But we must allow room for intellectual error, so I was not going to take the same blind bias in the realm of religion. On this go-around, I approached the issue thinking that perhaps I was wrong.

So is Christianity wrong? Here is how people of faith should approach this question. Since most people believe there is a higher power or supreme being, which is the approach of this book, we know He can't be mistaken, if indeed He is supreme. If we can prove what God has revealed, we are absolutely right because He is right. So what did He reveal?

As previously stated, at one point in my innocence I thought all religions added to some total truth about God. I would come to learn that this is not the case after examining world religions. Christianity proved to be the soundest as far as its founder, historical foundation, and reasonableness. Others think differently, of course, but the fact that a man believes his religion correct does not prove anything but that he thinks it is right. He who is correct is the one whose case is entrenched in evidence and reason.

Since my *verdict* is evident, let us touch upon key points that struck me most about these popular religions.

■ ■ ■

It is perplexing how folks can take a position or road and not claim it to be the prudent route. One would think the purpose of choosing one path rather than another is that it is the most correct or efficient route. We don't do what we do because we think it is wrong. Shall I follow the way of Christianity, or perhaps the atheist/humanist path? Maybe the Islamic way is most prudent? Of course, one can always argue that one road is not fitting for all people, just as one field of study is not appropriate for all students in a university. *But, again, this is NOT about subjective roads, but objective roads that apply to everyone*. We do what we do because we believe it is right, not for any other reason. This has nothing to do with personal upbringing or appeal to particular lifestyles. This is about figuring out *the* road of all roads. This is about grasping the tree trunk, not the branches that break off the tree. This is about delving into a deeper level.

Again it is undeniable that there are elements of truth found among other religions or beliefs. We can learn about the power of the mind, reverence toward nature, rich philosophies, discipline, meditation, etc. But we can't only be persuaded by the good aspects and become blind to the flaws. We can't stop at the halfway point because it's "good enough." Eastern religions and New Age-type faiths seem to hold this kind of position. Their prime allure is that one can avoid absolutism while believing what one wishes, regardless of its basis or merits. Hinduism is a chief example. Their openness to contradiction can turn into a migraine headache for one seeking logical consistency and rationale. "Truth is one; sages call it by different names," as Hindus say. Really? A Jewish rabbi and a Christian pastor would vehemently disagree with that statement. One can agree that all truth is one (or that it applies to all) only if it is true in the first place.

The bottom line is, there are cracks found in religious beliefs that cannot be ignored. Reincarnation, for instance, tells us we are not distinct individuals. As human beings, we are continuously recycled back into the world into who knows what—we are really no different than a cow, hippo, or anything else. As philosopher J.P. Moreland says, "Reincarnation says that I could come back as a dog, as an amoeba—heck, I don't know why I couldn't come back as an ice cube. If that's true, what's the difference between being J.P. Moreland and anything else? There's nothing essential to me. And just like being even is essential to the number two, so being human is essential to me—and reincarnation says that what is essential to me isn't really essential after all" (Strobel 265).

One has to wonder, if there is no self and we are but a mere illusion, as Eastern religions teach, what is reincarnating from one existence to another? Whose birth is it if there is no real self to be reborn? And if one is paying for bad karma in this life because of a previous life, what were they paying for in their first life (Strobel 212)? Also, in this cyclical process of purification is it not inevitable that more bad karma would attach to this person in future lives? It seems like an endless cycle. We don't even have memory of what we did in our past lives, so what are we being held responsible for? What should we be working to rectify? We are guilty and left in limbo as to the charges.

Another concern is how one would elevate themselves spiritually if one returns as an animal, without the faculties of a human being. Humans have the ability to discern and reason, to discard bad karma and work toward self-perfection, but how do you do this if you are a lizard? There are too many incongruities to be found. The Buddhist's goal is to rid oneself of all desires and wants. However, one must want to rid oneself of desires in the first place, which is a conflicting principle. Hinduism says we are god, yet we are so weak and fragile that we can't even remember we are god? We are one poor excuse for a deity, as one scholar wrote.

The core laws of logic we have been alluding to go a long way against religious deception also. The law of non-contradiction states that we cannot have both A and non-A at the same time. If I am in New York, I cannot possibly be in Florida. It can only be one or the other. This simple logic is a potent weapon against all "spiritualistic"-type faiths that claim that "What is true for me is not true for you" to explain their blatant violation of the laws of logic. If something is True (capital T), it is true for all, but whether one accepts it is quite a different story. Now, any religion that teaches there is no difference between A and non-A and that both exist side by side provides good enough reason to become skeptical.

Too any religions also conflict with a notion we have tackled already: that truth cannot fall upon individual men because of the obvious conflicts that arise. J.N.D. Anderson writes, "A God who speaks in an infinite variety of ways, but never decisively, really throws man back upon himself, for then it is up to man to determine how and where he can reach ultimate truth" (Lutzer 99). Unfortunately, many maintain truth *does* fall upon each man; this way, one can be "good" without having a god or any specific god, while using their own virtues as the standard and going about their business. Christianity sounds less attractive by demanding that we pick up our cross and follow the one referred to as King of Kings. But should we follow Christianity? Christ puts us in a difficult position with very little maneuvering room when answering this question. Why? Because of the exceptional credentials that we have touched upon. We know He claimed to be God, forgave sins, and accepted worship in conjunction with His sinless, miraculous life and resurrection. Those are some of the extraordinary qualifications with which we must grapple. We are forced to either agree with Him or deny Him. There are only three possible conclusions, as C.S. Lewis put it: Christ is either "Lord, Liar, or Lunatic."

∎ ∎ ∎

Since Christ presents a dilemma, let us examine Him more closely. As you may know, the Bible is divided into two parts, the Old and New testaments. In essence, what the Old Testament does is prophesy while the New Testament tells of the one who fulfills, Jesus Christ. For example, in the Old Testament, Micah 5:2, "But you Bethlehem Ephrathah, though you are small among the clans of Judah, out of you will come for me one who will be ruler over Israel." Then in the New Testament we read in Matthew 2:1, "When Jesus was born in Bethlehem in Judea, in the days of King Herod." Isaiah 7:14 states, "Therefore the Lord himself will give you this sign: the virgin shall be with child, and bear a son, and shall name him Immanuel." In the New Testament we find, "Now this is how the birth of Jesus Christ came about. His mother Mary was pledged to be married to Joseph, but before they came together, she was found to be pregnant through the Holy Spirit" (Matthew 1:18 NIV). The uniqueness of Christ quickly emerges with prophecies being fulfilled. Another of a multitude of examples is Zechariah 12:10 (Old Testament NIV): "... they will look at me, the one they have pierced, and they will mourn for him as one mourns for an only child, and grieve bitterly for him as one grieves for a firstborn son." In John 19:34 (New Testament NIV): "One of the soldiers pierced Jesus' side with a spear, bringing a sudden flow of blood and water."

The list continues with numerous prophesies fulfilled by Jesus Christ. How can a person accomplish what is out of his control? The chances are astronomical. Of course, however astronomical the chances, the skeptic would say another lotto ticket has been won. Other doubters would say it's nothing but a scam or setup, but that could hardly be the case when you have authors spanning centuries, independent of each other, who did the writing. The virgin birth of Christ puts Him in a league of His own. There are good arguments for this truth, including Mary and the apostles risking their lives. Even the Koran admits, in Surah 19:16-26, that Jesus was miraculously born of a virgin. This does not help the Islamic case against Christianity. How can a man born of a virgin be a mere man? His origin is unlike that of any other religious teacher. With just this premise, and not knowing anything else, how can any guru or prophet compare to Christ? The Koran even speaks of Jesus making a bird out of mud and breathing life into it and speaking as a baby also. The differences between the two are legion, at least one would think.

Consider Muslim author Sumbul Ali-Karamali, who writes in her book *The Muslim Next Door*, "Muslims believe that God entrusted Jesus with the same message as Muhammad, but that Jesus's message went a little awry and his followers began worshipping him instead of Allah" (40). In other words, Muslims believe Christ was miraculously born of a virgin (a spectacular phenomena which undoubtedly makes Him unique), yet was incompetent by failing to accomplish His mission. In the meantime, Muhammad, the mere man born of a woman, achieved it?! One is left scratching one's head. Muhammad was not even raised into Heaven, but Muslims claim Jesus ascended to the heavens (Surah 4:157-158). Meanwhile, Muhammad sits buried six feet under like all normal humans, but we are supposed to accept him as the greatest of prophets?

■ ■ ■

One can only stand impressed studying the life of Christ. It is one of the purest ever lived. What you get are flawless qualities. Great religious teachers and gurus acknowledge this. He has been described as one who has reached the highest level of "enlightenment." Mohandas Gandhi once said, "I shall say to the Hindus that your life will be incomplete unless you reverentially study the teachings of Jesus."

One of the bold claims Christianity teaches is that Christ lived a sinless life. Notice what others had to say about Him. Judas, who betrayed Jesus, admits, "I have sinned … for I have betrayed innocent blood" (Matthew 27:4). Pilate, the Roman governor, said, "I have conducted my investigation in your presence and have not found this man guilty of the charges you have brought against him" (Luke 23:14-15). Pilate's wife says, "Don't have anything to do with that innocent man" (Matthew 27:19). The thief next to Christ while on the cross said, "We are punished justly, for we are getting what our deeds deserve. But this man has done nothing wrong" (Luke 23:41).

People falsely defame Christ by looking at his followers. Some Christians are wretched. Although Gandhi praised the exceptional life of Christ, he also said that he is not Christian because Christians do not act very Christ-like. Similarly, Friedrich Nietzsche said, "I will believe in the Redeemer when the Christian looks a little more redeemed" (Strobel 210). These points must be recognized. With deep regret I recall some of the ways I responded to folks during debates. It wasn't very Christ-like. What ignorance, as I look back now. I was wrong and I was a bad representative of the faith. But, it does not follow that because some do not uphold the standard of the faith, that they should, therefore, ignore the claims of Christianity or Christ. Plenty of faults and sinful behavior can be found in individuals anywhere, but if we look at the founder of the Christian faith, one will find quite a different story.

Now, looking at the founders of other religions, they themselves underwent their own personal struggles. Christ did not struggle with sin; He went around forgiving sin. He was like men in all ways except sin. Buddha, for example, had multiple rebirths, suggesting he lived imperfect lives (reincarnation). Christians are taught that we live only once and holiness can be achieved in this one life through God, who makes all things possible. Also, if we look at Buddha's story, we find he left his home, leaving behind his family, wife, and son, in search for understanding he did not have. He was seeking a path to enlightenment and purity. One can only conclude that if he was in search of these attributes, he did not possess them. Christ never sought answers or insight; He was enlightened and pure from the beginning.

Similarly, another famous guru, Confucius, who attempted to establish peace within his culture and failed, only ended up perplexed. According to Dean Halverson, "Confucius asked himself: Does the failure to reconstruct a harmonious cultural order mean that the concepts of virtue or goodness are not eternal and transcendent? ... What is the foundation of virtue and goodness in an age of confusion?" (72) Confucius also acknowledges, "The way of the superior man is threefold, but I have not been able to attain it" (ibid79). There is no such inner seeking, confusion, or perplexity with Christ. He knew where He came from and where He was going. He wasn't seeking purity, fulfillment, or answers to philosophical questions. He was looking to fulfill and teach others and guide the disoriented.

Turning to Mohammad, "Although Muslims revere Muhammad as the embodiment of goodness and human perfection" (Ali-Karamali 34), he was told to ask for forgiveness in Surah 47-48. Christ never asks for forgiveness. Instead, again, He went around forgiving others, an assertion made by no other famous religious leader. One can only imagine the kind of life Mohammed led as a military commander, living life by the sword. Much criticism and debate can arise with his history of battles, slave ownership, morality, and marriages. Christ is not subject to any controversy except that of Him being more than a mere man.

Muslims claim Mohammed lived a courageous and virtuous life, and I do not deny he had good attributes, but the question is how he compares to Christ. Even the most devout Muslim will admit that when Mohammed first claimed to receive spiritual revelation, he was confused. He wasn't sure what it meant. He consulted his wife and companions to receive assurance of what he had experienced. *After Muhammad recovered from his shock on that night, he began preaching the glory of the One God* (Ali-Karamali 52). Again, there is no confusion or shock in Jesus' story. He knew His mission and accomplished it, or, as He said in John 17:4, "I glorified you on earth by accomplishing the work that you gave me to do." In Luke 2:49 he also states, "... I must be about my Father's business." When He was done with His business, hanging on a cross, He said, "It is finished." Although Christ claims to have accomplished his mission, Muslims believe He did not quite meet his goals, or that again, His message went awry.

A common thread tying major religions is that there is something spiritually wrong with humanity. We need some internal fixing, but why, and how do we go about it? Christianity says sin is the problem of mankind, while other religions basically maintain it is ignorance, attachments, unhappiness, a lack of love , or desires that cause our spiritual depravity. Regardless of the source, all spiritualists, prophets, teachers, and gurus exhibited defects in themselves. It follows, then, that we all need rescuing, and if we need saving, it cannot be from one who needs to be rescued. We have a situation where we have defective men instructing other flawed men. Christ is the only one who demonstrates no defect or need for rescue. For as He says, "The Son of Man has come to seek and to save that which was lost" (Luke 19:10).

Christ invited people to Him two thousand years ago and still does today like no one else. He knows we are in need and offers comfort in our trials and difficulties of life (2 Corinthians 1:3-4). He extends wisdom for decision-making (James 1:5), strength when we are weary (Psalm 29:11), and purpose in confusion (Mark 8:34). "I have come that they may have life, and that they may have it more abundantly," Christ said (John 10:10). Above all else, we are in need of salvation, and "Whoever believes in Him shall not perish but have eternal life" (John 3:15). This is the voice of someone who certainly needs no rescuing or internal fixing. This is the voice of our only hope.

■ ■ ■

Let me elaborate more precisely on the religion I have dealt with most, due to my profession and the events of 9/11: Islam. As a New Yorker there is no denying that incident struck a chord. I recall the tragic events vividly. The attacks by extremists are one thing, but watching Muslims overseas celebrating the fall of the towers on TV was quite another. This event prompted me to examine the Muslim faith like no other religion.

My initial research raised many flags concerning Islam such as how it spread throughout the Middle East, treatment of women, Sharia Law and other doctrines. But I was not only reading about Islam; I also had some firsthand experience traveling to many Middle Eastern countries. I noticed that showing or having a different faith in certain Muslim countries needed to be avoided. My observations were confirmed by my intelligence briefings. I recall a friend of a colleague was arrested and later released and given a day to leave Saudi Arabia simply because he had a Bible on his person. I have been to countries such as Pakistan, Afghanistan, Iraq, Yemen, and Saudi Arabia, and I have received a dosage of their perspective towards the West and those of different faiths. Walking around displaying a crucifix does not provoke a spirit of peace. There is no Christian country where one is concerned for their very safety for having a different faith, yet Islam is the religion revealed by God and referred to by many as a religion of peace?

There is no denying there are good, peaceful Muslims. I know some myself and would not dare label them extremist. But the ones I know display a devotion to their faith similar to Christians who say there is no need to go to church on Sunday. Due to this lack of devotion, I reverted to Muslim writers to get the real inside scoop on their beliefs, as I did with atheists. The authors were informative and devout. They shed light on many topics. They contradicted all my established knowledge. It seemed every conclusion I formulated about Islam was distorted or incorrect. The authors portrayed Islam as almost impeccable in its teaching and history. For example, Mohammed and his followers did not kill to spread the faith; rather, they killed because they "suffered persecution, treachery, and political strife" according to author Ali-Karamali. They were but "defending themselves" (173). Though there are elements of truth here also, my overall history and understanding of Islam and the Middle East was quite skewed. I mean, the "whole Arabian peninsula accepted Islam," according to author and professor of Muslim studies Abdel Haleem (*The Qur'an* xiii). Regardless of how Islam spread (though I disagree with Abdel Haleem), early Christianity also suffered tremendous persecution, but the faith did not spread through the sword, or require Christians to defend themselves. The Christian faith spread like wildfire due to believers living out their faith, and when persecution came they gladly died as martyrs, not by organizing battles. Christianity conquered not through the sword, but through hearts—a colossal difference.

Devout Muslim writers often refer to atrocities by extremists as "isolated incidents." One could understand this perspective, since the conniving ways of men can be found anywhere and everywhere, but why so many "isolated incidents" attributed to devoted Muslims who claim they are following the Koran or the will of Allah? With this obvious discord one can only isolate the problem to the interpretation of the Koran. Some claim certain verses no longer apply since times of old have changed, while others claim the contrary. Haleem writes, "The Qur'an is the word of God, revealed to the Prophet Muhammad ... and intended for all times and all places" (*The Qur'an* ix). Experience with the Muslim faith would suggest that many hold to the views of Mr. Haleem. That being the case, consider what are known as "sword verses," such as Surah 2:191, which reads, "Kill the unbeliever wherever you find him." Surah 8:7: "Allah wishes to confirm the truth by words, wipe the infidel out to the last." Surah 9:5: "Fight and slay unbelievers wherever you find them and seize them, confine them, and lie in wait for them in every place of ambush. But if they should repent, establish prayer, and give zakah, let them go on their way." In Surah 9:29 we read, "Fight those who do not believe in Allah or in the Last Day and who do not consider unlawful what Allah and His Messenger have made unlawful and who do not adopt the religion of truth." There are too many to mention, but to put an exclamation on this point, the Koran states that it is not the individual, but Allah himself, who is doing the slaying, using us as his instruments. "It is not us who slay them but Allah, in order that He might test the believers" (Surah 8:17).

Such verses can certainly be taken out of context, so interpretational problems can quickly arise and be of great consequence. As a friend told me, "Everything must be read within context, and some Muslims take many of these verses out of context and historical scope." That is a fair point. Being that the Koran is supreme in Islam, I attempted to find an authority on its writings in order to solve the problem of interpretations, so that I could make conclusions based on the *official* teachings of Islam, rather than on some cleric or other individual spreading his opinion. My search quickly ended in vain, since there is no defined authority on the contents of the Koran, but the mere interpretation of the one holding the book.

Ali-Karamali writes, "There exists no single Islam, no absolute interpretation of it—just as there is no single, absolute interpretation of

Christianity or Judaism or any other religion" (3). So how can one blame those who interpret the Koran differently when the individual is the authority? By the way, it is an *entirely false* statement that Christianity has no "absolute interpretation" or authority on scriptural interpretation, but we will discuss that matter in further detail in due time. Benazir Bhutto, in her book *Reconciliation: Islam, Democracy and the West*, writes, "Equally important to the context of interpretation of the Quran is who interprets it. Some Muslims, especially those belonging to theocratic regimes, try to assert that only a select few can interpret the Quran. This is not the case. Interpretation of the Quran is not limited to any one person or committee. The Quran did not establish a specific institution of group of leaders as its sole interpreters. Any Muslim is free to interpret the Quran. All Muslims are guaranteed the right to interpret the Quran. Muslim are told that each person is accountable for his or her individual behavior. No relative, teacher, or other can intervene for a Muslim on the Day of Judgment" (65).

It could not be stated any more clearly. These Muslim authors claim others are wrong in their interpretation of the Koran due to their conduct, and then go on to speak about "proper interpretations and teachings," making themselves the authority! It is outright perplexing.

With this lack of authority, no one can fault anyone for their personal conclusions, if this is how Allah has spoken to them via scripture. Take something as simple as taking photos. Ali-Karamali writes, "People get carried away in their efforts to be devout. I went to a Muslim wedding recently in which we were disallowed from taking photographs. This is the most extreme and expansive interpretation of this fear of idol-worship (photograph-worship in this case) that I have ever come across. Nearly all the guests at the wedding, mostly Muslim, did not agree with the view" (37). Since Ali-Karamali does not agree with those having the wedding and their view of photography, they, of course, are "carried away" for having such an outlook on idolatry. But surely those getting married would call themselves rightly devout, though disagreeing parties call them extremist. The author also writes that *nearly all the guests* did not agree with their perspective of idolatry, but what of those who did agree with not taking photographs? Is their interpretation not valid? If not, why not? Does not the interpretation of the Koran boil down to the individual? And what does "nearly" all guests mean ... 80 percent or 90 percent agreed with Ali-Karamali about photography not being idolatry? If there were one hundred people at the wedding and 10 percent viewed differently, that would make ten people not believing in taking photos. If there were one thousand, it would make one hundred siding differently. Now take more than a billion Muslims around the world—the numbers become significant. This can be applied to any Islamic doctrine, especially those questionable sword verses. It is no wonder such diverse opinions and "extremism" exist.

There are too many difficult doctrines to reconcile when Islam scripture boils down to individual opinion. One can debate at length the subject of whether women have equal rights to their inheritance or not. My interpretation of Surah 4:11-12 clearly states they do not have equal rights. Can a husband strike a disobedient wife? It appears he can, but read Surah 4:34 and make your own interpretation.

■ ■ ■

The bottom line is, many religions quickly grow shaky under scrutiny while logical consistency, empirical evidence, and existential relevancy persist in the Christian faith. Though Christianity is not without its critics, its founder is unlike anyone who has ever lived. That is *the* crucial point to grasp. Within Christianity one also finds all the big questions of life answered clearly, such as the purpose of man, his destiny, and how he ought to live. Others' belief systems are ambiguous in these areas. Christianity plainly teaches that each person has been created by God for a purpose, and what awaits us is either eternal life with God or eternal separation from Him. This teaching, by the way, clearly conflicts with many religions that believe God is not interested in the affairs of mankind (deism). Christianity states that God is personal and cares deeply for us, and wishes all to know Him intimately. This is one of the most unique teachings of the Christian faith. God is not some distant, abstract, silent, or unknowable being. He is not indifferent about us. He cares for us, hears us, and answers our prayers, unlike the complex voids found in religions whose primary goal is to rid oneself of the illusion of self, ego, desires, suffering, evil, and so on.

Also standing distinctively in the Christian faith is the concept of self-reliance. Christians are not alone in their spiritual journey as many are in other faiths. Instead, He says He will never leave us or forsake us. Jesus said, "Come to me, all you who labor and are burden, and I will give you rest. Take my yoke upon you and learn from me, for I am meek and humble of heart; and you will find rest for yourselves. For my yoke is easy, and my burden light" (Matthew 11:28). With other religions, one has a relationship with certain rituals, mental disciplines, or philosophical ideas, but with Christ we get personal with a loving God. He guides us and talks to us, while other beliefs primarily teach self-actualization by telling us to pull ourselves up by our meditative and moral bootstraps, to reach some level of perfection or self-actualization. Christianity declares that no matter what we do, all human effort falls short of the perfection of God. Thus, we must lean on the saving works of Christ to get us to the finish line, because we cannot do it ourselves. We are spiritually dead, and the dead cannot help themselves.

Christ's uniqueness simply cannot be swept under the rug. The signs and wonders of His life are beyond human and can only be attributed to divinity. Confucius, Buddha, and Muhammad performed no miracles and cannot claim they rose from the dead. Many critics, in order to deny Him, attempt to peel Christ down to a mere man or another spiritual guru, but studying His life and works makes that position very difficult to accept. The high priest said to Him, "I order you to tell us under oath before the living God whether you are the Messiah, the son of the living God." Jesus said in reply, "You have said so. But I tell you: From now on you will see the Son of Man seated at the right hand of the Mighty one coming down from the clouds of heaven." (Matthew 26:64). If He is not who He claims, that statement is as blasphemous as they come. That is why the high priest tore His robes when he heard these words. This claim is ultimately why Christ was crucified. But such "blasphemy" cannot be attributed to a man who is revered for His character and virtues. Such a statement can only come from a liar or lunatic, and there isn't the slightest hint that Christ was either. The claims of this Jesus of Nazareth are staggering. Everyone was shocked by Him—from His disciples to His enemies and everyone in between. "Never has anyone spoken like this" (John 7:46). The fact is we must face the very question He presented two thousand years ago: "If I am telling the truth, why do you not believe me?" (John 8:46)

No leader throughout history, whether secular or religious, had the audacity to say, "I am the bread of life; he who comes to me will never hunger ... he who believes in me will never thirst." The Christ who came into the world two thousand years ago claimed to be the light of the world: "He who follows me ... shall have the light of life" (John 8:12), yet other spiritual leaders die seeking light. Mohammed claimed to be a prophet and descendant of Abraham, but Jesus said, "Before Abraham was born, I Am" (John 8:58). One is indeed left in shock at His statements. New Age religions continue seeking and long for peace and tranquility, while Christ says, "Peace I leave with you; My peace I give to you; not as the world gives do I give to you" (John 14:27). Many religions and their leaders claim reincarnation, various versions of the recycling of life, but none say, "I am the resurrection and the life; he that believes in me, though he dies, he shall live" (John 11:25). One can only remain speechless and in awe. While all other teachers claim to be speaking the truth, Christ claimed to be *the* Truth (John 14:6).

Now if Christ is the redeemer, He is not only the redeemer in Brazil; He must also be the redeemer of the rest of the world. If He is the Truth (capital T), as He claims, then He is the Truth for everyone, not just some. If He is not who He claims, He is the Truth for none; His claims are false and He is the savior to no one! We must think seriously about who this man is and ask ourselves the very question He posed to His apostles: "Who do people say that I am?" (Mark 8:27)

WORLD RELIGION/CHRISTIANITY COMMENTS AND RESPONSES

The following is a compilation of related chats popularly brought to light on this topic:

Comment: Do you mean to tell me those who have not heard or known Christ are destined to damnation? One can only be held accountable for personal experiences or knowledge, not foreign ideas.
Response: God knows where we will be born and raised, and those who do not know the facts through no fault of their own will not be condemned. People will be held accountable to the degree of knowledge they have been exposed.

Reverend Carty writes, "The merits and grace of Christ were applied by God to men of goodwill ... Those who through no fault of their own did not know of a Redeemer to come were saved if they obeyed the natural dictates of their conscience, and repented of their failings. Every single human being has the moral standard that what is apprehended to be morally good must be done, whilst moral evil must be avoided" (1: 42).

Whatever the outcome for those who have not heard of Christ, we can trust God will do what is right, for He cannot commit an injustice, so let us leave the ultimate fate of those who have not heard of Christ to the God who judges righteously.

Comment: Then it really doesn't matter what path one takes to God if one is saved anyway.

Response: That is an extravagant conclusion. If God has set out a path for us to follow then it does matter. You want to plead ignorance when you know more is required of you. There is nothing noble about ignorance. Knowledge is better than ignorance. You, like many others, want to meet God under your conditions, not His. But, it is for the Almighty to determine what path we shall take to Him, and we are called to respond to His plans.

His plans included sending His only begotten Son into the world to suffer, bear our sins and to show us the right path to Him. If God went to such extreme, it must be important to Him that we follow His teachings, rather than whatever we can imagine. To say what God has done really doesn't matter is an offense to Him.

Comment: I prefer the philosophy that all roads lead to the same destination.
Response: You should prefer what conforms to reality, since reality cannot adapt to your preferences. Why is it that so many think that truths should be adjusted to their ideas? Again, all roads are *not* the same, and even if some arrive at the same destination, a paved road is better than a dirt road filled with rocks and holes. Let us at least attempt to get on the prepared surface for a smoother ride. Your mentality doesn't seem to be interested in real wisdom and understanding. It seems indifferent about truth and error.

Comment: I grew up in an evangelical church, I'm married to a Catholic, I myself am a Zen Buddhist, I've considered Taoism and Unitarian Universalism along the way, I've read many religious texts. I've just gotten different answers than you. The difference is you think your beliefs are superior because that's what you chose or prefer. Not having the same spiritual needs as you does not make others stupid.
Response: First, I have not called anyone stupid. Secondly, I don't "prefer" Christianity because I choose it, but because it is where reason leads. The only reason one should believe anything in this world is because it's true.

If Christianity is not true, it should be disregarded and so should the religions you mention. But, you open a lengthy subject in comparing religions, to which we cannot do any justice over an Internet chat. I will say this much: Christianity surpasses other religions based on the credentials of its founder, historical basis, teaching, and reasonableness.

Comment: We do not know the whole truth about anything so how can one group have the nerve to claim they possess it in religious matters?
Response: We do not know the whole truth about God, but this does not mean we don't know anything about Him. What He has revealed can be known and deciphered. He certainly has not revealed countless religions contradicting themselves, sending each and every man in all sorts of directions.

Comment: In the end, God knows our sincerity, and that will do.
Response: Sincerity is good, but it may not go far enough. All the sincerity in the world will not do for the one who wants to lose weight, yet sits on their couch watching TV and eating all day. We can apply this concept to anything in life. Sincerity demands action. You believe in God but ignore His claims. Why should your sincerity in religious matters suffice while you go about your daily business? Don't hide behind "sincerity" to avoid the hassles of finding religious truths.

The only way your "sincerity" argument can hold is if you honestly believed that sincerity is all that is required of us and nothing else. Then your lack of knowledge may be excused, since no one is called to violate their conscience. If you should suspect more is required than just sincerity, than you are not free to remain in your "sincerity."

Comment: Eastern spiritualism works well for me. Christianity works for you, so let it be!
Response: There is a significant difference between what works and what is true. A lie, for example, may have temporary benefits, but only temporarily.

I noticed you have a tendency to speak of "spiritualism" as if it is something exclusive to Eastern religions. Christianity is very much about spiritualism and has attained giant mystics throughout the ages. The issue is that in our spiritual endeavors and advancements, we must focus our energy in its rightful place. Not the Earth or Mother Nature. Not just our minds nor the universe or any created thing, but the creator Himself. God created all these good things to lead us to Him, not to focus on them alone. Indeed the activities of spirituality such as meditation are great tools to elevate the mind and spirit. It is a very commendable undertaking, but what we need most is not just rising above the sensual realm, but the using of spiritual tools to obtain the higher plain of the salvation of our souls.

Comment: Why do you hate other religious folks and their beliefs?
Response: I do not hate other religious folks and their beliefs. I appreciate everything good and true about other religions, but I am not going to be blind to errors. This is about analyzing theories, not insulting people. If no differentiation between concepts can be made, then we are no different than brute animals; but we are endowed with intelligence, and intelligence makes distinctions between ideas.

Comment: The exclusivity and bigotry of Christianity will be its downfall.
Response: One would expect a religion to make exclusive claims if indeed they be true. Truth excludes its opposite, falsehood. But claims of exclusivity don't fall on Christianity alone. Take one of the most popular religions, Islam. In the Koran we read "True religion in God's eye is Islam" (Surah 3:19). Surah 3:85 states, "If anyone seeks a religion other than Islam, it will not be accepted from him: he will be one of the losers in the Hereafter."

The idea that Christianity makes exclusive truth claims ignores the fact others do the same. Also, it is important to recognize that Jesus Himself claims to be the Truth, not Christians about themselves.

Comment: What we need to do is concentrate on living good happy lives and treating each other with kindness and respect instead of debating. When this is done, all else will fall into place.
Response: One can treat others with respect while not subscribing to their theories. But you are mistaken if you think this life is just about morality and being happy. Christ did not simply come to make bad people good

or happy, but to make dead people alive. If this life were just about being good, we would be in a world of hurt since we all fall short. No one can live up to the standard and character of God.

Ravi Zacharias states, "How a person lives and how he treats his neighbor is very important. But it is not more important than what he believes, because the way he lives is reflective of what he believes" (Strobel 218).

Comment: If Christ is God, why did He have to die for forgiveness of sins? Why didn't He just forgive sins and be done?
Response: Because actions have consequences. We have sinned against God and, as a result, we are separated from Him. To restore this relationship, forgiveness is necessary. The only one who can forgive is he who is offended. *Now forgiveness is not without cost.* It has its price. When someone sins against you personally and you forgive them, you take the hurt and the results caused by their wrong actions (sin). So in essence we are taking upon the wrongs of the person on ourselves. That is what Christ did by dying. He represented the one who was sinned against, being that He was both God and man. He is the only one who is suitable to bear our wrongs, making forgiveness available to all.

Comment: Islam is the true and complete revelation of God's religion. It's the world's fastest-growing religion. That speaks volumes for itself.
Response: Islam may be the world's fastest-growing religion due to geopolitical considerations and birthrates that dwarf others in order to fulfill Islamic agendas. Regardless of the number of Muslims, it has no bearing on the question of whether it is true or not. Islam did not suddenly become true when it surpassed the number of Hindu or Buddhist adherents. Truth (capital T) is not dependent on how many people believe it.

Comment: You show grave ignorance concerning many facets of the Islamic faith. You spoke of Jihad, and it does not relate to war or strife, but the internal spiritual struggle to do God's will.
Response: The word Jihad can mean a couple of things. It can represent a believer's internal struggle to live out the Muslim faith or the struggle to defend Islam (holy war). Many modern Muslim writers claim the primary

meaning of Jihad is an internal spiritual struggle. But, there are so many references to Jihad as a military struggle in Islamic writings that it is obvious as to why many would interpret it that way. Take for example Surah 9:39: "Unless we go forth [for Jihad], He will punish us with a grievous penalty, and put others in our place." Also, "Believers, when you encounter the armies of the infidels, do not turn your backs to them in flight. If anyone on that day turns his back to them, except it be for tactical reasons, or to join another band, he shall incur the wrath of Allah and Hell shall be his home: an evil fate" (Surah 8:13-17). These sound more like Jihad the holy war version.

Comment: How about concentrating on some commonalities such as the fact that Islam and Christianity worship the same God to begin building some bridges.
Response: Let's put that statement to the test. If Christ is God, we should worship Him. Jesus Christ proves and claims to be God, therefore Christians worship Him. Muslims do not worship Christ and reject his divinity. It stands, then, that Muslim and Christians do not worship the same God. To build bridges is noble, but it cannot be done under false premises.

Comment: You talk a lot on behalf of Christianity when it can be compared to the butchery of Sharia law. You seem to be conveniently forgetting about the atrocities of your Christian God in the Old Testament.
Response: The Bible as a whole in conjunction with Christ is night and day compared to the Koran and Mohammed. To put it simply, the God of the Old and New testaments are the same. He is immutable. All His actions are justified; nothing He does violate His attributes. What we must extract is that God is not just a God of love but of justice. There is no injustice with God, as Romans 9:14 states. It is not for God to adjust to our ideas of justice.

One would be hard-pressed to find anything in the New Testament or teachings of Christ, who is the center of Christianity, similar to Sharia Law. Christ said, "Let the first one without sin cast the first stone." He also said, "You have heard it said take an eye for eye, tooth for a tooth, but I tell you the truth, pray for those who persecute you and love your enemies." The apostles asked Him, if someone sins against a person how many times should we forgive him? Christ said, "Not seven but seventy-seven times" (Matthew 18:22). He said to turn the other cheek, and speaks of loving your enemy. "If your enemy is hungry, feed him; if he is thirsty, give him something to drink; for by doing so you will heap burning coals on his head. Do not be overcome by evil, but overcome evil with good. Vengeance is mine, says the Lord" (Romans 12:17-21). No one can use Christian teaching to justify stoning, hanging, lashing, beheading, flogging, amputated limbs, etc., as they can with Sharia laws.

The bottom line is the founders and teachings of these religions are day and night. Jesus Christ stands out in all aspects. Meanwhile, one can go to Turkey today to view the sword of Mohammed. One has to wonder how many fell under the sword of the prophet. Should he have used a sword in the first place? Christ did not. He loved every one into His kingdom. He simply said, "Come follow me." Love is an invitation; it is never forced.

Comment: Christianity derives from paganism and ancient myths. It is but a compilation of borrowed ideas.
Response: That is a popular comment amongst atheists/humanists with no other basis but hearsay. Can you be more specific, since that's as far as most nonbelievers go? What about the evidence for the faith? Is that made up too? If you actually did some investigation, you would find the evidence for revealed religion far outweighs your notions.

You must understand there are practices or similarities that transcend all cultures. There are *commonalities* in life that are unavoidable, being that we come from the same great architect. Even a saint has commonalities with an evildoer. False belief systems have specks of truth in them also. Commonalities are a natural phenomenon of life. We borrow and advance ideas from other people and cultures. New concepts and innovations, for instance, derive from the observation of world fashion, technology, art, and music. How often do we hear folks mention how so-and-so influenced or inspired them? Similarities and overlaps of certain ideas are undeniable.

Do you suggest Christians not make New Year's resolutions because the concept goes back over three thousand years, to the pagan origins of the ancient Babylonians? Should Christians abstain from using water for baptism since ancient pagans used it in ceremonial rites? Similarities do not deny the facts of the faith. You can rest assured all pagan notions have been purified to reflect real Christianity.

Comment: Hogwash. The Christian Trinity, for example, has its origins in Indian myths.
Response: Anything anti-Christian is suitable evidence for the nonbeliever regardless of substance. I will quote Rev. Carty on this issue. He writes, "In the Vedic philosophy there are traces of a trinity, but not of *the* Trinity. The idea of Father, Son, and Holy Ghost is not to be found in it. That philosophy taught a pantheistic notion, all things being a kind of emanation from God to be reabsorbed into Him. It has no distinction such as ours between the creator and the creature, and Brahma, Vishnu, and Siva bear no real resemblance whatever to the Christian doctrine of three divine and equal personalities sharing the one divine nature ... You might just as well try to account for the notion of the Trinity from any notion of triplicity wherever it occurs" *(*1: 135*)*.

Comment: That does not refute that Christianity is full of myths and fantasies. They finessed their own and embodied it in the fairy tale book called the Bible.
Response: With so many independent authors in the Bible, how did they coordinate this lie spanning centuries? Who made up the lie and why? Was it to get tortured and put to death to defend what they knew was a lie? What you should be considering is what took Christians into the lion's den singing hymns rather than denouncing their faith. I don't attribute the spread of Christianity to a fictitious Christ, but to a living Christ who transformed man's interior disposition.

Also, myths are not just fictitious stories or without substance. They are used to convey truths metaphorically. In other words, a story doesn't have to be literally true on the outside to be so on the inside. We are supposed to grasp the substance rather than each and every detail of a story, such as God creating the world in seven days and then having to rest due to being "exhausted." To illustrate further, you may have seen or read *The Lion, the Witch, and the Wardrobe* by C.S. Lewis. Though the characters and events in the movie are fictitious, it does not mean the story has no foundation or basis in truth. It has strong symbolic implications: God is good and sacrificed Himself for others. Rest assured there is nothing fictitious about Christianity.

Comment: Many theologians and church leaders acknowledge the paganism found in Christianity.
Response: I don't know what theologians or church leaders you are referring to, but because Christianity may have some similarities with false religions, it does not mean they are of the same source or origin. Again, even Paganism with its errors has particles of truths that can be extracted. As Christianity developed and evangelized, it retained only truths while filtering all errors and pagan notions. There is nothing wrong with using purified truths to spread and express the faith.

Comment: The Bible refutes itself with all the inconsistencies found in it.
Response: There are no real inconsistencies, and what appears to be contradictory, can be reconciled. Each writer of the Gospel gives a partial story from their experience while others give complementary details. If you took a road trip to Florida from New York with friends you don't have to mention your stop in North Carolina, though you can certainly remark about your experiences in Virginia. Another friend could speak of your North Carolina experience, which was neglected by you, and add more details to the adventures you've mentioned in Virginia. An outsider might find inconsistencies, but after further examination he would find you actually went to both places. One fact does not omit the other. You will find this same phenomenon in the Gospel.

If you want to learn about this matter in detail, I recommend reading *The Case for Christ* by Lee Strobel who goes into a thorough investigation into the documentary and historical evidence of Christ.

Comment: How do we know the New Testament is reliable history? For all we know the stories may have been corrupted and manipulated. Are there any writings outside the Bible of these events?

Response: We know they are reliable in the same way we know any other historical piece of information is reliable. You don't question the historical foundations of other classical material, yet there is plenty more evidence for the events in the Gospel. It surpasses all criteria of historical criticism applied to other books. If the New Testament is unreliable, then there is little to no reliable history to our knowledge.

Historical and archeological evidence demonstrates the trustworthiness of biblical history and withstands the most detailed scrutiny. The degree of accuracy in the New Testament exceeds 99 percent, which is greater than that of any other book from the ancient world (*The Compact Guide to World Religions* 259). From the voluminous number of ancient manuscripts, to the very early dating of documents written during the lifetime of eyewitnesses, to the multiplicity of the accounts (nine authors in twenty-seven books of the New Testament), Christianity sets the bar in terms of providing proof to back up its claims. Archaeologist Nelson Glueck writes, "No archaeological discovery has ever controverted a Biblical reference." Archaeologist Millar Burrow states, "More than one archaeologist has found his respect for the Bible increased by the experience of excavation in Palestine" (Halverson 256).

You also seek evidence outside the Bible? Although the Gospel writers are reliably informed eyewitnesses who can also be called historians, the Roman historian Tacitus speaks of Christ as well as Josephus the Jewish historian. Tacitus makes it clear that Christ was the founder of the Christian movement. He records that Christ was executed by Pontius Pilate during the reign of Tiberius and that Judea was the origin of Christianity. Much can be said about this topic, but you can be quite sure these are not invented or manipulated stories. If they were, the writers themselves are evil for their deception. But, wicked men could not have written the New Testament, for it condemns them. All these men showed nothing but the highest standard of ethics and integrity. Again, I highly recommend reading The Case for Christ by Lee Strobel.

THE CHRISTIAN FIASCO

"We shall return to proven ways—not because they are old, but because they are true."

— Barry Goldwater

With all we have considered thus far, it follows that *if* Christianity is True, God has made provisions for His religion. The task now is deciphering to whom and how He has revealed this knowledge. Who is the steward of the Christian faith? To answer these questions, we must narrow our focus down from the multiplicity of world religions and delve further into Christianity. In doing so, another massive hurdle manifests: the hundreds of Christian sects conflicting with each other, claiming to possess the "truth of Christianity." We have within the ranks of Christianity much falsity to be found, and an abundant number of sincere but mistaken individuals. So which branch of Christianity is correct? Let me share my story of how I came to my Christian verdict.

■ ■ ■

Catholicism has been at the forefront of my debates and discussions. I can only attribute this to the misunderstandings or blatantly wrong information many people have about the Catholic Church. The things I hear as a Catholic Christian make me scratch my head in disbelief. Catholicism, unfortunately, gets prosecuted before it is even heard out. Typically, those who attack it have no real grasp of what the Church teaches in the first place. Their study or knowledge of Catholicism is almost or totally nonexistent. Their position is based on hearsay and blind prejudice alone, not genuine inquiry. If I had the ideas they subscribe to I would be just as outraged. This is why I intend to clarify some misconceptions. A clear explanation of facts carries tremendous weight with unprejudiced minds.

■ ■ ■

"He is not the God of disorder but of peace."

—— *1 Corinthians 14:33*

As a cradle Catholic growing up, I never thoroughly questioned or understood my faith, until I began my personal search for spiritual truths. As I sought knowledge and understanding, it was inevitable that I come across other spiritual seekers. I encountered Baptists, Southern Baptists, Presbyterians, Mormons, Evangelicals, Jehovah's Witnesses, Methodists, Pentecostals, Calvinists, and other nondenominational individuals. Not that I hadn't encountered people of faith before—I just did not pay them any real mind. But in my personal quest I became more cognizant of believers. I was eager to know their experiences and what they had come to learn in their walk in the faith. I enjoyed chatting with and soaking up knowledge from those who had already walked the path I was only beginning to venture down, but this would prove short-lived. The more I associated with Christians, the more uneasy I felt. It dawned on me that the multitude of denominations did not add up to some total truth of Christianity, just as I mistakenly thought world religion comprised some complete truth of God. The more I mingled with other Christians, the more pronounced an incompatibility became with my Catholic upbringing.

During one occasion, I was informed that it is ridiculous that I confess to a priest. I had always been taught that the normal means of forgiveness was to confess to a priest, so what was the Catholic Church talking about? I was even familiar with John 20:23: "Receive the Holy Spirit. Whose sins you forgive, they are forgiven; if you do not forgive them, they are not forgiven." OK, so which one was it? I grew confused and agitated.

As time passed my ears became even more keen to negative and sarcastic remarks floating through various churches. Having been bred Catholic, the comments about Catholicism in particular hit home. People spoke as if I had been taught and had believed in a lie my whole life. I was accused of being part of an "unbiblical church." Now, according to these critics, I had come to some sort of enlightenment concerning true Christianity, since I had left the Church. Though I never officially left the Catholic Church; I simply went where I was invited. I did not know any better in my gullibility and ignorance. The Kingdom Hall of Jehovah's Witnesses was no different than the Baptist church down the street. My mindset was that Christianity was Christianity no matter where I went. All that mattered is that we acknowledge Jesus—or at least that's what I thought.

But it became apparent to me that there was more to the faith than just saying "Jesus." As I gained more exposure to various sects, I could no longer deny or ignore the inconsistencies. I came to grips with the reality that there was no unity in Christian teaching. Every group essentially does what it believes to be right according to the Bible. Being an officer in the military, I was used to standardization, which I found lacking in Christianity. In discontent, my flourishing faith hit a tailspin and became stagnant. Even some skepticism loitered in my mind. How can one Christian church teach that there is no Hell, while another declares differently? One holds that the consecrated bread and wine is the actual body and blood of Christ, while another claims it is only a symbol. I heard varying doctrines about the Trinity, baptism, and salvation, so on and so forth, which left me bewildered. In the meantime, each entity unwaveringly claimed they were the true followers of the Bible while flagrantly contradicting each other.

Though I met exceptional folks wherever I attended church, this could not be used as the basis of validity. One can find exceptional individuals in all walks of life, but that does not prove their beliefs true. If that were the case, a "good" Jehovah's Witness cannot negate the "good" Southern Baptist, and vice versa. Certainly the good Baptist does not possess the truths of Christianity if the good Jehovah's Witness does. Or should we take the position that Christ, truth Himself, revealed all these contradictions? No, because we know the hallmark of truth is consistency.

When I began to inquire into these irksome issues, I received responses from both ends of the spectrum: indifference and passion. The passionate fervently referred to biblical passages to support their claims, while other motivated individuals quickly negated those statements using scripture of their own. For the time being, I was at a loss. It appeared solid answers were out of reach.

The indifferent were not too concerned about the exact teachings of the faith. I was told on one occasion by a fellow Christian at work not to "get so hyper; it is a matter of opinion." I was referring to him for insight, but that was all he basically had to say: "it is a matter of opinion." But how can that be? Christianity cannot be based on personal conjecture. My opinions have no weight against what Christ actually taught. Did He not make Himself clear, or did He purposely leave us in uncertainty? If He did, no wonder we have such a fiasco. But no person who believes that Christ is the son of God, a divine teacher, could accept that confusion and disorder was His vision. Not from a God of order. Christ was the wisest and greatest of teachers and to say that what He taught is uncertain is not a position I was willing to accept.

Many of these indifferent people, in essence, conclude that since all groups can demonstrate "evidence" for their positions, then it is all a matter of perspective. In other words, let's agree to disagree and call it a draw. But that is ludicrous. That apathetic mentality about Christian teachings was enough to confirm to me that their church was not "the one" left behind by the divine teacher. True Christianity cannot be indifferent about the teachings of Christ. The problem of the varying perspectives, angles, and views on the faith must be solved! God is not a democracy, where we vote for what we want. He has never asked for our suggestion. If we Christians are to truly call Him Master, we must find out what He actually taught, and then accept it.

To add to my frustration, legitimate questions were brought to my attention about Catholicism, and I did not have a firm handle on the answers. I was intimidated by the confident claims coming from those of other denominations. I could not give a solid explanation for my faith, a failure which runs contrary to what scripture demands (1 Peter 3:15). Every rational man should understand what he does and why; but I was not such a man. That would eventually prove to be a great motivation, but at the time I was ill-equipped to give adequate responses.

Honestly, on occasion I did not know what to think about the Catholic faith. Maybe the Church was wrong. The non-Catholics I came across appeared to present sound theories. They had great preachers and gave the impression of knowing their Bibles well. I certainly did not want to be associated with a church that did not follow the Bible. So for a time I also grew indifferent and laid the controversy aside, attending several Protestant churches with companions.

■ ■ ■

Initially, like many of us when dealing with religious matters, I did not put forth the effort required to figure things out. We always have too much on our plates or assume the matter is not serious enough. Though we have tons of questions, we stop short of investigating. Even knowing, deep inside, that something is not right, we rationalize those feelings away. I personally settled for the flimsy mentality that all that mattered were my good intentions. Though, I have heard it said that the road to Hell is paved with good intentions. Regardless, I believed what I believed and God was to be satisfied. But should we be telling God to be satisfied with whatever we choose? Since He is God, we should probably follow what He has laid out, rather than following our own ideas. At least, that's where reasoning was leading me. My breaking point came while in training at Little Rock Air Force Base. I was attending a weekly Bible study session at a local

Baptist church. In one particular gathering, I heard some discomforting comments directed toward Catholics. "Here we go again," I thought! I did not know my faith to the level I should, but what I heard was absurd. "Catholics elevate Mary to the level of Jesus." Huh? Since when has the Church taught that!? Other eye-raising comments would eventually reach my ears. "Catholics worship statues." I knew the Church had many statues and images, but I didn't recall ever being taught to worship any such statues or images. Such remarks got my blood boiling, so I said, "Enough is enough!" I got off my lazy, indifferent behind, and I put aside every excuse in the book and decided to investigate the claims made against the Church thoroughly to finally figure out this Christian fiasco. It was time to connect the dots for the sake of clarity. We can't straddle the fence all our lives. We must eventually take a position. As General Ulysses S. Grant said, "Take a position and hold your ground."

There are masses of Christian denominations claiming to be "the one," teaching the Gospel as Christ Himself intended. Many make the claim, but can they back it up? The knowledge was out there and I was going to get to the bottom of it all. I was tired of my ignorance, frustration, and confusion. It is no wonder that so many are losing their faith or couldn't care less about the Christian religion when Christians themselves can't be in accord. There is much division amongst God's people. Division does not come from the Lord. He tells us that a divided house cannot stand. The fact is, God is the author of unity, not confusion (1 Corinthians 1:10). I could have stayed indifferent or lost my faith altogether, but I responded differently. Sometimes when one is tired of being tired, that is when one acts. I was exhausted of not only my lack of knowledge, but of my own refusal to think.

The Investigation Begins

"Falsehood has an infinity of combinations, but truth has only one mode of being."

— Jean-Jacques Rousseau

I began my exploration by simply looking at objective history. I did not get bogged down with details initially, since one can easily be overwhelmed. I only wanted historical truths, such as, the Japanese bombed Pearl Harbor on December 7, 1941—historical, fundamental, verifiable, proven facts, to get the ball rolling. What are the origins of Christianity? Who are the founding fathers of the church? Did Christ establish a church? If He did, is it still here today? Who put this book called the Bible together? And so on. I was genuinely looking for answers to these rudimentary questions. I figured that wherever these fundamental questions led is where I would find truth. I simply did not know or was unsure. Most of the faith reading I had done to this point was about other religions, atheism, and God; not Christianity specifically.

In a short investigative period, I came across some eye-opening information. At the time, I thought the material I encountered was profound, as if I had discovered something new, but history is available to anyone who cares to peruse it. I was staggered to learn that, *literally*, all these churches I had visited came into the picture fifteen to eighteen centuries after the establishment of Christendom. Five hundred years ago they were all nonexistent. This is where I familiarized myself with Martin Luther and the Protestant Reformation. I recalled these concepts vaguely from school, but had never considered their implications. Going further back in history, at around the ninth century, I stumbled into the Eastern Orthodox churches where I came upon the East/West schism. Dwelling hundreds of years before Orthodox churches, I came across various heretical sects that do not exist today. Finally, centuries before these sects, came the Catholic Church, which stood alone. An unprecedented two-thousand-year-old historical institution still standing today.

As I enthusiastically continued to examine the pages of history, the winds of time accounted for the Catholic Church playing an integral role in Christian history. The Church could retrace its steps back to the apostles of Christ, while everyone else was incapable of doing so. Certainly not the Church of New Hope, founded by Reverend William in 1955. Historically speaking, the Church seemed indisputable. History was screaming Catholicism, but why all the bashing? Wasn't this information remarkably credible? Shouldn't true Christianity be founded on the original apostles? I applied this newfound knowledge to examine what others had to say. I immediately came across reluctance, such as my barber, who claimed the Church of Christ was the original church, established on the day of Pentecost. With genuine interest, I asked for evidence to support his claims, since all I can find in the history books is a Reverend Alexander Campbell, who founded this church in the early 1800s. I figured he would have an abundant amount of evidence, since his church has been around for two millennia. His answer, I kid you not, was, "You can find it posted on our Internet site." Curiosity led me to peruse his church's website; I stared in disbelief at the sea of ancient evidence. He did warn me I would find historical cracks or "lost periods" in his church's history, due to real Christians (those of his church) operating underground to avoid persecution. Ironically, the only place I could find his church's theories was on their website or out of his mouth. I could only shake my head in disbelief.

In our ongoing discussions while he was clipping away, he proceeded to inform me that to him it was unbelievable that I should believe my own findings. Well, it shouldn't be unbelievable, since it is verifiable. Truth can be defined as verifiable facts, not assertions such as his. His explanation of my findings would eventually boil down to a conspiracy theory. All the proof or documentation I came across, all this so-called objective history, is fixed. Church history is incorrect, just like school textbooks are wrong by stating Christopher Columbus discovered America (since the land was already occupied). His implications were simply that the Catholic Church had mangled history to assert for itself an advantageous position from which to claim apostolic procession. Unfortunately, there is no room for such speculation. His position is like those who deny the Holocaust or that we ever landed on the moon. The discussion with this person is not even worth noting in any further detail, but I mention it briefly to demonstrate how far a person will go in order to substantiate their position. Everyone has a theory to support their theory.

■ ■ ■

Immediately after this event I decided to go for the jugular and examine who was responsible for putting together this holy book Christians call the Bible. Certainly, whoever put the canon together knows Christianity thoroughly. The answer, once again, was the Catholic Church. I came across the Fourth Council of Rome (382 AD), the Councils of Hippo (393 AD) and the Council of Carthage (397 AD) held by the Church, which essentially put the Canon of Bible together as we know it and declared the selected books to be inspired by God. I never realized the Church preceded the Bible. For whatever reason, I thought the Bible went back to the times of Christ and his apostles, but that was not the case. Again, it would be the Church under the inspiration and guidance of the Holy Spirit that would differentiate between inspired writings from heretical writings or what is scripture from what is not. To quote Henry G. Graham, the New Testament belongs to the Church "because she wrote it by her first apostles and preserved it and guarded it all down the ages by her Popes and Bishops; nobody else has any right to it whatsoever, any more than a stranger has the right to come into your house and break open your desk and pilfer your private documents. Therefore, I say that for people to step in 1,500 years after the Catholic Church had had possession of the Bible and to pretend that it is theirs, and that they alone know what the meaning of it is, and that the Scriptures alone, without the voice of the Catholic Church explaining them, are intended by God to be guide and rule of faith—this is an absurd and groundless claim" (27). It suddenly dawned on me what I heard long ago: "To be ignorant of history is to be non-Catholic." Surely if people knew this information they would think differently. The facts continue to support Catholicism. That being my mentality, I continued to question other friends. "Do you know who is responsible for putting the Bible together?" I asked. They explained to me it was the Holy Spirit. I countered that the Holy Spirit usually works through individuals to make things happen, not "Shazam, here is your Bible out of thin air." History does not show the Bible falling out of the sky. It seemed that any theory besides the Church sufficed for these individuals, some of whom regarded themselves as "truth seekers" and yet ignored the facts.

One colleague did acknowledge the Church's work in putting the Bible together, but explained that the Catholic Church has gone astray from the teachings of the Bible. That is certainly a plausible answer. Perhaps that was the root of the problem—I had to keep that possibility open—but the issue remained to be decided.

With these discussions and others under my belt, I began formulating conclusions. The very reason all these churches even have a Bible today is because of the Catholic Church, yet they refer to the Church as unbiblical? How can that be? I recollect the words of Philosopher Peter Kreeft who was cited during a radio talk show: "How can a 'rotten' Church produce such a Holy book? Christians regard the Bible as the very word of God. It is impossible to squeeze fresh apple juice out of a rotten apple." His statement is a very logical proposition, leading to a stench of unreasonableness amongst my peers.

■ ■ ■

As I continued to excavate through history, I looked up the founding fathers of the Church, much like one might search for the founding fathers of the United States, to see where they stood on the faith. I reviewed writings going back to the first and second centuries. All the great saints and theologians I heard about were Catholics: Clement of Rome, Ignatius, Papias, Irenaeus, Tertullian, Augustine, and Jerome, to name a few. Like a detective cracking a profound case, I continued to share my findings. One female acquaintance found my research interesting and told me, "Just because the Catholic Church is the oldest doesn't mean it is right." I said, "That's true, but isn't this a better starting point than the church founded in 1870 by 'Pastor Jack'?" She didn't appear to like my remark, and immediately the tone of our conversation altered. I inquired as to why the Catholic Church is wrong. Why are you in this church and not another? She tried to gather a response, but seemed uncertain. She finally admitted what I would eventually hear from many others: that this is where she'd grown up and felt at home. I had to collect myself after such a response. These people who I thought had it all together were as vulnerable as I was. They couldn't give an intellectual reason for their faith. On the surface they appeared so confident, but digging deeper confirmed that there was another story. Reasoning would prove to be a most uncomfortable position. Most were merely content with their church or maintained a certain loyalty. So the notion of "cradle Catholic" doesn't just apply to Catholics; we also have plenty of "cradle Protestants."

Such incidents revealed a glimpse of human stubbornness. No matter what evidence or reasoning I presented, it didn't matter to many folks. They would not accept it! We are so convicted by the "rightness" of our position that we dismiss anything that goes against it. The element of pride is never far behind. Even a person who knows their argument to be flimsy maintains being correct in order to avoid admitting error.

With this foundation in mind, I intend to further explain my position. I am not simply a product of my environment, as a coworker declared. That cannot be the case when members of my family deny the Catholic faith. I was a wanderer who eventually returned to his roots through discernment. Many are those whose philosophies concerning the Christian faith are entirely different. Their first priority is to feel good via choir, congregation, and church activities, while disregarding sound doctrinal teachings. We must do what we do because it is, above all else, true. Also, the philosophy of "I am, therefore I'll be" has no place in the journey of a truth seeker.

Long ago I learned that more often than not, truth is on the persecuted side, and there was one church I knew that was as persecuted and rejected as Christ.

Did Christ Establish a Visible Church?

> *"May the God of endurance and encouragement grant you to think in harmony with one another, in keeping with Christ Jesus, that with one accord you may with one voice glorify the God and the Father of our Lord Jesus Christ."*
>
> — Romans 15:5-6

Here is a crucial question that needs to be answered: Did He or did He not establish a church? Did He deposit the knowledge of the faith under the care of His close companions, or was it for each man to decipher this knowledge? One would think the purpose of Him grooming, teaching, and establishing an apostleship was to leave a mouthpiece, representatives to speak on His behalf. If not, division and disarray among hundreds of separated sects with conflicting doctrines working independently of each other could be the only result. Christ must have left behind provisions. He must have left a point of reference for us to consult and guide His flock. So I confidently err to the side that He commissioned a visible church to continue His mission and teachings, and to represent Him in matters of faith and morals.

It is often said that "the Church" is not an erected edifice, but spiritual, made up of all those who believe in Christ. What needs to be understood is that the word "church" can be used to designate two different entities. Church can be a congregation of men united in prayer, identical belief, authority, and worship. That is what is meant by spiritual church. A church can also be referred to as a building used for the purposes of worship by members of the church. Now, however sweet it may sound on paper that the church is all those who believe in Christ, that idea cannot be admitted. There are Protestants who tell me that I need to renounce Catholicism and become Christian, yet we are "the church?" That is preposterous. Others bluntly call the Church wretched and evil. If we were "the church," they would be condemning themselves at the same time. Christians who call Catholics idolatrous for having statues or images of saints would have to declare that they belong to an idolatrous church as well. The Seventh-day Adventist teaches that the pope is the Antichrist while Catholics maintain he is the vicar of Christ. If we are "the church," we must declare the pope as our spiritual leader, yet to some he is the devil's advocate! At times a church will excommunicate a member and that member will then join another church. You have the same church accepting and rejecting the same man at the same time! That is absurd. The fact is we are not a "church" with our different creeds. Some claim we just have different angles of truth, similar to the world religion debate, but that cannot be accepted either. Catholicism, for instance, teaches confession, purgatory, sacrifice of the mass, sacraments, etc., and if these ideas are true, to teach the contrary is not a "different angle" of truth but a denial (Rumble and Carty 1: 49). The fact is, we must admit there are *false churches* when we have variant beliefs and authority. To top things off, denominations or sects disown even each other. Therefore, we cannot be blindly calling ourselves a "church."

I am reminded of a colleague who held to this "We are one 'church'" concept; "We are all one, united in faith," he said. Then he boasted about how he can write several pages explaining why his wife left Catholicism. I am wondering why she left in the first place, if we are one united "church"? The bottom line is, there is a true Church founded on Christ and His apostles, then there are "manmade substitution churches," as my Mormon physical therapist used to remark. We must distinguish between the impostors and the legitimate one. As Revelation 2:2 states, "You have tested those who call themselves apostles but are not, and discovered that they are imposters."

■ ■ ■

For the life of me, I can't understand the difficulty of comprehending that contradictions cannot be true. We cannot purposely resist reason in order to accommodate every idea the mind can imagine. While being mindful and respectful of others, we must get down to the facts of life. We know Christ lived, that He claimed to be God and left us a beacon for guidance. If we find this beacon, we find Christianity in its purest form.

It must be mentioned that Christ is not indifferent about what we believe. He did not come to be ignored or have His teachings perverted. Therefore, He must be biased toward the true church, not any other church. If He revealed the Baptist church, He cannot possibly be pleased with someone who deliberately chooses otherwise. What matters from this point forward is what Christ did and taught.

Though many, for the purposes of avoiding spiritual authority, altogether reject the idea that Christ established a visible church, let us look at the plain and simple evidence within the history book also known as the

Bible, although external evidence speaks volumes on the subject. Christ began formulating His church by selecting His legislative body. Matthew 10:1 tells us, "He called his twelve disciples to him and gave them authority." According to Matthew 28:20, He made them teachers and leaders of His church: "[Teach men] to observe all things I have commanded you." Their mission was to carry Christ's mission: "As the Father has sent me, I also send you" (John 20:21). He warned them they should expect many hardships and danger: "I am sending you out like sheep among wolves" (Matthew 10:16). Due to these difficulties, He said He will always be with them as they carry out their mission: "And behold, I am with you always, until the end of the age" (Matthew 28:20). Amongst His disciples, He selected Peter as head of the church. "Thou art Peter, and upon this rock I will build my church" (Matthew 16:18). He gave them power to legislate as necessary: "And I will give to you the keys to the kingdom of heaven. Whatever you bind on earth will be bound in heaven, and whatever you loose on earth will be loosed in heaven" (Matthew 16:19). Christ gave them power to purify or consecrate: "Baptize them in the name of the Father and of the son and of the Holy Spirit" (Matthew 28:19). The Lord told them to forgive sin: "Receive the Holy Spirit. Whose sins you forgive, are forgiven them; if you do not forgive them, they are not forgiven" (John 20:23). He commanded His followers to offer sacrifice: "This is my body which is given up for you; do this in memory of me" (1Corinthians 11:24). He gave disciplinary command: "He who hears you, hears me, and he who despises you despises me" (Luke 10:16). Also, in Matthew 18:17 we read: "If a man refuses to listen even to the church, then treat him as you would a Gentile or a tax collector." He said his flock would be one fold with one shepherd, though many sheep (John 10:16). All the above characteristics can only be attributed to the Catholic Church, which speaks with authority in the name of Christ (Rumble and Carty 1: 77).

This and much more He said to His apostles, and they exercised their delegated authority from the beginning, as seen in Acts 15:24-29: "Since we have heard that some went out without any mandate from us have upset you with their teaching and disturbed your peace of mind, we have with one accord decided to choose representation and to send them to you along with our beloved Barnabas and Paul, who have dedicated their lives to the name of our Lord Jesus Christ. So we are sending Judas and Silas who will also convey this same message by word of mouth: It is the decision of the holy Spirit and of us not place on you any burden beyond these necessities, namely, to abstain from meat sacrificed to idols, from blood, from meats of strangles animals, and from unlawful marriage. If you keep free of these, you be will doing what it right."

All of Paul's epistles are evidence of the seed planted by Christ that would eventually grow into a large tree. We find Paul administering as he writes letters to the churches flourishing in Corinth, Ephesus, and Colossae. In the Book of Titus, Titus is referred to as the person tasked with evangelizing and developing the church on the Mediterranean island of Crete. Paul writes, "For this reason I left you in Crete so that you might set right what remains to be done and appoint elders in every town, as I have directed you" (Titus 1:5). The Book of Timothy is all about Paul instructing Timothy on pastoral duties and church organization. *The seed that began with twelve men was bound to mutate into a visible institution; it was the inevitable.* As the faith grew, structure, organization, leadership, headquarters, etc., developed.

Common sense also tells us that to qualify as the church founded by Christ it must have continuously existed since His time. History is quite clear in demonstrating that the Catholic Church has existed since the time of Christ, so she alone can be apostolic, and critics cannot dismiss this crucial point. If we examine history, we will learn that Martin Luther founded the Lutheran Church around 1517, which he left to his successors. The Church of England was established by King Henry VIII in 1534, and he left it to his successors. The Presbyterian Church was founded by John Knox in 1560; he left it to his successors. The Baptist church emerged in 1606 by John Smyth who launched it in Amsterdam. The Episcopal Church was founded by Samuel Seabury in the seventeenth century. The Methodist Church came to the scene in 1739 via Charles and John Wesley, so on and so forth, to the modern-day megachurches led by Joel Osteen, Rick Warren, and T.D. Jakes. Any church today can be researched to see who established it and when. One thing is certain—it was not Christ! And there is a titanic difference between the Church founded by Christ versus that founded by Pastor Joe.

Another critical characteristic of the true Church includes it being universal, since Christ commissioned His apostles to teach all nations. That is precisely what the word Catholic means—universal. No church brings men together from all walks of life regardless of race, culture, or language like the Catholic Church. I have witnessed this universal spirit in my travels around the world. The Catholic Church is not national or local, but international. Looking at this universal trait closer, logic dictates that the original apostles themselves could not have gone to all the ends of the earth, as Christ commanded, nor could they be on earth until the end of time, as the Lord promised His Church would be, so their authority obviously had to be delegated. That's what defines a church bishop. They are direct successors of the apostles. The evidence was becoming clearer and clearer.

How about the aspect of standardization? The one true Church and its members must follow the same set of teachings and guidelines. There must be uniformity throughout, whether one is in Canada or South Africa. Location does not change the facts of the faith. Each member cannot be running around believing or doing what they please. The Catholic Church is exceptional in doctrinal unity, an element lacking gravely in other churches. On every continent, there are no surprises as to its expectations or teachings. Christ prayed that His Church would be one, as the Father and He are one. Yet outside the Catholic Church, discrepancies in doctrines are all one finds, except, of course, for the belief that there is a savior of some kind. The bottom line is, all the above characteristics of the *true Church* are present only in the Catholic Church.

After pondering and digesting this information, one realizes the fantastic position denominations or sects hold. They in essence profess that Christ failed in establishing His Church, since it has gone "astray." Though Christ said that Hell will not prevail against His Church, non-Catholics say it did! So since Christ did not quite meet the target, Martin Luther took it upon himself to rectify the problem by establishing his own "infallible" church. Since Luther didn't quite get it right, John Knox then decided to do some tweaking of his own, and so on. That the Son of man botched His Church is a difficult position to take. But yet, you have folks like my Mormon physical therapist, who says we should be grateful Joseph Smith came along in the 1800s to redeem the Gospel of Christ and rectify the teachings of the Church. Unfortunately, Mormonism is about 1,830 years too late to be the true Church. To believe Christ is the very nature of God, as Christians believe, and then assert that He failed in establishing His Church, goes beyond comprehension.

So as we proceed, one conclusion can be firmly made; nowhere in scripture do we find the concept of denominations or local or national churches—it is completely unbiblical. The entire New Testament gives a resounding "Amen" to unity. There is no evidence of independent churches in the writings of church fathers or tradition either. In other words, there is a definitive Christian faith. No one has the right or authority to establish their own church other than what has been prescribed by Christ Himself. We as Christians have a duty and obligation to be united. And we cannot take the position as believers that what Christ taught really doesn't matter.

The "Wretched" Church

Where secular and non-Catholic opponents focus to degrade the credibility of the Church is in its supposed "history of wicked and scandalous behavior." Undeniably, in my studies I came across wretched Catholics, so this was a subject I felt uncomfortable with, if indeed this was the church Christ left behind. The general thought process deriving from people is that since there have been and are still corrupt men within the Catholic Church, it cannot be the church founded by Christ. But are wicked men the ultimate test? If so, those who recommend I depart the Church due to sinful men should, using this logic, immediately leave their church as well. If sinful men are the test of truth, there exists no true church or religion on the planet.

Let me be clear: by no means do I defend the scandalous behavior of any clergy, or anyone for that matter. There have been those who have been abominations to the faith, but their atrocious behavior is not due to the Church's teachings, but in spite of them. If these hypocrites actually lived according to their Catholic faith and were wicked, by all means blame the Church; but they have not. That is why I defend the Church as a Church in regards to her teachings, not the misconduct of individuals.

Church leaders are not perfect. They suffer from the same human frailties we all do. Undoubtedly, they are rightfully held to higher standards. Much is expected from men who are supposed to be representing Christ. But, even so, members of the Church can fail and will fail due to the human element. She does not have men or women immune to sin. All of us must fight for our salvation, not just those sitting in the pews, but all the way up the chain, including the pope. The one who is flawless is Christ, not members of His Church. He came for the sick, not the healthy. His Church is a hospital for sinners, but we must differentiate between the human and divine elements of the Church. Christ said that scandals will come, but woe to that man by whom the scandal cometh (Matthew 18:7).

When speaking of scandals I am reminded of a senior military officer who was involved in a prostitution ring. Using the rationale against the Church in this incident, we should condemn the entire military for the repugnant behavior of this officer, but that cannot be rational. The disgraceful individual and those responsible should be condemned. They are not representative of all the other fine men and women in our service. The problem is not the military, or the integrity it upholds and teaches. This officer was wicked through his own fault, not through that of the institution he represents or its core values.

The military as a whole must be viewed as distinct from its failed leadership or members, and believe me, it has its share of rotten apples, but that does not mean the whole batch is bad. In the same way, the Church must be judged distinctly from its failed clergy. The Church has never taught the embezzlement of money, child abuse, theft, or lying to any of its members. Too often it is said that "the Catholic Church did this or that," but the Church did not do anything—the individuals involved did. Such blanket statements condemn all innocent faithful abiding by true Christian principles. Like scandalous military officers, who do not represent me or the uniform I wore. Nor do appalling clergy represent my faith, except in name. Unfortunately, the innocent are guilty by association, but only when it comes to the bad; ironically, all the good it does is simply dismissed. Again, I do not deny misconduct. People should be upset and rightly appalled when abuses occur, but that righteous animosity must be focused on its rightful place.

Even with some detestable members, for lack of a stronger word, the Catholic Church can still be the true church. The Church claims infallibility in matters of Christian faith, teachings, and morals, not in making every Catholic live up to those standards. Her infallibility and holiness do not deprive individuals of their free will. Any believer will admit that God is infallible, yet His children (us) violate His commandments every day. The reasoning used against the Church is like saying that since sinful and wicked men exist, therefore God is not holy! But He is holy. God has not failed, despite the wretchedness of some men. Likewise, Christ's Church has not failed, despite the wickedness and corruption of her subjects. He said the gates of Hell will not prevail against His Church, which implies He knew His Church would go through tumultuous times and experiences, but would always stand. It is the evil disposition of men that is forever present and unavoidable; that is the root of the problem. Not even Christ himself could overcome a person (Judas) who was set on his evil disposition. Truly, even in Christ's close-knit circle there was a scandalous one.

Indeed, religion has been the subject of abuse for ages. Some have used it for God's glory while others have used it for their gain. The vices of men will never disappoint, but we are here to analyze teachings, but more specifically credentials, not conduct, whether bad or good. Ultimately, one can't use the behavior of a megachurch's member to prove their church wrong, but one can certainly prove its errors in Christian doctrine. Doctrines and credibility must be examined independently from a church's members. If conduct were the way to resolve this, all I would have to do is produce a "good" Catholic to prove Catholicism true, and there are abundant amount of saints to choose from.

I recollect reading about the legendary Catholic social activist Dorothy Day and Mother Teresa and their impact on those in need. Not bad for products of a "wretched" Church. What a witness they are of the Lord and the Church they represent. Like Dorothy Day, Mother Teresa and countless others, the Church will continue to produce spiritual giants, as she has done throughout the ages, even in her darkest times, precisely because they have followed their Catholic teachings. Mother Teresa was once asked what steps can be taken to fix and make the Church better. She answered, "The first step is for you and I to fix ourselves."

The bottom line is, it is not reasonable to condemn the Church for the deplorable conduct of a small minority. Catholics have sinned, and I acknowledge it. But wretched Catholics must give up what is bad—their evil and hypocrisy—not surrender what is good, their Catholic faith.

Quite honestly, the biggest issue I have with the Church is the lofty standards it calls its members to live by, but I respect her for that as well. Anyone who dares live up to Catholic teaching will surely be a better man for it. There is no higher standard in the Christian faith. Many have left the Church precisely because of the lofty standards she demands, and have settled for less demanding churches.

As we continue forward, one has to recognize that non-Catholic churches produce some good fruits, yet the fact remains, it is not as Christ arranged. This is about the *whole* of Christ's teachings, not just fragments. *If we are not obligated as Christians to follow the totality of Christ's teachings, then why believe or follow Christ at all?! That is imperative to understand.*

Christian Fiasco Comments & Response I

"I urge you, brothers, in the name of our Lord Jesus Christ, that all of you agree in what you say, and that there be no division among you, but that you be united in the same mind and in the same purpose."

— 1 Corinthians 1:10

The following are some of the most popular dialogues dealing with the Christian Fiasco:

Comment: The Roman Catholic denomination was founded after Emperor Constantine made Christianity the official religion of his state. I don't know where you get your history, but I suggest going back and reviewing it.
Response: Neither do I know where you get your history. Your statement is simply not true. The Church goes back directly to the time of Christ. The word Catholic was applied by St. Ignatius of Antioch around 110 AD as a sign that Christ came to all people several centuries before Constantine. There is also a misuse of name. The term "Roman" is not part of the Church's official name. That attachment derives from the Church having its headquarters in Rome. Today the term "Roman Catholic" is also used to differentiate between sects, but it is not part of her official name. She is simply the Catholic Church. Lastly, the Catholic Church is not a denomination. Denomination means part of the whole. The Catholic Church is the whole from which separated sects come.

Comment: I do not have time to discuss this but trust me your church can be proven wrong. There are plenty of reputable churches.
Response: Plenty of reputable churches? That makes no sense. Christ said His Church would be one fold, not many folds. He said I shall build *my Church*, not churches. If you ever prove the Church false, you will face an extraordinary challenge proving your own particular brand of Christianity correct.

Comment: I believe Christ meant Protestantism to renew his church that fell astray or else it would not be.
Response: Protestantism is not something God intended, but its possibility must be so, due to the free will and distortions of men. Your reasoning is like saying since evil exists, therefore God intended it to be. God did not create evil, but rather the possibility of it by allowing man to be free. But, even in chaos He has a way of extracting good; hence, the good fruits of Protestantism.

Comment: My sincere advice to you, if you want to find real Christian teaching, depart the Catholic Church.

Response: You are mistaken in your sincere advice. Truth is consistent and never contradicts itself. Protestantism is inconsistent and full of contradictions. Jean-Jacques Rousseau was right, "Falsehood has an infinity of combinations, but truth only has one mode of being." And by the way, to which brand of Protestantism do you recommend I turn to so I can follow up with some questions?

Comment: The key is to follow a Bible-teaching church.
Response: The problem is that a so called Bible-teaching church is called *not* Bible-teaching by another who claims to be a Bible-teaching church.

Comment: Are you blind to the need for reformation with all the corruption in the Church during the time of Luther?
Response: Action was needed, but it is one thing to reform practices of bad clergy and quite another to reform Christian doctrines, which is precisely what the Protestant fathers did. Christ described His Church like a picnic basket holding good and bad apples. Instead of working to eliminate bad apples, reformers began to make their own baskets. That is their mistake. Christ made the original basket and He said it would *not* fail, and it has not. Reformers said it did fail and took matters to another level by reforming and eliminating vital doctrines, traditions, and disciplines with human-invented alternatives. They used the failures of clergies to abandon the Church altogether, like one who is married using any possible means to terminate the relationship; but marriage is for life and problems must be worked out. Similarly, the Catholic priest Luther, though rightly upset with certain abuses, broke away from the Church to pursue his own passions. Did you know he took a wife from a convent because he did not agree with the teachings of celibacy? That's the way it essentially works today: If you don't like a particular teaching, start your own branch of Christianity.

Most Protestants view Martin Luther as a hero. The way I see it, he is a sincere, although mistaken, unauthorized agent who is the author of Christian indifferentism. We can talk about abuses of Church members, but it still does not change the fact that no one has the right to establish their own church, aside from that which was founded and assured by Christ.

Also, Protestant churches might have credibility if only one form stood against Catholicism, but there are countless mixed with their own particular errors. Protestantism can't even stand united in their protest against the Church. *For every doctrine taught by one Protestant church one can find another teaching the contrary.* The only real commonality within denominations is that there is some sort of Christ.

If Luther and the fathers of the reformation were here today, they would regret the fiasco they began. Since their time, churches have continued to split like a malignant virus. Denominations are scattered like lost sheep running in all sorts of directions, making a wreck out of our faith. Believers are becoming atheist, agnostic, and indifferent about Christianity. Confusion and frustration abound. That has been one of the results of the so-called "reformation."

Comment: It's incredible how you turn a blind eye and follow a church with such dark history.
Response: I do not turn a blind eye, nor is that what history demonstrates. What history does illustrate is that there have been corrupted men within the Church. And because some monsters have called themselves Catholics does not mean that they are in practice. What's even more "incredible" is that you should think a two-thousand-year-old institution consisting of hundreds of millions throughout history would not be exposed to wicked men and their misconduct! It is a given that any institution will have its share of bad apples especially the bigger and more influential they are. You must understand I am defending the Church as a Church, not individuals.

Comment: What about the Crusades the Church launched! That has nothing to do with individualism, but everything to do with the Church.
Response: We must ponder the big picture. First, launching the Crusades was justified, though I agree there were wrongs committed. Men will

never disappoint in injecting their evil in any endeavor in life. But, let me explain what the Crusades were all about since most people don't even know the answer to that question. The Crusades were a calculated tactical decision by Christian Europe to counter the hostility of Islam. If it were not for the crusaders, we Christians would probably not be here today. So in a way we should be indebted for those men who left everything behind to fight for their Christian brothers in the East.

There is no denying that wrong was done in the Crusades, but that does not make the wars themselves wrong. There exists the notion of just war. Augustine addresses the just war problem in his Christian philosophy book *The City of God*. He asserts that an army with right intentions is not responsible for unforeseen ill consequences of individuals within as long as the good outweighs the negative outcome (Rooney 168). If war crimes make wars wrong, there isn't a single just war in history. The Crusades are justifiable because they were a joint effort for the survival of Christianity.

Again, some crusaders gave Christians a bad reputation, but just like you can share appalling stories about the Crusades, I can share noble ones as well. I give crusaders tremendous respect for the good they did and condemn all atrocities and evils committed, but as a whole the decision is justified. The Crusades saved Christianity from being wiped out.

I hope there will never be another Crusade, but the way things are shaping up in this day and age, there will probably be a modern-day Crusade. Christians are already being persecuted and will be required to fight once again for the right to be a Christian. Rest assured that even then, abuses will be done by "Christians."

Comment: Catholics must be brain-dead to accept the teachings of their Church.
Response: I acknowledge many Catholics do not know their faith as they should, but experience has taught me non-Catholics are just as bad or worse. The non-thinking Catholic does have one significant advantage over a non-thinking Protestant, that is, they are not being taught the wrong thing.

Comment: If your church is right, why don't Christians see their mistake?
Response: First of all, Catholics are Christians. And men will not see the nature of their errors due to pride, peer pressures, loyalty to their persuasion, ignorance, etc. One would think men would realize the nature of their error when it comes to politics and economics, but men differ in opinions, with many believing what one would consider to be outlandish. Similarly, many will not realize the truth of Catholicism. Many in their personal loyalty, laziness, and indifferentism, are not sufficiently interested in finding out whether their Christian beliefs are right, let alone study Catholicism. The fact that they believe what they do is good enough to call it a day.

Comment: Others are entitled to their view, so let it be! I'm Baptist and don't go around claiming I am right.
Response: Everyone is entitled to their view indeed, so let me share mine like everyone else. But why do you claim to be Baptist rather than Methodist or anything else? I assume you are Baptist because you believe it is the correct form of Christianity. The reason we do things is because they are correct, right? If you don't admit the Baptist claim to be right, you have no ground to stand on when rejecting the brands of Christianity you will not accept. How do you even defend Christianity against any other religion?

Also, it is imperative to understand that Christianity is not to be left to mere sentiments and opinions. Christ spoke with authority and power, proclaiming a definitive Christian faith. He came to change people's minds from wrong ideas to right ideas and commanded His apostles to teach all nations those exact ideas; it was not a suggestion. Instead of sidelining the issue as personal assumption, let us solve the problem.

Comment: To what specifically do you attribute the many Christian sects?
Response: One word—ignorance. One has to stand in awe at the gullibility of men. If it reads good and sounds good, it must be true! So long as an individual is charismatic, an excellent speaker, endowed with

some leadership qualities running around waving a Bible across a stage he will steal sheep from the one intended flock. Anyone with a little knowledge of human psychology would not be surprised at this phenomenon. Also, the nonsense people read and believe on the Internet is downright painful.

We must recognize men are religiously inclined by nature and those who do not know the facts about the true faith invented their own. Others, who have known true Christianity, departed the faith in pursuit of their own agendas. The conniving ways of men are never far behind; particularly those who feed on the ignorance of others to service themselves. The apostle Paul warns us to be vigilant in Acts 21:30, "From your own group, men will come forward perverting the truth to draw the disciples away after them."

The greatest safeguards against denominations are Catholics who thoroughly know their faith. We should not be jumping headfirst over the sofa when a Jehovah's Witness knocks on our door.

Comment: You must be upset Protestantism is flourishing while Catholicism is struggling in the United States.
Response: The faith as a whole seems to be struggling in the United States due to secularism. But if Protestantism is "flourishing," it is because it is quick to water down Christian teaching to suit societal appetites. On controversial topics, many Protestant pastors rather remain silent or cave to societal pressures altogether. They don't want to "stir the pot" and hurt their revenue flow. Protestantism shows laxity in Christian teaching and caters to indifferentism. The "old and outdated" Catholic Church stubbornly teaches the full doctrine of Christ regardless of how comfortable or uncomfortable it may be. That is one of the purposes of an institutional church; to preserve the Christian faith, not to cater to individual desires or what sincere but mistaken men may think.

Comment: Why don't I ever read anything good about the Church?

Response: When was the last time you read anything good about any church? That's the media for you; ready at a moment's notice to trash the Church. It is only interested in advertising failures of members who have failed to live up to Christian ideals. They love discrediting religion and faith so folks such as you follow suit in bashing and dismissing religion since it does not align with their agendas. But if you want to see the good being done, just walk over to your local parish and learn more about what the Church does every day in your community and around the globe for all those in need.

As a matter of fact, when the Church was founded, there was no formal schooling for the average citizen. Today, the Catholic Church teaches droves through more than two hundred plus Catholic Colleges and Universities, in its thousands of elementary and Catholic High Schools. Also, since its foundation, there were no hospitals, but today countless receive services from Catholic hospitals around the world. Every day, the Church feeds, clothes, shelters, supports and educates more people than any other organization on the Planet. The good it does is unprecedented.

Comment: The Church would be much more useful to the world if they stopped spending millions on lavish cathedrals and artifacts. Have you been to the Vatican? How does one justify such lavishness with the simplicity of Christ? Sell them all, I say, and give the proceeds to the poor.
Response: Such "lavishness" can be justified with the spirit of Christ. Remember God ordered the Jews to build an extravagant temple. Christ also rebuked His apostles after a woman poured and "wasted" an alabaster jar of expensive ointment on His head. The point is we are to give God our best in all we do. Our first fruits. These "lavish cathedrals" and their contents are there to glorify Him and have been given to the Church by the likes of Michelangelo and other great talents. What you must understand is that the faith can be expressed by believers through various mechanism including paintings, sculptures, music, architecture, and literature. They are a signs of God's presence and his creative activity. But even if you sold the contents of St. Peter's Basilica, it would

not solve the problem of poverty. Christ said we would always have the poor with us.

I'll leave you with a quote from renowned theologian Father Rumble, who writes, "It takes two to make a religion, God and man. God is a pure Spirit, but man is not. Man is a composite of the spiritual and the material. And He must worship God according to his twofold nature. Man not only possesses spiritual thoughts; he gives them expression in speech, writing, music, art, and architecture. And, where God is concerned, he dedicates all these things to God's service in religion ... God wants the service, not of half our being, but of our complete being" (1: 277).

Comment: What about all the wealth the Pope owns?
Response: The Pope owns nothing in the Vatican. Pope Benedict, who stepped down, is receiving a pension of just over three thousand dollars a month. That does not sound like wealth. The Vatican is simply the headquarters of the largest institution on Earth and is where the Pope resides, but popes do not own anything, just like the CEO of Bank of America can't claim he owns the company's buildings or its contents.

Comment: You should stop debating so much. That is not what Christianity is all about.
Response: Though we should have our faith in our hearts, we should also have it in our heads. We should be able to give an explanation of the faith we possess in Christ (1 Peter 3:15) and reason with folks as the great Apostle Paul did (Acts 17:2, 17:17, 18:4, 18:26).

Comment: It doesn't matter where one attends church. There are many good Protestants and Catholics out there. What matters is a personal relationship with Christ, not being a member of a man-made church.
Response: There are good Muslims, Hindus, Mormons, Jehovah's Witnesses, etc., out there also, but that has no bearing on whether their beliefs are correct. And no one wants you to be a member of a man-made church. Examine the claims before discarding them on blind prejudice.

Comment: I believe there are many good things about the Catholic Church, and I would say about 70 percent of its teachings align with Christianity. But, I am curious, what are your thoughts on Pope Alexander?
Response: Pope Alexander was a complete abomination to his office, but that is, of course, why you bring him up. It would do your thesis no good to mention a great Catholic or pope. But, indeed, he was a complete scoundrel who perverted and abused his authority. He is an embarrassment to every Catholic who has walked the planet. He, like others, has been dishonorable, scandalous, wicked, unworthy, despicable, wretched, and every other negative word you can bring to mind. They were monsters, despite Catholic teaching, not because of them.

But still, this pathetic pope's behavior has no bearing on the truth of Catholicism. Catholicism is true despite his gross tenure. Catholicism is neither true because of the great popes or countless saints it has produced. It is true despite the 70 percent you may accept. It will still be true in the future, when other scandalous and virtuous individuals arise.

Comment: It's impressive, the amount of disagreement found in Christianity.
Response: What's also impressive is that those condemning the Church don't even know what she teaches. She is wrong simply because "The Catholic Church must be wrong." But the Church is not just any church. When she speaks on matters of Christianity, it is worth listening.

Anyhow, there may be a lot of disagreement, but it does not follow that there is no true church. It is a fact that Christ lived, claimed to be God, and established a church two thousand years ago that would be the one holy, universal, and apostolic Church. If you find those qualifications, you will have found the religion of Christ.

Comment: I will do my own thing, you just worry about yourself.
Response: It seems like you are your own master. If you honestly believe Christianity entails doing your own thing, you are quite mistaken. Christ said, "If a man refuses to listen even to the church, then treat him as you

would a Gentile or a tax collector." The question is, what church He is talking about?

Comment: So everyone who does not belong to the Catholic Church is a heathen Gentile!?
Response: No—those who have come to know the truth and reject their obligations to the truth are heathens. NOT those who do not know the truth through no fault of their own and are trying to serve Christ as best as they know how. One with a sincere and good disposition towards Christ cannot be called a heathen. The one who knows better and does otherwise is the heathen.

Comment: What have you to say about the Greek Orthodox churches?
Response: The same as Protestantism. They are national churches, not universal. There is no defined authority. Each is independent of the others. You have the Eastern Churches of Alexandria, Russia, Romania, Ukraine, and so on. Though more similar to Catholicism, they still differ with the Church on essential Christian doctrines.

Comment: I no longer attend any Church with the hypocrisy that goes on. My spiritual relationship with the Greater Power is perfectly fine. I can read my Bible on my own. By the way, God has never once asked me for money.
Response: It does not follow that because some churchgoers fail to live up to their duties towards God, and their fellow men, that you should refrain from doing so. We are still obliged to serve God regardless of the sinfulness of others. We must not use the failures of others as an excuse.

And how do you know your relationship is "perfectly fine"? How do you know what you do is pleasing to Him? Is there no possibility of error? As far money is concerned, if you read your Bible, as you say you do, you will notice God loves a cheerful giver (2 Corinthians 9:7). There are plenty of verses that support the idea of tithing, including Leviticus 27:13, Numbers 18:26, and Deuteronomy 14:24. To do God's work around the globe requires resources.

THE FIASCO CONTINUES

"In giving this instruction, I do not praise the fact that your meetings are doing more harm than good. First of all, I hear that when you meet as a church there are divisions among you, and to a degree I believe it.

— 1 Corinthians 11:17-18

<u>Church Hierarchy</u>

Aside from the points covered, the Church's hierarchy is another area often attacked, as if there is something inherently evil about a chain of command. Opponents often say, "Hierarchy and structure in the Church is tyrannical." This perception must derive from problems recognizing authority, let alone spiritual authority. "The Church's structure is all about control, power, and personal agendas," I am told. It's always intriguing how non-Catholics insist on educating me about my faith, and insist that as a Catholic, I have little or no say in the matter.

Anyhow, from my experience, all non-Catholic churches I attended acknowledged a chain of command within their organization. I have observed greeters, assistant pastors, pastors, and bishops. It would be logical to assume the person running the children's ministry does not possess the same authority as the senior pastor. I am sure also that the head usher has to answer to someone, as do the secretary and the youth leader. The point is, if hierarchical mutation is possible in a congregation of eight hundred people, then why is this phenomenon not possible in a church of more than a billion? Simply because it is the Catholic Church, I gather.

In the corporate world or the military, tens of thousands of employees and soldiers compose a chain of command. Though no condemnation is found in these areas, the point should be obvious as to the necessity of structure, that is, to facilitate order and organization. The larger denominations avoid condemning hierarchy, since they acknowledge its necessity, but if the denomination is small enough, such a system is often seen as tyrannical. Condemnation is appropriate—until the sect grows large enough that it becomes necessary and then, of course, it's not tyrannical. The bottom line is, as an entity grows in size and influence, so must organizational structure. The principle applies to the Church as well which has over 2,400 dioceses divided by regions and countries. In the military, terms such as squad, flight, squadrons, company, brigade, battalion, European Command, and Pacific Command, are used to distinguish between groups, regions, and levels of authority. Hierarchy is as typical as it is in the natural world. We go from microorganisms to plants to the more complex animal life to humans. There is an unavoidable food chain.

Though we are all equal in the eyes of God, we are not equal in responsibilities. To whom much is given, much is expected. Presidents, prime ministers, and chancellors are men like everyone else, but they are not equal to the common citizen in authority. The concept is not difficult to grasp. The Burger King employee must answer to the shift boss. The shift boss must answer to the store manager. The store manager must answer to the regional manager. The regional manager must answer to the corporate office. The same concepts exist in all other arenas, including an international church whose job it is to teach and uphold the Christian faith beginning from the laity (people), to deacons, priests, bishops, archbishops, cardinals and pope. Scripture reads, "Everyone must submit himself to the governing authorities, for there is no authority except that which God has established. The authorities that exist have been established by God. Consequently, he who rebels against the authority is rebelling against what God has instituted, and those who do so will bring judgment on themselves" (Romans 13:1-2). Hebrews 13:17 states, "Obey your leaders and submit to their authority ... so that their work may be a joy, not a burden." In 1 Thessalonians 5:12 we read, "But we request of you, brethren, that you appreciate those who diligently labor among you, and have charge over you in the Lord and give you instruction." Christ thought it was necessary to commission men to teach in His name, and He appointed Peter as head of His Church, which has morphed into the hierarchy we see today to handle more than 1.3 billion members.

Teaching demands structure and organization, as it does in secular education. Although wherever two or more are gathered politics will be present, the church's hierarchy is not about tyranny, but is a natural organizational process to accomplish its mission. Christ established a living church that would grow from a small seed to a giant tree. A tree that continues to grow today.

<u>Scriptural Interpretation</u>

"I urge you, brothers, to watch out for those who create dissensions and obstacles, in opposition to the teaching that you learned; avoid them.

— Romans 16:17

Some years ago a most infamous discourse concerning the issue of scriptural interpretation took place between me and a fellow "Christian." We should always be mindful that Christianity, above all else, begins with love and repentance, not with how much book knowledge one can hit someone over the head with. We should also be cognizant that we have two ears and one tongue so that we might listen more than we speak.

Our verbal altercation began in the early afternoon at his house when I stopped by while running some errands. We already had a history of discourse, but this one took the cake when he claimed Catholics aren't even Christians and are Hell-bound because we don't operate in accordance with the "Good Book." He suggested that I "begin reading the Bible so you can start doing some Christian things." These comments immediately put me on the defensive, leading to a clash concerning scriptural interpretation. I accused him of being both unbiblical and unreasonable. Scripture clearly teaches that faith is not subject to individual interpretation. Christ said, "Go forth and teach all nations ... what I have commanded you." He did not say to His apostles, "Go forth and teach men whatever you think." Everyone can formulate opinions concerning scripture, but how do self-appointed experts know they are not in error? And who appointed them authorities in the first place?

My friend explained there is no need for an authoritative interpretation: "The Bible is easily understood and anyone who picks it up can figure out its content." Really? Why then do we not come up with the same conclusions if it is so clear? Why do we even debate? 2 Peter 3:16 states that *scripture is not subject to private interpretation because the unlearned can distort it to their own destruction.* We couldn't even agree about this single verse, but all is "easily understood."

Most people do not realize the difficulties that can be found in scripture. We can't judge ancient writings only by our knowledge of today. Knowledge of one age can very much differ from that of another. For correct biblical interpretation, one must be familiar with the times, culture, and customs. One has to be familiar with Hebrew or Greek, also, to avoid translation distortions and obtain the original intent. There aren't many who are inclined or have the time to pursue such thorough studies. That is why I leave certain matters to qualified experts and proper authority. Such comments provoked from my friend a furious sermon on how the only thing I do is "listen to a bunch of men in Rome and refuse to think for" myself. The way I see it, this so-called thinking has unfortunately become a license to think whatever one wishes about Christianity.

He then went on to demonstrate his in-depth knowledge of history by implying that the Church purposely kept people ignorant of scripture. When folks were finally able to acquire Bibles, they were able to determine the falsity and oppression of the Church. This newfound knowledge eventually led to a breakaway from the misconstrued notions of Catholicism, hence, Protestantism, a protest against the Church.

In a nutshell, he was stating that what should follow from reading the Bible is a departure from Catholicism. Though I have read the Bible multiple times of my own accord, my conclusions are obviously not in sync with those of Protestants, so they suggest I go back and reread the "Good Book," since I apparently did not grasp its teachings. In other words, I need to reread the Bible until I come to their conclusions. To make matters worse, Protestants can't agree themselves on what conclusions should be made about the Bible! It is the strangest phenomenon.

Regarding his historical claims of the Church keeping the masses ignorant, we simply cannot take the privileges of the present and blindly apply them to the past. The Bible was not available to everyone by nature of the times. It was not affordable or cheaply distributed, as it is today, since there was no printing press or computers. It had to be cautiously handwritten on expensive paper (papyrus) that not everyone could afford. Besides cost, literacy was also an issue amongst the uneducated. Due to these issues, the Bible was carefully read and taught in Mass and readily available for anyone who wanted to read it in church. The mass production of Bibles did not come until the *Catholic* Johannes Gutenberg invented the printing press in 1545. The first order of business was to print the Bible; not a good strategy for keeping people ignorant. My friend's argument is like blaming the Church for not having displayed the Bible online before the Internet was invented, or blaming the Church for not having a Bible app before smartphones.

How easily people forget, for their convenience, that the Church was a cornerstone in educating the common man. In a time when education was for those with wealth or nobility, the Church recognized the dignity of everyone receiving an education; hence, the countless Catholic schools and Universities in place today around the globe. Yet, the Church attempts to keep people ignorant?

■ ■ ■

"If you believe what you like in the Gospel, and reject what you don't like, it is not the Gospel you believe, but yourself."

— St. Augustine

A simple, but apparently complex, point concerning scriptural interpretation is that guidance is needed to prevent people from coming up with their own fantastic conclusions, as evident throughout history. Christ's method was to establish a teaching church. I am frowned upon for seeking counsel in an arena where I lack expertise. I am a pilot and investor, not a biblical scholar. It's a paradox how those who maintain that interpretation is solely between the Bible and the reader invite me to their churches' Bible study to have their pastor teach scripture when they could have stayed home and interpreted it themselves!

There must be a set of standardized teachings to remedy this Christian fiasco. As an instructor pilot in the Air Force, we held standardization meetings so that the entire flying community could be of one accord. All issues and misunderstandings were brought to senior leadership, instructors, and evaluator pilots to be discussed and dissected. While tackling problems we considered a broad range of issues and their implications, including FAA and training regulations. All findings and conclusions were annotated and disseminated throughout the commands, keeping everyone on the same page. The Christian faith has a similar system—well, at least it does in the Catholic Church. Outside the Church is a different story; it's everyone for themselves.

A standard of authoritative knowledge is necessary to avoid chaos and confusion. Who then has the most appropriate credentials or resume? No entity is more qualified than the Church personally founded by Christ and responsible for putting the Good Book together. It can only be the one church which scripture calls the pillar and foundation of truth (1 Timothy 3:15), the one commissioned to instruct all (Isaiah 2:3). Not all have been charged with such duty. Christ said He would send out His Holy Spirit and be with His Church. This same Holy Spirit has guided the apostles and their successors "into all truth" (John 16:12-13). Historically, logically, and scripturally, that church can only be the Catholic Church. Only the one that has watched and preserved the Christian faith since its foundation is most qualified, not one that came into the scene nine hundred, fifteen hundred, or two thousand years after the fact. If Christ had commissioned everyone, we would all come up with the same doctrinal conclusions, but we do not. The Holy Spirit does not contradict itself, leading men to different conclusions. Christ's method, once again, was to leave behind an imperishable teaching church to teach all nations whatsoever He has commanded, since He knew so many would be mistaken.

So as with any military, government, or civilian entity, standardization and operating procedure manuals facilitate order or a point of reference. Similarly, the Church has its official teachings, which are standard to all Christian Catholics. If two Catholics or even priests disagree on a certain topic, they refer to the official teachings of the Church to clarify or resolve the matter. The problem of Christian doctrines cannot be left suspended in the air. We have not been left in doubt and confusion about the faith.

According to my acquaintance, I can take any standardization and "Shove it." With him, as with many others, the standard is the Bible and its holder, and nothing else, period. Why people do not see the danger of this position is also perplexing. It is like individual Muslims being the sole authorities and interpreters of the Koran. We have already talked about those predicaments, and it ends badly. Unlike Islam, which has no entity that speaks on behalf of Mohammed or the writings of the Koran, Christianity *does* have a voice that speaks on behalf of Christ and the Bible. People have got to grasp that if it were up to the individual, we would be making up our own faith relative to our own mental capacities and desires. Ultimately what we are saying is that we believe in ourselves. But the teaching of the faith must be explicitly taught by a proper authority, as seen in Acts 8:30-31: "'Do you understand what you are reading?' the apostle Philip asked. 'How can I,' he said, 'unless someone explains it to me?'" Acts 18:24-26 is another example. The Apostle Paul's companions, Priscilla and Aquila, find themselves correcting Apollos, who was a studied and eloquent speaker, because he did not have all his information correct. Verse 26 reads, "But when Priscilla and Aquila heard him, they took him aside and explained to him the way of God more accurately." As it was two thousand years ago, so it is today. The faith must be taught by an accurate authority to prevent discord and misunderstanding. The flock of believers and its teachings must be watched over as Paul states in Acts 20:28.

To further emphasize this critical issue, let's use the Constitution of the United States. It can be subject to much interpretation, but the duty of discernment rests upon the highest court of the land, the Supreme Court. The law of the land is not subject to each citizen's interpretation. This is so with the Bible as well. It is the Church's job to dissect scripture and its exact teachings, which they have done a remarkable job of since putting the Bible together. The Church is the pillar and foundation of truth, not individuals waving around Bibles (1 Timothy 3:15). I am no authority concerning biblical interpretation, nor do I have the audacity to claim I know more about Christianity than a Christian institution that has been around for two thousand years.

Finally, during another similar discord, after expressing my logic about the Constitution with a Seventh-day Adventist, he stated he was just speaking what the "Holy Ghost" had revealed. But what about countless who disagree and also claim to be guided by the same "Holy Ghost?" People too often confuse divine guidance with foreign elements such as pride and stubbornness. Or are we to accept that the "Holy Ghost" only operates within the Seventh-day Adventists and not those differing in doctrinal views? With our headstrong perspectives, he declared our debate a stalemate and uttered the ever-famous, "It is a matter of opinion." Again, these were precisely the kinds of words that led me away from Protestantism. This "stalemate" mentality was enough to demonstrate to me that their church is not the one left behind by Christ. That is why at the end of the day, outside the Catholic Church, you end with uncertainty, doubt, division, and a loss of religious faith altogether.

Comments and Response II

> *"But there are some who are disturbing you and wish to pervert the gospel of Christ. But even if we or an angel from heaven should preach a gospel other than the one that we preached to you, let that one be accursed!"*
>
> — Galations 1:7-8

Here are popular comments and responses concerning biblical interpretation:

Comment: The only rule of thumb we need is the Bible and nothing else.
Response: The Bible as we know it did not come together until almost four centuries after Christ. Until it did, what was the rule of thumb? What was

the rule of thumb in the year 55 or 75 AD, when all the books of the New Testament weren't even written yet? Could it have been the Church? It certainly was not the Bible.

Comment: Why do you insist on giving the Church more authority than she already gives herself?
Response: The Church does not delegate herself any authority or power. It would be as ridiculous as a man walking into a boardroom and appointing himself CEO. Proper authority commissions or delegates power, as Christ did when He said, "I shall give you the keys to the kingdom of heaven. Whatever you bind on earth shall be bound in heaven. Whatever you lose on earth shall be loosed in heaven." The Catholic Church is the only one that can be credited for receiving the authority and jurisdiction delegated by Christ.

Comment: The only reason you remain Catholic is due to your failure to think.
Response: Catholics are not prevented from thinking. In fact, the Church encourages thought like no other. Her method is to first instruct and then members can verify their learning. She lays out her teachings which can readily be examined and dissected. I can do all the studying and thinking I wish concerning the faith, but unlike you I have a Church to reference for guidance to keep me from thinking wrong in matters of faith and morals. Other church members think as they wish with no protection from errors, and the results are what we have today—believers running any which way!

It is amazing how in any endeavor in life it is prudent to seek counsel in matters of law, economics, medicine, computers, etc., but when it comes to matters of religion it is wise to consult only oneself. I know we live in a generation where the notion of error does not exist, but this so-called freedom to think without any protection, defined authority, or point of reference has led to a license to think anything one wishes. You continue to make my case as to why Christ left a teaching church in the serious matter of faith since many sincere men would be mistaken. As St. Hilary said in 357 AD, "The Lord has not left this in uncertainty" (Johnson 7).

Comment: So when you want to know something about Christianity, you blindly accept the teachings of the Catholic Church?

Response: When I want to know something about computers I go to a computer tech. If I wish to learn about fixing a car I go to a mechanic. When I want to know something about investing I consult an investor, and so on. If I should have a question or am unclear about any Christian doctrine or teaching, I go to the Catholic Church, which is the appropriate authority to crosscheck my readings and learning. I don't just simply grab a Bible and consult myself to end up inventing my own Christianity with my limited capacity and comprehension.

Comment: What people need to focus on is Jesus, not organized religion.
Response: The Christian faith must not be without "religion," that is, the Church. If so, it changes as the individual sees convenient. This colossal foundational point must be understood. The institutional Church must oversee and govern the faith so it maintains its fidelity and purity, if not, errors will quickly infiltrate and corrupt it. We can see the Church governing from its origin in Acts 16:4 for instance: "Now while they were passing through the cities, they were delivering the decrees which had been decided upon by the apostles and elders who were in Jerusalem, for them to observe." The Church continues to govern today. He who has faith in Christ and has no religion goes against the very teachings of Christ. "Give me Jesus but no Church" is like going to play baseball with no balls or jumping in a vehicle with no gas. If someone wants the teachings of Christ, who himself fulfilled His religious duties in synagogues and the temples, they must accept His provisions, not their own.

By the way, don't you attend a mega-church? Can you explain how that is not organized religion?

Comment: You are a lost soul if you seriously think the Bible is only subject to the interpretation of a few.
Response: The interpretation and dissecting of scripture is subject to the magisterium of the universal church, just as the Constitution is subject to the Supreme Court of the United States. No one is called to listen to any particular individual, but to the Church as a whole. Indeed scriptures

can instigate different thoughts in individuals. I am not referring to subjective matters, but to doctrinal or dogmatic teachings of the faith. The faith teaches definite guidelines on confession, trinity, divorce, faith vs. works, authority, purgatory, etc. Is the Eucharist the body and blood of Christ or is it the symbol of Christ? One thing is certain—it can't be both!

Comment: The Supreme Court consists of fallible men. They have erred in the past, like all men. What makes you think the fallible men in your church aren't mistaken themselves on crucial doctrines?
Response: And what makes you think you are not mistaken with your own conclusions? The Church is not a mere human institution, it is a Christ-made institution. It is a divine institution by virtue of the promise made by its founder when He said He would leave His Holy Spirit with His Church until the end of age. The Holy Spirit guides and protects against errors when the Church sets conditions in doctrinal matters. This is why the Church is referred to as infallible in matters of faith and morals. The Church of Christ, He who is truth Himself, cannot be going around the globe teaching error in His name.

Comment: Christ's sacrifice at Calvary saved all men. Religion and churches obstruct the most important issue here: All of our souls have been saved. Focus on what matters.
Response: That is your personal interpretation, which I certainly reject with my interpretation. Christ, a religious man (Jew), thought religion and His Church to be necessary. Also, Christ's sacrifice did not save all men; rather, He made salvation available to all men. Do you really think no man can lose his soul? Just do as you wish, and one's soul is automatically saved by Christ? Living a good life or bad life makes no difference? According to you, there is no reason to believe in Hell, since we are all going to Heaven. Though salvation is a free gift, it must be accepted. God does not force salvation. That is my interpretation of the Bible, and rest assured, one of us is quite mistaken with these conflicting views.

<u>Bible vs. Tradition</u>

> *"When anyone came along who had been a follower of the apostles, I would inquire about the Apostles' discourses: what was said by Andrew, or by Peter, or by Philip, Thomas, or James ... It did not seem to me that I could get so much profit from the contents of books as from a living and abiding voice."*
>
> — St. Papias

"Bible Christians" insist no one can prove them wrong so long as they stick to the Bible. That statement would be true provided they actually adhered to the Bible, but the problem is, they do not. I have not met the non-Catholic who can prove their position using the Bible without contradicting or stumbling all over themselves. Why? Because their fundamental notions and ideas are nowhere defended in the Bible.

Many Bible Christians have a misconstrued notion that the Bible is the sole beacon or guidance of the faith, but that is only a partial truth which can be very dangerous if one is not vigilant. The Good Book does not stand alone when it comes to defining the fullness of the Christian faith, but stands side by side with sacred church tradition, which I will shortly explain. Protestants often quote Martin Luther's "sola scriptura," meaning scripture alone is truth. The problem with this concept is that nowhere in scripture is this idea found or taught. It is a self-contradiction. The primary verse used to support this claim is 2 Timothy 3:16-17, which states, "All scripture is God-breathed and is useful for teaching, rebuking, correcting and training in righteousness, so that the man of God may be thoroughly equipped for every good work." Amen to that! No one denies how useful and valuable the Bible is, but the Bible does not say that it is the only truth or the source of truth.

When one mentions "tradition," those who don't understand it immediately get skeptical. We are not talking manmade traditions such as getting together for a yearly family picnic or gathering to watch a football game. I am referring to Tradition with a capital T. Tradition is knowledge rooted to the core of one's being. It is something someone knows, and this knowledge, or tradition, can be handed down via statements of beliefs, information, and customs through generations by word of mouth or practice. Christian traditions set the groundwork for many of the ways we go about our daily lives. For instance, the celebrations of Easter, Christmas, and attending church on Sunday are not explicit in the Bible but stem from Church tradition, as do other practices.

Tradition is the body of unwritten knowledge given by Christ to his apostles and handed down through their successors, the Church's bishops, who teach to everybody else (Johnson 36). This is how the Church got started. The Church did not spread like wildfire because of the Bible. There was no such book until centuries later. Many mistakenly believe the Bible has been around since the time of Christ. It has not.

There is no denying that the Bible helped spread the faith, just as it does today, but let us use facts in their appropriate time frame and give credit only where it is due. If we examine the time from immediately after the death of Christ until the last of the epistles were written some fifty years after the crucifixion, there weren't thousands of manuscripts. The lavish number of copies would come later in time. FedEx and Kinko's were not around at the time (no sarcasm intended). Again, we cannot apply the privileges of today to the year 50 AD. The farmer tending to his pigs did not receive the *Mesopotamia Times* or the *Jewish Daily News*. When Jesus taught the five thousand, He wasn't handing out flyers, or emailing, texting, and tweeting. Neither were His apostles. *As a matter of fact, Christ never wrote a single word of His teachings!* It is interesting to note He never wrote down a single word. Great intellects in history have also done the same. Plato often said that his purest philosophy was never written down and he shared it only orally with close and trusted friends and colleagues. He said the written word was not an appropriate medium for important and difficult material, as it could not be explained or defended in the author's absence (Rooney 89).

The bottom line is the rule of thumb in the first century concerning the faith was, *the Church or body of believers via the power of word of mouth*. As time passed, the number of manuscripts multiplied, which is the natural evolution of things. The thousands Christ and his apostles preached to and converted went back to their particular towns and spread the good news, creating a chain reaction.

The Jews were a very oral society and took their customs very seriously. They memorized their teachings and if someone spoke something contrary to their traditions, that person was immediately corrected. There was nothing else to lean on but their oral culture without the technology we enjoy presently. Unlike today, there was a time when a man's word meant something.

The point is, too many accelerate the sequence of events, not allowing proper evolution to take place. The Bible was *NOT* the initial spark of the Christian faith; therefore, it cannot be the only source of truth. After Christ, the apostles continued His work, converting thousands by word of mouth; that is, tradition. Paul tells us while talking to the Galatians, "I would like to learn one thing from you: Did you receive the spirit by observing the law or by believing what you heard?" (Galatians 3:2)

The New Testament is essentially a byproduct of church tradition. The writings in the epistles include preaching, instruction for converts, and denunciations of heresies. These writings would later become part of what we know as the Bible. To write something down supposes an existing knowledge. The apostle Luke, for instance, wrote his accounts while observing, hearing, and journeying with the apostle Paul. The New Testament slowly begins to form as the disciples, specifically Paul, started to write down traditions to preserve the faith.

There should be no amazement that there are unwritten parts of Christian revelation, because that's how it's always been. God did not send down textbooks, printing presses, or other technologies. The revelation to the Jews contained in the Torah, for example, includes a written part, and the oral tradition handed down by priests and rabbis was never written down. Malachi 2:7 states, "The lips of the priest shall keep knowledge and they shall seek the law at his mouth." In Isaiah 59:21, the Lord says, "My spirit, who is in you, and my words that I have put in your mouth will not depart from your mouth or from the mouths of your children, or from the mouths of your descendants from this time on and forever."

As the Old Testament revelations are not entirely written down, so it is with the New Testament revelations. No one claims the New Testament doesn't have an enormous amount of information. St. Jerome rightly said, "Ignorance of scripture is ignorance of Christ." The Bible is the Bible. But we cannot skip over scriptures that are inconvenient to our theories, such as those that support traditions:

- 2 Timothy 2:2: "And the things you have *heard me* say in the presence of many witnesses entrust to reliable men who will also be qualified to teach others."
- 1 Corinthians 11:2: "I praise you for remembering me in everything and hold fast to the traditions, just as I handed them on to you."
- Mark 4:34: "Without parables he did not speak to them, but to his own disciples he explained everything in private."
- John 16:12: "I have much more to *tell* you, but you cannot bear it now."
- 2 Timothy 1:13: "What you have *heard* from me, keep as the pattern of sound teaching, with faith and love in Christ Jesus. Guard the good deposit that was entrusted to you—guard it with the help of the Holy Spirit who lives in us."
- Luke 10:16: "He who listens to you listens to me."
- 3 John 1:14: "I hope to see you soon, when we can talk face to face."
- Luke 1:1-2: "Many have undertaken to draw up an account of the things that have been fulfilled among us, just as they were handed down [tradition] to us by those who first were eyewitnesses."
- Acts 20:35: "... remember the words the Lord Jesus himself said."
- 2 Thessalonians 2:15: "Therefore, brothers, stand firm and hold fast to the *traditions* that you were taught, either by an oral statement or by a letter of ours."
- 2 Thessalonians 3:6: "We instruct you, brothers, in the name of (our) Lord Jesus Christ, to shun any brother who conducts himself in a disorderly way and not according to the *tradition* they received from us."
- John 21:25: "Jesus did many other things as well. If every one of them were written down, I suppose that even the whole world would not have room for the books that would be written."

So on and so forth. Why continue? Protestants err when they hold Catholics to the other extreme of "sola scriptura," that is, *"sola ecclesia," or "church alone."* The Church doesn't claim truth on the basis of scripture alone without referencing tradition, nor does she claim any truth on the basis of tradition without scripture (Johnson 5). Divine tradition and scripture, therefore, never oppose each other. They must complement each other and be in total harmony. If one wants an accurate interpretation of the Bible, examining Church tradition is necessary, or else one ends up distorting scripture. The Church uses this oral deposit of faith to examine all Christian teachings and biblical passages (Johnson 5).

As mentioned, scripture is not subject to private interpretation; there are things that are difficult to understand, that the unlearned and the unstable distort, just as they do the rest of the scriptures, to their own destruction (2 Peter 3:16).

■ ■ ■

Critics often say the Church has changed or "gone astray." What has changed is the knowledge concerning tradition and scriptural revelation. Our understanding of the faith has grown, just as we learn more about the material world through physics, astronomy, or biology. These sciences don't change, but our comprehension of them continues to grow. In the same way, the Church's understanding of God's revelations continues to develop gradually as the Church faces new issues in the metamorphosis of time, cultures, and environment. But she does not add anything or take away any of Christ's teachings. An institutional Church is not just needed to teach, but to keep all teachings and revelations intact as stated. It is the Church's job to take on the ever-changing affairs of humankind such as capital punishment, homosexuality, abortion, stem cell research, contraception, human cloning, and so forth. The Catholic Church is the reliable source, guided by the Holy Spirit, needed to speak on behalf of her founder. She was established to tackle the questions of good and evil, right and wrong, truth and heresy, wherever they surface. Someone must speak on behalf of Christ, and it is certainly not every person holding a Bible (Johnson 7).

Fiasco Conclusion

Hopefully, my Christian verdict has been clarified. I was tempted to explain Catholic doctrine here via the Bible and tradition, but there is too much material, plus that is not the intent in these writings. I depart this Christian fiasco with an arrow pointing toward where Christianity can be found in its purest form—the Catholic Church. I recommend reviewing *The Essential Catholic Survival Guide* by the staff of Catholic Answers and *Radio Replies* by Leslie Rumble and Charles Carty as a starting point. There is no suspicious or unbiblical teaching deriving from the Church. It all complements the Bible and sacred traditions. Keep in mind also, if you want to know about Catholicism, ask someone who knows the faith. Many who oppose the Church don't get their information from the appropriate source, which is like asking your landscaper for medical advice. Hearsay does not avail against facts. Ironically, the Catholics I have learned the most from are Protestants who set out to disprove the Catholic faith and ended up converting!

What causes great frustration is that I am told I am wrong by some Christian brethren and don't receive any guidance on where I should turn to find genuine Christian teachings. My perspective is simply wrong and I "need to go read" my Bible. Being accused of error supposes my accusers are in the right. Are Methodists correct, or the Seventh-day Adventists? Pentecostals, perhaps? Mormons claim to possess the truth about Christ. Should I become a Mormon? Is the solution to attend True Word Bible Church in Florida? Or the Church of Christ, which tells me I am part of the biggest cult on the planet? Why these and not another denomination? Who is guiding the flock? Surely such crucial information is not to be hoarded by those who claim Catholics err. "To whom shall we go?" as Peter asks in John 6:68. To whom?

Considering the circumstances, I will stay put, since the only answers to the question of where can one find true biblical teaching seem to be "Go read your Bible" or "Come blindly join our church." What I do know is that Christ prayed His Church would be one, as He and the Father are one. Since the foundations of Christianity, many sects have called themselves the true church. These breakaway churches rose and died because they lacked the promise of Christ to remain on earth until the end of time. For two millennia, kingdoms have fallen and risen, cultures have come and gone, the world has changed with the winds of time, and these sects have all slowly faded away into history, but the same Catholic Church stands today, despite all her attackers, internal or external. Today she stands with a string of new sects, and they too will die, and new churches that don't even exist today will rise tomorrow claiming to be the "true church," and in their midst will stand the universal church that has stood the test of time.

This denominational problem cannot be swept under the rug; it is a crucial issue every intelligent Christian must eventually deal with.

WANDERING CATHOLICS

Many Catholics are sitting on a treasure chest and don't even realize it. Most of us take our faith for granted. This is why I must address with tough love my fellow Catholics staggering in their faith, especially the apathetic who entertain such notions as, "It is not necessary to attend church to pray to God," or if they do go they say, "I get nothing out of Mass." I speculate that these comments derive more from the motive of excuse rather than sincere reasoning. Going to church on Sunday interferes with such activities as sporting events, afternoon ventures in the park, or sleeping in. If folks prayed as diligently as they claimed, they would feel quite differently about their Mass attendance. They would at least attend one of the numerous services on Saturday or Sunday.

We can agree there is no need to be in church to pray to God. Pray wherever and whenever possible, but the reason we attend Mass is *to give God the proper worship He deserves in the way He demands.* "Do this in memory of me," Christ said. It's not just about saying a small prayer on the way to the football game. The one to be worshiped has made specifications on how He should be worshiped. We attend Mass not because we like it, but in obedience to and reverence for Him. Nonetheless, we do get something out of Mass. The Church has always taught that Christ is truly present in the consecrated bread and wine. He said, "This is my body." At Mass, we acknowledge the most significant event in history and receive what we need more than anything in this world: Christ Himself in the Eucharist. We may not feel any different, but it nourishes our soul in the same way multivitamins nourish our bodies. Keep in mind, this process is a two-way avenue. We need to bring more spiritual hunger and faith to Mass to feel its transforming power. We must approach the Eucharist with more zeal and faith.

We also attend church for fellowship. God calls us to community, not individualism. It also keeps us focused on our spiritual walk and helps us "stay in the zone," if you will. We attend church to find a suitable environment away from the noise of the world and for a much-needed moment of peace in which to be still and listen. We go to church to learn about our faith. We go to serve and love others. We go to church to continue to work on our personal relationship with God. The reasons are numerous, and attendance is a necessity for any and all believers.

Avoiding Mass because it's "full of hypocrites" does not fly either. Though hypocrites may be dwelling in a congregation, that is exactly where they need to be. Church is not just for the righteous, but is a hospital for sinners, as my pastor, Father Bob, would say. Church is precisely where hypocrites need to be, rather than elsewhere and doing who knows what. A house of worship is a great place to inspire change. Besides, I am willing to bet that more hypocrites are found outside of church than God-fearing men inside church.

■ ■ ■

We as Christians also need to review some fundamental doctrines of Christianity. Christian teachings are often thrown into a blender with all sorts of divergent dogma and called Christianity. Many people redefine terms and use words loosely. We must be on guard against such sugar-coating. Mentioning Christ here and there does not make one a Christian. Let's go back to the basics. What is a Christian? Christianity 101 has taught for two millennia that a Christian is one who accepts and spreads the full teachings of Jesus Christ. They acknowledge Him as the son of God and believe in a triune God, but one entity: God the father, God the son, and

God the Holy Spirit (the Trinity). Christian basics profess that God came in the flesh as the person of Jesus Christ, who suffered, died, and was buried. He rose for our salvation and whoever believes in Him will not perish. That is Christianity 101 in a nutshell. Anyone who claims otherwise has invented their own "Christianity." I challenge all believers to do an inventory of their faith to see where they stand with these basics.

A vast number of organizations have problems harmonizing even with these fundamentals. They lure people in by preaching a false Christ. On the surface they teach what appears legitimate, until closer examination, where one finds, for example, denials of: the deity of Christ, the Trinity, the Holy Spirit, His physical resurrection, and Hell. They alter the Bible by changing passages and adding to the Word of God. They refuse to read verses in their biblical contexts, and instead insert their own theological presumptions to alter biblical text to suit their needs. Some of these organizations have predicted multiple times that the world's end was imminent. We must be cognizant of what we are being fed and taking in. That is why we must know our faith.

The spirit of deceit runs rampant. Ignorance has many falling astray. "Do not trust every spirit but test the spirits to see whether they belong to God, because many false prophets have gone out into the world" (1 John 4:1).

THE ISSUE OF HOMOSEXUALITY

"Speak the truth by all means; be bold and fearless in your rebuke of error, and in your keener rebuke of wrong doing ... but be human, and loving, and gentle, and brotherly the while."

— *William Morley Pushon*

"All men are equal; it is not birth, but virtue alone, that makes the difference."

— *Voltaire*

We have covered much about God and religion to this point. My methodology for finding certain truths is evident. Objective truth and morality cannot be left for each individual to determine. Therefore, I force the issue on the most qualified: the man who claimed to be truth Himself via the institution He left on earth. Because of this, we boldly move forward to touch upon some controversial and delicate social issues frequently in the spotlight: homosexuality and abortion. Let us examine what happens when these controversial issues are filtered through this system. It is only right that we tackle these issues in such a book. We continue forward with the premise that there is a God and an objective right and wrong.

■ ■ ■

Homosexuality and same-sex marriage are topics that have spread much tension across the country, and have been some of my most-debated topics. This is an arena where the words "bigot" and "hater" are thrown around often—unless one agrees with the homosexual position, in which case one is as "open-minded" and "loving" as they come. The so-called unjudgmental gays and their supporters judge others for disagreeing with them, though those who do so are merely standing by their principles, as homosexuals do theirs!

The word "judging" these days is used quite loosely. Disagreement does not mean one is narrow-minded, prejudiced, or maliciously judgmental. There is a notion of wrong judgment and right judgment. We have rationality so as to live and rule by right judgment. The one who stands for right principles in the correct manner demonstrates right judgment. Such judgments are exercised every day by parents, judges, teachers, military leaders, politicians, and others. The question is not whether one judges, but whether one is judging rightly or justly. It is a natural phenomenon we practice even unconsciously. Should one be a Democrat, liberal, Independent, Republican, or conservative? Refusing to be part of an ideology or movement is a judgment call one must make based on what a party represents.

Judging distinguishes between ideas. We should judge actions not to discriminate, but to *distinguish* between right and wrong, so that we may know and do what is right. Judging is wrong when one does not know the facts, but rather is arbitrating based on speculation in an attempt to put oneself on a pedestal. Though bad judgment is often exercised, it does not diminish the fact that there is right judgment. So this is not about being judgmental in the belittling way people often use the word. It is my sincere and honest judgment that I disagree with homosexuals and their supporters, in the same way that they *judge* my position as incorrect. One man can certainly disagree with another man without hating that man. The goal here is to demonstrate logically why the disagreement exists and to make an informed decision as to where one should stand.

■ ■ ■

Homosexuality grasped my attention with a riveting experience on the subway station in New York City. Across my platform I noticed a couple showing a public display of affection. Something seemed at odds, so I squinted and maneuvered for a better angle, from which I discovered two men "going at it." I honestly didn't know what to think, as I caught myself staring. All sorts of emotions rallied through my mind. I have been around homosexuals before but never had I seen two men caressing and kissing each other. I expeditiously took a seat to contemplate the happenings. How would I explain this scene to my five-year-old? I thought of nature and human anatomy. Could this be normal behavior? What was I missing? Do not a man and woman complement each other like light and darkness, cold and hot, happy and sad? I thought the norm was yin and yang; now there is a version of yang and yang, yin and yin, making its way ferociously across the country. This incident would open the door to another arena full of contentious new debates.

After considering and questioning the reasoning behind homosexual relations, I initially received half-baked answers. The usual commentary was along the lines of, "What matters is that they are happy together," or "Since they love each other, it's OK," or "To each his own." Of course, the classic "It boils down to what the person believes is right and wrong" argument never fails to present itself. Even a scoundrel would like to believe that what he does is right, but our personal choices are not the final test. Many are the things a man would "love" to do that are not necessarily right. Some folks would justify the seven deadly sins simply because they "love" to commit them.

Eventually, more objective theories came to my attention from someone who claimed homosexuals are born the way they are due to genetics. That would be a potential game-changer if there really were a "gay gene," but for every article I found concerning a "gay gene" there was another condemning the theory. I found no real evidence. The accumulated analysis suggests that homosexual orientation is a complex issue in which biological, social, and psychological factors combine to play a role in the ultimate sexual orientation of an individual. Factors such as environment, poor parenting (specifically the father), peer group influence, developmental factors, sexual experiences, violence or abuse, sickness or disease, psychological trauma, and more may all play a role, but there is *no* sole "gay gene" that commands homosexuality, like a gene that directs brown hair. Now, if being gay is not genetic, at the end of the day it is a choice.

We must admit there are those who, through no fault of their own, have been exposed to circumstances that make them more prone to homosexual desires, such as those who are more prone alcoholism. But let us also acknowledge that there are those who make the choice to participate in such activity out of curiosity or sheer perversion, such as a friend of mine who experimented because it seemed like the cool new thing to do, but eventually reverted to her old heterosexual ways because, she admitted, "There was something not right." We cannot make blanket statements that say *all* who participate in homosexual activity are homosexually inclined, just like a person who chooses to indulge in drugs does not necessarily have to have a history of substance abuse. For those who are homosexually inclined, the orientation in itself is not wrong, but what is done with those feelings and thoughts is what can be wrong. All of us carry burdens in life, and for a homosexual that may be their burden. A person who suffers from depression, drug addiction, physical deformity, etc., has their own grievances and hardships to deal with. We all carry burdens, and some are naturally heavier than others, but we must play the hand we have been dealt. Even a bad hand, when properly played, can be a winner.

It is easy to justify and rationalize that for which we have a strong passion and desire. Passions and cravings blind us from what we ought to do. But we must cease our blind tendency to pursue our animal appetites.

■ ■ ■

Before venturing into natural law and reason, let us first tackle this issue from a moral perspective. When speaking of morals one has to bring God into the discussion. As discussed, morality is above the authority of any individual. No one can say that something is moral simply because they think it is. Not surprisingly, most homosexuals (not all) I've encountered are atheist/humanist, and do not want to hear "any noise about a fairy-tale man in the sky." Their lack of faith seems to be rooted in avoiding any moral restraints. As with any unbeliever, I attempt to make a case for God because if there is no God, then anything goes. We should be indifferent about homosexuality, or any moral issue, but we know there are many things that are not permissible. Therefore, a standard of morality exists. What, then, does the author of all moral standards have to say, through the filtering mechanism we just used? He is quite clear on this subject, and it does not favor the homosexual position.

Indeed, Christian denominations vary even on the homosexual issue. There are some that marry gay couples, but to avoid venturing on another escapade dealing with denominations, I will simply state that *one cannot be a genuine disciple of Christ and sanction homosexual unions without advocating a clear contradiction to the Christian faith*.

Christians only want to hear the nice, warm fuzzies taught by the faith and dismiss everything else not in accordance with their ideology. "Love thy neighbor" sounds comforting, but "Repent or you will die in your sins" sounds too uncomfortable. Though the Good Book teaches that we should love everyone, it does not say we should love or support other's mistaken notions. There is a great distinction.

One homosexual pastor I encountered on HuffPost Social News comes to mind who explained, "Christ never specifically spoke against homosexuality but commanded us to love everyone instead." Christ neither spoke about human trafficking, pornography, or other perversions, but we know quite well these things are sinful and against Christian principles. Scripture makes very clear that homosexual acts, not the orientation, are wrong. "You shall not lie with a male as with a woman; such a thing is an abomination" (Leviticus 18:22). "If a man lies with a man as one lies with a woman, both of them have done what is detestable … their blood will be on their own heads" (Leviticus 20:13 NIV). Some dismiss such verses as old and outdated Old Testament scripture that should not be accepted, but the New Testament leaves no room for maneuvering. It states that the sexually immoral, the adulterers, the homosexual offenders, thieves or drunkards will not inherit the kingdom of God (1 Corinthians 6:9). In Romans 1:26-27 we read, "Therefore, God handed them over to degrading passions. Their females exchanged natural relations for unnatural, and the males likewise gave up natural relations with females and burned with lust for one another. Males did shameful things with males and thus received in their own persons the due penalty for their for their perversity." It cannot be made clearer than Matthew 19:4-6, where Christ says, "Have you not read that from the beginning the Creator 'made them male and female' and said, 'For this reason a man shall leave his father and mother and be joined to his wife, and the two shall become one flesh?' So they are no longer two, but one flesh. What God has joined together, let no man separate." Clearly, from a moral and biblical perspective, we were designed to find sexual fulfillment with the opposite sex.

The pastor dismissed my claims by bringing to light that we are all sinners and fall short. That is true, but we cannot use any logic that says that since we are all sinners anyway, let us sin away. We are not exempt from our responsibilities.

Many would then tell me that I am no authority in matters of Christian teaching. That is true, and neither is the individual holding a Bible, or your local pastor. The Church is the authority, and she says the following:

"Basing itself on Sacred Scripture, which presents homosexual acts as acts of grave depravity, tradition has always declared that 'homosexual acts are intrinsically disordered.' They are contrary to the natural law. They close the sexual act to the gift of life. They do not proceed from a genuine affective and sexual complementarity. Under no circumstances can they be approved.

"The number of men and women who have deep-seated homosexual tendencies is not negligible. This inclination, which is objectively disordered, constitutes for most of them a trial. They must be accepted with respect, compassion, and sensitivity. Every sign of unjust discrimination in their regard should be avoided. These persons are called to fulfill God's will in their lives and, if they are Christians, to unite to the sacrifice of the Lord's Cross the difficulties they may encounter from their condition.

"Homosexual persons are called to chastity. By the virtues of self-mastery that teach them inner freedom, at times by the support of disinterested friendship, by prayer and sacramental grace, they can and should gradually and resolutely approach Christian perfection" *(Catechism of the Catholic Church, 2357-2359).*

The bottom line is that from a Christian perspective, homosexuality is improper, but there is a distinction between having homosexual desires and acting on them. Temptations do not make us who we are. Therefore, there is no such thing as "gay Christian," "alcoholic Christian," etc. Rather, a person who struggles against homosexual desires and temptations and sincerely tries to rectify his ways is simply a "struggling Christian," just as other Christians struggle with their own issues or vices.

Again, homosexuals carry the burden of resisting the abnormal sexual temptations within them, so I caution heterosexuals not to condemn people, but rather, actions. "Let the first one without sin cast the first stone." Do not take this to mean that we should be defending the homosexual lifestyle. We must employ discernment and wisdom. We can treat others with dignity and respect while disagreeing with their creed, but the key is to strike a right balance of love and truth. With the transcendent power of a right example, we can inspire change.

Though the majority of Christians claim they do not agree with homosexual activity, their silence on the issue supports the homosexual cause much more than they think. My aunt, for example, insists there are "bigger fish to fry," but if the dignity of marriage and family is not a priority precisely when it is being attacked the most in history, it will never be a priority. Here is a scripture people of faith can appreciate: "I have made you a watchman…When you hear a word from my mouth, you shall warn them for me. If I say to the wicked man, You shall surely die; and you do not warn him or speak out to dissuade him from his wicked conduct so that he may live: that wicked man shall die for his sin, but I will hold you responsible for his death. If, on the other hand, you have warned the wicked man, yet he has not turned away from his evil nor from his wicked conduct, then he shall die for his sin, but you shall save your life" (Ezekiel 3:17-19).

■ ■ ■

Now why is homosexuality against the natural law? Let's put it this way. We know food is for nourishment. If we were to decide *not* to eat, we would gradually wither away and die of hunger. That is the law of nature. Now, if someone decided to eat for pleasure and purposely vomit to keep from gaining weight, such action goes against the natural course of eating and digestion. Mental professionals categorize this as a disorder, known as bulimia. Why is this an illness? Because the organs of digestion are designed to take food on a one-way trip.

In the same manner that the digestive tract has its purposes, the sexual organs are designed for particular functions, and by light of common sense or human anatomy, we can tell what those are. Penises and rectums have inherent functions that do not cooperate with what homosexuals imagine. When someone uses their sexual organs for reasons other than those for which they were designed or intended, such action is classified as inherently disordered. Just like bulimia, homosexual acts are disordered because they are contrary to natural law. It does not matter if one enjoys having sex with the same gender or eating food to throw it up; it's still a disorder.

Fundamental ethical intuition speaks volumes on this matter. We recognize spontaneously that the natural sex partner of a man is a woman, and not some lower animal. In other words, nature calls for the union between two human beings of the opposite sex to make a sexual whole, not between a human and a dog or any other animal. If one can argue that bestiality is unnatural, using the same logic and intuition, we can also say that the natural partner of a man is a woman, and of a woman, a man.

Homosexual activists don't want to hear any "nonsense" about violation of natural law. They think it is perfectly normal, and that the American

Psychiatric Association will vouch for them. Although for decades, the American Psychiatric Association considered homosexuality a disorder, pro-homosexuals have let sexual politics trump science and logic. In his book *Homosexuality and American Psychiatry: The Politics of Diagnosis*, Dr. Ronald Bayer makes a case for how the decision to remove homosexuality from the official list of psychological disorders was based on power politics, not science.

Deep down, everyone knows there is a fundamental difference between the union of a man and a woman and that of any other kind. Even a child can discern the problem with the homosexual equation. But many have allowed themselves to be distracted from this fact by ingesting a narrative of false compassion and empathy, especially from the media, which leads people to ignore what they know to be true.

I am not trying to be cold or cruel, but telling others that homosexual behavior is OK is not genuine compassion. Nor is telling others that incorrect conduct is fine simply because they enjoy the activity. We are all broken people in many ways, but the solution is not to reinforce and indulge in our brokenness. In the end, that will leave us more broken.

Homosexual Comments and Responses

*"Wrong is wrong even if everyone is doing it.
Right is right even if no one is doing it."*

— St. Augustine

Is homosexual activity against reason? I believe the following debates answer the question. They also demonstrate the passions boiling over this issue.

Comment: You use the word "abnormal" to describe gays as if they are less than any other human, bigot!
Response: That is not true. I do not use the word in the derogatory way you imagine. I use the word in the sense, where if it snowed five feet in New York City, one would say it is "abnormal." I am not trying to diminish the dignity of anyone. I am here to examine actions, and I maintain that homosexual actions are inappropriate. It is no more bigotry than noting that falling objects have a downward trajectory rather than sideways.

Comment: It is none of your business what people do behind closed doors. Repeat: Mind your business!
Response: Correct, but it's no longer an issue kept behind closed doors which is why I cannot mind my business. The homosexual agenda is pushing to restructure family and the sanctity of marriage. That is nothing more than an intrusion, which makes it everyone's business.

Comment: Why don't you believe in personal freedom?
Response: I believe in personal freedom, but even freedom is within boundaries. The homosexual agenda crosses those boundaries. Besides, there really is no real freedom—one is either subject to vices or virtues, and there is nothing virtuous about homosexual activity.

Comment: Studies show same-sex couples can be just as good or better parents than heterosexual couples.
Response: Even better parents than heterosexual couples? Where do you derive your conclusions? I am sure the "study" you reference has no bias, right? Human history speaks for itself and stands against your study. The reality is, same-sex "marriage" ignores a child's best interests, depriving the child of a mother and father role model. Homosexuality denies the obvious psychological and physiological differences between men and women which come together in marriage for the benefit of the child. Two completely different things cannot be considered equivalent. This is a simple matter of honest observation as to what is and is not directed by natural law.

Comment: You talk about the complements between man and woman. What about single parents who do a great job and the piss-poor job heterosexual parents do, with their abysmal rate of divorce? And studies do show that same-sex couples can do a better job of raising kids.
Response: First, no one denies that some single parents do an excellent job under certain circumstances, but because this is so, it does not mean a woman or man should raise a child by themselves. That is not normal. Second, bad heterosexual parents do not justify redefining marriage and family; we must strengthen the definition and values of marriage and family, not redefine them. Or do you mean that same-sex marriage is the cure for infidelity, bad parenting, abuse, etc.? You give your imagination too much credit. Thirdly, same-sex couples do not make better parents than the complementary man and woman. Fatherhood and motherhood play very distinctive roles which cannot be provided in a homosexual relationship. Historically, the government imparted benefits on married couples because by its very nature and design, marriage provides the normal conditions for an established balance and moral atmosphere that is beneficial to the upbringing of children. This strengthens our society and supports the continuation of the human race by replenishing the population.

It is important to understand that family is the cornerstone of society. All around we see broken homes, divorce, drug abuse, births out of wedlock, abortions, teens that are disrespecful and out of control and so forth. The majority of these problems stem from the negligence or breakdown of the family. If we focus on the family and restoring traditional values these issues would not be as prominent as they are in our society. We cannot continue to ignore the core issue that will alleviate many of our concerns, that is, the structure of family, and marriage is closely interwined with the success of the family. Unfortunately today marriage between a man and woman no longer holds a special place in society, at least amongst the secular. This only continues to chip away at the foundation stone. Today marriage has been warped; morality has been thrown aside, while politics, political correctness, and the subordinate appetites of men have taken precedence.

Comment: I don't get it. Homosexual couples have opened their hearts and homes and provided a loving environment to adopted children. What is the problem with that?
Response: These men and women are covering a distortion in their redefining of marriage and family. They disguise their actions with what outwardly seems good to justify their behavior, but no one is justified doing wrong as a means to an end of doing "good." What we need to do is strengthen the institution of marriage and family to avoid more kids being in the situation they find themselves.

Children, unfortunately, are the biggest losers in this homosexual agenda. They are deprived of the uniqueness of experiencing real fatherhood and motherhood. Kids have become an accessory to satisfy the lifestyle choice of individuals of the same sex. Children are losing their dignity and rightful place. They are becoming like an item or thing that people have a right to obtain in this wild society.

Comment: Can you tell me flat out what is wrong with homosexuality?
Response: Besides it distorting the real institution of marriage and family, it is against natural law, moral law, logic, and reason, and repels common

sense. Therefore, it can't be considered as some sort of "goodness." Not everything that is pleasurable is good or beneficial. We cannot let our lower appetites take over our better judgment.

Comment: It seems you are the illogical one. You mention homosexuality is against Reason. Well, humans are often not reasonable- Flawed point. You say it is against Natural Law…Wrong again. Homosexuality occurs in nature and found in hundreds of species- Flawed theory. Then you mention Moral Law- Morals are not universally agreed upon. Another flawed point. Your opinion cannot be reasonably justified, logically justified, theoretically justified, or morally justified and lacks any thoughtful facts.
Response: "Humans are often not reasonable," you say, but it does not follow that there are no reasonable humans. I assume you are attempting to be reasonable, or why else would you be commenting? Or are you writing for the sake of writing, hoping that it is not nonsense?

It is against natural law because of self-evident impossibilities and flawed design. No matter how you look at it, two male or two female bodies are physically incompatible. The penis was not designed for another man's rectum. Your notions vary greatly from the proper penis/vagina complement.

As far as homosexual activities amongst various species, we are not brute animals that there should be a logical parallel, as you pretend. If we were brute beasts you would have an argument, but we are of a higher domain. We are "glorified" animals endowed with intellect, consciousness, soul, reason, self-control, discipline, etc. Therefore, we don't act on instincts and our lower cravings like brute animals. Darwinism is against you too, since two people of the same sex do not fit the survival of the fittest doctrine or natural selection. Two people of the same sex cannot procreate, so why would nature favor such conditions?

Lastly, you bring up moral relativism, which will only leave us in a vicious circle, concluding that nothing is right or wrong. Relativism is a lengthy subject we can't entertain here. I will say this much: You contradict your relativistic mind by demanding homosexuality be universally supported or accepted. That doesn't sound too relativistic.

Comment: Technology is not a part of natural law, so by your logic, technology should be wrong.
Response: No, there is nothing immoral or non-virtuous about certain technologies, depending on how they are used. Homosexual activity is immoral and non-virtuous, regardless of how it is used.

Comment: First, we are part of the animal kingdom. Second, I am a heterosexual in a committed relationship, and both my boyfriend and I do not feel the institution of marriage is being threatened by same-sex marriages.
Response: I did not say we are not part of the animal kingdom, I said we are not at the level of mere animals. We are of a higher domain. We are endowed with many qualities that a brute animal does not possess. Our similarities with animals are due to the harmony or unity of life, but we cannot argue that because a superior principle (human beings) is capable of lower operations, that an inferior principle (animals) is capable of higher operations. We are of a greater dominion and cannot be bluntly compared to animals. The creatures of this world do not have our capabilities because of the higher mental and overall abilities necessary to belong to an entirely different order of being (human beings)—therefore we don't act like animals (3:12).

As far as you and your boyfriend not "feeling" the institution of marriage is being threatened, remember there are others who "feel" quite differently, so that cannot be a logical argument.

Comment: Homosexuality is NOT against nature since it has been around since the beginning of creation. Sex is not always about procreation either. If it was, then why should an 80-year-old couple be allowed to marry? They cannot procreate. Lastly, if you truly believe in the Bible then how can you believe in Darwin and evolution? Darwinism goes directly against and contradicts religion.
Response: It is an anomaly of nature. There have been all sorts of diseases, physical and mental disorders since the beginning of time, but we do not call them "normal." Like with any irregularity, we seek help such as counseling, medication, and therapy. You suggest we call homosexuality normal simply because you like it.

And the ultimate purpose of sex is procreation; however, no 80-year-old couple or any couple should be denied marriage, because procreation is not the sole purpose of marriage. A man was not made to be alone but given a suitable partner (Gen 2:18). There are other principles at force here that are just foreign to you, but regardless, one man and one woman (whether 30 or 80 years old) still satisfy the requirement and definition of a real marriage, thereby respecting natural and moral law.

Finally, evolution, science, and faith go hand in hand when rightly understood, so there are no issues putting science and religion side by side, for their source is the same.

Comment: If marriage is about having kids, then let's not allow young couples who can't have children to marry.
Response: Homosexual activists always have a tendency to appeal or lean towards the abnormal to make a case for anything. A young or old couple unable to have kids in marriage is not the norm. Exceptions do not disprove the rule. Regardless of fertility, there are physical and psychological differences that help one man and one woman thrive like same-sex couples cannot. And it remains that even though they are unable to have a child, they are still a woman and man respecting the real definition of marriage, natural law, moral law and reason.

Comment: Nature will bring about more homosexuals, which shows that it is natural.
Response: There will be more homosexuals in the future, but not because it is normal, just like the many other disorders we know now will present themselves in the future. But tell me, how much more unnatural can it get than having to depend on heterosexuals to produce homosexuals?

Comment: What do you not understand about homosexuality not being a choice?
Response: We can admit that some may be more homosexually inclined than others through no fault of their own, but to act on those desires is

ultimately a choice. We are not robots without will. We must practice some tough virtues. Also, it is a fact, there is no such thing as a homosexual gene; therefore, it is ultimately a choice.

Comment: The pressing matter here is human equality for all. Many conservatives believe a century-long battle to reform health care should have taken a back seat to job creation in 2010 (though the two go hand in hand). During World War II, freedom and security was a "pressing matter" for the entire planet. Was addressing the plight of the Jews a distraction from that urgency, or part of the solution?

In the '60s, the Cold War and threat of mutual assured destruction via nuclear exchange with the U.S.S.R. was a "pressing matter" for the entire planet. Was addressing civil rights legislation in the U.S. and the women's liberation movement a distraction from that urgency, or part of moving our nation forward despite it?

There is NO such thing as a less important matter when it comes to moving humanity and democratic ideals and principles forward, regardless of what continent or nation we're discussing. In a "free world," it's part and parcel of the same goal: recognizing and supporting the full worth and self-actualization of all free citizens. Gay rights are one small part of human rights and human rights are, generally speaking, THE most pressing issue facing every nation and continent on our planet. Efforts to deter inequality must continue at all cost.

Response: Well said. You make points with which I agree, but the case we are entertaining is not equivalent. You are operating under the premise that homosexual activity is a virtuous thing to fight for in the first place, but it is not. If it were, your argument would stand. Homosexual activity is against natural law, moral law, reason, and common sense. Therefore, we cannot compare it to the plight of the Jews, civil rights legislation, and so forth. Movements that are virtuous cannot be compared to those that are not.

Also, you are mistaken in framing this as an inequality issue. For there to be inequality, two things must be the same. Homosexuality and heterosexuality are fundamentally two different things, and pretending they are the same is indulging in a fantasy.

Comment: Yes, I gathered your personal opinion of homosexuality was just as you describe it here and that you and those who you agree with fail to acknowledge equality as a "pressing issue" because of personal objections to homosexuality—opinions, incidentally, that are often (though not always) grounded in religious "convictions" born from misinterpretations of antiquated dogmatic texts.

But you misunderstand me. I don't fight for homosexuality itself as "virtuous," because homosexuality in the simplest sense is merely a personal orientation—an inclination to be (or not to be) attracted to one person versus another. One can neither fight for nor against another's personal orientation or feelings, only for or against the consequences of ensuing choices and behaviors. I, of course, do not see homosexual orientation or behavior as immoral, and I certainly don't see it as beyond reason. But neither of our personal opinions bear on individual liberty and freedom to self-actualize, for those are universal human rights that exist independent of your personal objections or my personal support. All members of the human family are entitled to life, liberty, and security of person—not merely "breath, non-incarceration and non-torture," but the inalienable right of individuals to CHOOSE destiny, pursuit of happiness, and self-*actualization. This right to make these choices IS liberty and life.*
Response: You allude to my opinions being personal, but even if they were, what makes you think your personal opinion pulls more weight than mine? Whether my views derive from "religious convictions," natural law, or reason ... I have to ask where your convictions come from and who made you the authority? And if you want to speak of "universal human rights that exist independent of" us, you will force this issue into a theological one. You don't realize the implications of what you're saying. Why ought we allow same-sex marriage? Ought supposes a law. Laws derive their authority from a lawgiver. This again will force us to bring God into the equation, since morality is above the authority of everyone. The bottom line is, our innate rights do not come from government; they are from a much higher domain. There is a difference between what is legal and what is capital-R Right, and what is Right is what we are trying to tackle here.

Now, one must be against "another's personal orientation or feelings" precisely because of their consequences as you've have mentioned. That is why we have detention centers for all sorts of other conducts. No one should have the right to do what is wrong, though they certainly can choose it. In this case, the result or consequence of accepting homosexual marriage will weaken or destroy the true definition of marriage and family, while bringing about another enormous wave of indifferentism and laxity in principle that give way to whatever craving men desire.

Do you not see the danger of your position? Even rights have limits, or what you call the choosing of destiny and pursuit of self-actualization. "Art, like morality, consists of drawing the line somewhere," as G.K. Chesterton said. There are many personal orientations we desire which we do not act upon or shouldn't. We restrain ourselves, rather than let our lower nature take over. This issue is like mold on bread that eventually spreads to the whole loaf. As mentioned earlier, there is no absolute freedom. Ultimately we are either subject to virtues or vice. I am all for pushing human rights, that is, virtuous human rights (the plight of the Jews, voting rights, etc.), not invented "rights" stemming from whatever the lower passions of men crave, disregarding their consequences. Now, there is nothing virtuous about fighting for homosexuality. "Virtuous" supposes things such as righteousness, purity, morality, self-control, holiness and discipline, none of which can be credited to homosexual activity. *And if there is nothing virtuous about homosexual activity, its results cannot possibly be good. Goodness cannot be extracted from vice.*

As Confucius once said, "The superior man thinks always of virtue, the common man thinks of comfort."

Comment: Same-sex marriage is a civil rights issue, just like African Americans had to fight for their rights. You as a minority should know better and should be ashamed of yourself.

Response: Same-sex "marriage" is *not* comparable to the struggle for racial equality in the United States. I know African Americans who take insult to such comparison. Sexual preference and race are not logical comparisons. They are two different realities. A man and woman who want to marry may differ in many ways. One may be black, white, or brown. One can be African while the other is from China, or one may be obese, the other skinny, one wealthy and the other poor. But, the two individuals are *still one man and woman*, therefore, nature and the true definition of marriage between a man and woman are respected, not redefined. Two persons of the same sex, irrespective of their race, origin, wealth, etc., do not satisfy the requirements.

Again, *for there to be any inequality homosexuality and heterosexuality must be equal, and they are not. They are fundamentally two different things.* That being the case, there is no "discrimination" or "inequality," but an intrusion. You are smashing apples and oranges together. For your argument to work, you must redefine the definition of marriage, which is the goal of homosexual activists, and one they have accomplished, at least legally.

Comment: You say "Homosexuality is not the same as heterosexuality; therefore we cannot treat them equally." That's like saying women don't deserve voting rights because they are different from men. It's completely arbitrary and it discriminates based on an innate characteristic.

Response: That does not follow. You might as well continue saying since men and women are different; women shouldn't drive, be politicians, fly airplanes, mow lawns, etc. There are ways in which men and woman are equal by virtue of being human, and as humans we have common privileges, but not in marriage. Marriage is the exclusive union between a man and a woman. Fighting for such things as the right for women to vote was honorable. No wrong can be found there, but there are multiple errors found with homosexual activity.

What is "arbitrary," as you say, is having a woman and a man in various duties and professions. Parenthood and family are not arbitrary. The uniqueness a man and woman bring to the table unites to bring about the qualities of real family and parenthood. Family and parenthood is the nucleus and backbone of society and should never be taken lightly.

Comment: You are thinking of this as woman and woman or man and man. What you need to do is think human to human and then you will see the discrimination.

Response: You cannot ask me to ignore reason, the obvious dictates of nature, and biological differences. You are smashing apples and oranges together as well. Although they are both fruits, if you want an apple pie, you use apples, not anything else. Right ingredients must be used for right outcomes. If you want true marriage, the ingredient or recipe is the distinctive union and uniqueness brought together between a man and a woman. As the right ingredient for an apple pie is apple, that does mean one is being discriminatory towards oranges.

Comment: What matters is that two adults are consenting.
Response: Two adults consenting to do an incorrect action does not make it right.

Comment: Between these adults exist a real love is what you do not grasp.
Response: There are countless things we would *love* to indulge in, but we refrain from them. We must love what is good and righteous, not vices and distortions.

Comment: Only God in the end can judge me.
Response: That's true, but I speculate you make that statement with the presumption many take with all sorts of activity. That is, "I know what I am doing is incorrect, and I don't care anyway."

Comment: I cannot change.
Response: Indeed you can, though I am not saying it is easy. You believe in an almighty powerful God who created all, yet you believe He can't help change you? Many under the weight of pornography addiction, alcoholism, sex, drugs, etc. have been delivered with grace and help. You can too.

Comment: Listening to you debate sounds like you think all homosexuals should be locked up in a psychiatric ward. You see God made men and women that way. Are you arguing with God?
Response: No reasonable man can argue with God, but one can argue about false ideas of God. Although homosexual activity is not normal,

I am not saying all homosexuals should be in therapy or counseling. We are all born with our own imperfections. We have conditions that make us more prone to violence, anger, promiscuity, etc. Though these behaviors occur, it does not mean we all need therapy. Most of us function fine, despite our imperfections, by practicing self-control and discipline. Homosexuals have an imperfection heterosexuals don't have. If homosexuals let their orientations depress them or control them, then help is by all means advisable.

Your argument that God made man and women "that way" cannot stand either. That's like saying that since evil men exists, therefore God intended evil. Or that since there are those born with mental issues or physically deformity, that therefore that is the norm. Mental illnesses and deformities occur due to laws in the natural order set forth with the operations of which God does not have to interfere, because our limited minds cannot understand them. While God created us, we can counter the desires of the flesh through His grace and the practicing of good habits. I am not saying it is easy, but it is certainly attainable. That is something no one wants to hear, the mastery of self. Mind over matter, as the saying goes.

Comment: Many are abandoning your way of thinking.
Response: Perhaps many are doing so because your route is the path of least resistance, as far as thought and virtues. To demand people think and practice mastery of self is not popular in a Hollywood society. It is all about satisfying the flesh, fulfilling political agendas, etc. It is easy to say love justifies homosexual activity, but it is hard to say love does not excuse error for what it is—error—and then defending that statement.

Comment: Do you have any clue as to what civil rights are? Marriage is a legal binding contract between two people, it has nothing to do with religion! It is my civil right.
Response: Marriage is the unique binding union between one man and one woman for the procreation, education, and upbringing of children. It has been so since before recorded history around the globe, regardless of

culture. What you are asking for is the redefinition of the term to include things that are not marriage.

Now, although the case of *Loving v. Virginia* established marriage as a civil right in 1967, what you must comprehend is that at the time of the decision marriage was understood in its historical essence, between a man and a woman, excluding what you imagine to be marriage. What you are doing is playing verbal gymnastics with the definition of marriage and the decision of the court. The word marriage cannot be redefined or bent as we wish to suit our desires any more than one can push to change the meaning to fit marrying four partners or an animal.

Comment: "We hold these truths to be self-evident that ALL men are created equal." Period.
Response: All men are created equal in dignity and value, but not all behaviors and choices are created equal.

Comment: Personally, I don't believe the government has any business dictating morality. They should stop meddling in people's affairs and be more concerned about running the country.
Response: The government has a duty to enforce standards. Prostitution, perjury, cruelty to animals, stealing, and human trafficking, for example, are all moral issues that the government involves itself in for the betterment of society. Should we eliminate or ignore these laws so we won't intrude in people's business? How dare the government impose their moral values on a sexual predator! Why even have jail cells?

Comment: This is precisely why we need to work harder for separation of church and state, to keep lunatics like you in check.
Response: Politics and religion will always be tied together to an extent, it is inevitable. One reason is that politicians frequently distort God's laws. Secondly, politics deals with the application of power, and power has moral obligation, which is in the sphere of the Church. Thirdly, do not expect people to simply separate what they believe with what they do. Lastly, the intention of separation of church and state is intended to

prevent government from infringing on people's faith (i.e., their religious freedom), not the other way around.

Comment: Homosexuality will be universally accepted as the norm within the next half-century or so. Get on the right side of history.
Response: A half a century or a thousand years from now, the principles of natural law, moral law, reason, and common sense will remain immutable. They will forever stand as a beacon of how far men have gone astray to suit their lower appetites.

Speaking of history, we are living in lax moral times and widespread ignorance. The youth of today can be categorized as a Hollywood/MTV generation who are more interested in the affairs of the secular world and in pleasing their appetites. It is no accident the homosexual agenda has been harbored in such an environment and has taken full force in these perverse times.

Comment: I am a Christian pastor in a loving and beautiful gay relationship. The Roman Church does not understand that homosexuals are people in need of love, relationship, and salvation.
Response: The Church comprehends quite well that homosexuals are people in need of love, relationship, and above all salvation. The problem here is that many Protestant pastors, such as yourself, study the wants of man first, and then interpret Christianity to fit those needs. Isaiah the prophet had this to say about your type: "You call evil good and call good evil. You turn darkness into light and light into darkness. You make what is bitter sweet, and what is sweet you make bitter" (Isaiah 5:20).

As mentioned, you cannot abide by true Christian teaching and endorse homosexuality or any other pseudo-sexual relationship without supporting a clear contradiction to the Christian faith.

Comment: Christ taught that we should love one another.
Response: He did, and with that same authority he taught much else too. Love your neighbor, not his mistaken notions.

Comment: We are all created in God's image and have equal dignity.
Response: We are created in God's image, but that does not make us the same in every other aspect. Man and woman are two different expressions of the human form established to complement each other.

Comment: Christ was more open-minded. He would definitely be more left-leaning if He were alive today.
Response: Christ is alive today, and if He was liberal why was He preaching in the name of truth to convert minds from false ideas to right ones, instead of letting others pursue their passions, as the left-leaning tend to do. Though Christ preached a gospel of love, His love for us did not excuse our errors for what they were. He went around forgiving sin but warned to restrain from further sin.

God is no liberal. Nor is He a democracy. He has never asked for our recommendation or opinion. God is God. It is His will be done, not ours. That doesn't sound too liberal.

Speaking about Christianity will not help your homosexual position. There are good reasons why homosexual activists don't mention Christianity in their apologetics—it doesn't help their case at all.

Comment: I may not agree with homosexuality, but we must be tolerant even if we believe they err.
Response: We must be tolerant but even tolerance has its limits. We must speak out lovingly and tactfully should circumstance dictate. It is interesting though how you think homosexuals err, yet you want tolerate their error? Why stop there? Let us tolerate all those who err in conduct. That doesn't make much sense. Too much tolerance leads to cowardice, and I believe you are more concerned about confronting the problem. It's impressive, though, how we have all the tolerance in the world for error, but very little for what is right.

Comment: Gays have a heavy cross they did not ask for and have no control over.
Response: Not one of us asked to carry a cross, but we must bear our crosses. There is no escaping that reality. We can but through grace and

help make the burden lighter. Christ Himself was not relieved of His cross. Our Christian faith teaches us not to fear or run away from our crosses, but that He shall help us should we turn to Him. We do not have to carry it alone. We can control our flesh. Our Lord said, "If anyone wishes to come after Me, let him deny himself, and take up his cross daily, and follow Me."

Comment: You deny bigotry, but it shows quite well.
Response: Bigotry is a word used very loosely and inaccurately these days, but my disposition is very similar to yours. You stand up for what you believe is right. I also stand up for what I believe is right. You may say I should keep quiet if I don't support the homosexual agenda. I would say no, in the same way you wouldn't stay quiet about what you thought was wrong. You and I DO NOT believe in others believing in error, as it should be, that is why you attempt to correct my position and are very outspoken. I don't blame you for what you do, because NO ONE should be indifferent about what is right or wrong. But, I maintain, although you are sincere, you are quite mistaken.

Comment: People simply fear or hate what they don't understand, for no logical reason.
Response : Hopefully you will allow me to be the judge of my own inner disposition. A Facebook posting I saw by Rick Warren states, «Our culture has accepted two huge lies. The first is that if you disagree with somone's lifestlye, you must fear or hate them. The second is that to love someone means you agree with everything they believe or do. Both are nonsense. You don't have to compromise convictions to be compassionate."

Comment: I am a straight man with my own family and could care less if two of the same sex want to get married. Who cares and how does it affect you?
Response: Your attitude nurtures the mentality of indifferentism and laxity in principles sweeping across this country. It is bringing about a devastation that you can't imagine. What society pushes has implications on all of

us, so we must make sure it is pushing right principles and proper conduct. All our actions overlap and influence others from a societal scope. It reminds me of good parents censoring what their kids watch on TV or the Internet. They constantly find themselves sheltering their children, competing with the vices and acceptable misconducts society embraces. How does a parent protect their child from the indoctrination of homosexuality and the false ideas of marriage and sexuality? Particularly in some public schools where it is being taught and endorsed? Parents are already losing the right to protect and direct the upbringing of their children. Kids will be required to learn that homosexuality is good, equal to heterosexuality, and get the idea that perhaps they should even try it. That is why it matters what society pushes—it affects all of us. Nothing stands alone. We are all interconnected or in relation to each other. Whether it is our neighbors letting their grass grow three feet high or individuals killing innocent in a mall or church, it affects us. The quietly mounting debt our nation's leaders are accruing, affects us. A smoker in a restaurant affects others. If a rock is tossed on one side of a pond it will affect the other end. If our pinky toe hurts it affects the rest of the body. The promotion of promiscuous behavior, pornography, etc., weakens our moral fabric. Everything is in relation to everything else. People only see what's right in front of them, while failing to see the in-depth problem of the issue. What may not seem like a big deal really is. Even a small hole sinks a giant ship. The endorsement of homosexuality is another ailment slowly leading to further moral decadence. That being the case, we must make sure only right principles and virtuous conducts are being pushed forward, since what we do as society affects us all.

Your attitude of indifferentism reminds me of a cartoon I once saw. It had a man standing in front of the gates of Hell holding a sign that read, "Welcome to Hell where nothing is wrong or right, just do whatever works for you."

Comment: According to you we can expect the country to implode once gay marriage is legalized nationwide.
Response: Gay marriage is not a silver bullet that will cause an implosion, but you can certainly expect it to contribute to our moral depravity as a

nation. In the same way, adding another $20 trillion to our staggering debt may not be the cause of an implosion, but you can rest assured it is adding to a pending financial implosion.

Comment: I can't get this conservative mindset. Not everyone has your views. Why is it so hard for that to sink into your head? Not everything is an absolute right and wrong!
Response: Is that an absolute statement? And why is it so hard for you to understand that not everyone has your views? Anyway, I don't believe all is absolute. Some things are while others aren't. We must respect the freedom of people to choose within the boundaries of the common good. Homosexual marriage crosses those boundaries.

Comment: You right-leaning hardheads need to get with the times! What kind of heart do you have that shows no sympathy for the discrimination gays endure?
Response: Get with the times? Many justify behavior because "many are doing it." But if everybody was sick, that doesn't make sickness health; therefore one does not blindly need to "get with the times."

Also, I've noticed the ill treatment some homosexuals endure and I condemn those actions. Abuses are wrong, but we cannot use one wrong to justify another wrong. Sympathy is fine. We may have some even for a criminal on death row, but sympathy does not change his wrong conduct to right.

Homosexual activists are great at exploiting the aspect of "sympathy" to have others help join their cause, but we must be mindful of the difference between being sympathetic and condoning an action.

Comment: There is no basis for your opinion. In this country, we stand by the Constitution of the United States, not the Bible. The Constitution guarantees me the right to marry anyone I wish. Thank goodness for its founders.
Response: I am all for the Constitution. It protects the innate rights of man. Homosexual marriage is an invented right manufactured by perversions of men. Also, the Constitution does not guarantee you a right to marry a

man. I believe the founders would have been stunned at such a notion, as would the citizens who passed the 14th Amendment, which is the instrument through which this invented right is being crammed down on the country. Progressive liberal judges will impose your view on the nation, but that's because rather than applying and interpreting the law they will write politicized opinions that are all about pushing liberal ideology. But, the law is whatever the justices say it is, even if they make up constitutional rights out of thin air. However, the idea that there is no rational basis for defining marriage as between one man and one woman is an outcry from the standpoint of logic, reason, and history.

Comment: What are you talking about? All rights are "invented" by men.
Response: Our innate, God-given rights don't come from man or the Constitution. They come from a higher domain. Your innate right to life or to defend yourself, your liberty, and your possessions, for instance, do not come from a group of men or women in Washington, D.C. who decided you should be able to.

Comment: If rights are not protected they do not exist. Try to think realistically, not metaphorically. If we have no laws or government to enforce laws, rights are only something in your mind. There is no higher domain when it comes to reality.
Response: You make some fantastic conclusions. You defend homosexual "rights" that did not exist, but now they suddenly exist because they have become a topic of debate? If these "rights" did not exist prior, how can we even be discussing them now? You sincerely believe a man who was enslaved had no right to freedom because there were no laws to protect him or no government to enforce them? You think a man suffering under slavery is just imagining his right to liberty and fair treatment? You need to think this one over. Innate rights are of a higher domain.

Comment: Hopefully, one day it will sink through your thick skull that all men are created equal.

Response: That is true. All men are created equal, but all conduct is not created equal. It is injustice to treat completely different things (homosexuality and heterosexuality) as if they were equal.

Comment: You have some nerve being in here calling homosexuals evil. Your lack of tolerance and acceptance shows why droves are leaving the Church.
Response: I have not called anyone evil. You must understand, Christians are not called to be tolerant of error, they are called to love others, and love mends error, it doesn't tolerate it. And the reason many have left the Church is because it is easier to satisfy the flesh, rather than the spiritual. Also, the Church is not here to cater to the desires of man but to fulfill the commission implanted on her by Christ, whether they are comfortable or not.

People do not depart the Church for greater ideals or virtues, but to fulfill their own appetites. "Pick up your cross and follow me," as Christ said, is too uncomfortable to bear.

Comment: This comes from a Church littered with homosexual priests and believes pedophilia is noble.
Response: People always exaggerate. The Church is not littered with homosexual priests. And for those who are homosexuals, any homosexual activity on their part is not excused simply because they are priests. Homosexual desires are not a sin, but homosexual acts are. It is one thing to be tempted, and another to entertain and act on those temptations. And pedophilia will never be noble. It will forever be an abomination.

Comment: You religious people and your hypocrisy are sickening.
Response: Religious people may fail, but they do not call their sins virtues, nor do they celebrate them by organizing parades.

Comment: You make valid points, but we must cherish and appreciate our differences.
Response: We should always cherish and respect the good and virtues of others, NOT their vices and distortions.

Comment: Love is love. That's all that matters at the end of the day.
Response: You are thinking with your emotions. Love is love and error is error. Love does not excuse error for what it is…error. The love you have for your kids does not excuse them from taking what does not belong to them, or any other mistaken notion. We must distinguish between the person and the action.

Comment: I'm a gay parent, and a gay grandparent. And I have to point out your error. Just accept it as my love for you.
Response: You support my point. Love attempts to correct error, not support it, just like your "love" for me is correcting my "wrong position" on homosexuality. That love corrects error is indisputable. The question is, who is in error, those who support homosexuality or those who don't?

Comment: Your views are based on a religion that I do not believe in and cannot be forced on me.
Response: Homosexual activists always revert to religious talk as if this is just about religion. Though religion/God/moral law is a powerful case against homosexual activity, we don't have to talk about it. We just have to look at basic human nature and biological impossibilities. All one needs is natural law, reason, and logic seasoned with a little common sense to dismantle the homosexual argument.

Comment: You are still living in the Middle Ages. Times of old have changed. Get with the program. Learn to grow with the times.
Response: Right principles are immutable and permanent throughout the variations of history, they do not get old.

There is no denying we all have room for growth, but one can argue that not all growth is constructive. Are we growing in vice or virtue? "Growth for the sake of growth is the ideology of a cancer cell," as Edward Abbey said; therefore we must focus on proper growth.

Comment: You are so going to be on the wrong side of history.
Response: I may be on the wrong side of history with all the accepted distortions of this Hollywood generation, but I will always be on the Right

side of history. As Cardinal Francis George similarly stated, "The world divorced from the God who created and redeemed it inevitably comes to a bad end. It's on the wrong side of the only history that finally matters."

Comment: There are as many people who believe homosexuality is not a problem as there are people who do. But as history has proven, what is right and wrong is merely subjective and changes over time; morals are relative to the time period, and not at all absolute.

Many years ago it was perfectly moral to discipline a woman for disobeying her husband, yet today that wouldn't fly. Sexuality, much like race and gender, is but one of the many facets of human lives. One day the culture will have changed enough (it has changed a lot already) to accommodate LGBT sexual orientations, because they have been proven time and time again to be completely OK and non-problematic.

Response: Moral law and right principles are immutable. If a thing was Right (capital R) a millennia ago, it is Right today. Beatings one's wife was never Right even though it was practiced by some in their ignorance. Forced slavery was never Right (capital R) even though it was also practiced. Many were ignorant and sincere about their actions, but that does not make their actions right. It is like a student who thought he did his homework correctly, only to have his teacher correct his work with a great deal of red ink. Eventually, people come to know Truth (capital T) and hopefully leave their mistaken notions. Homosexual activity will remain a distortion so long as the dictates of reason and intelligence prevail.

Comment: No, see, that's where you are wrong, if you had lived in that time period, your moral compass would not have even flinched (unless you were the victim or were really empathic). There may be universal truths, but it would be arrogant of us to claim to know them.

If you believe that you do know them, then explain the differences in religions, and cultures, or will you sit here and actually tell me that other countries that mistreat women (for example) just have not seen the light of your belief system and that they are morally incorrect despite what their mainstream religion tells them?

Response: I agree that my moral compass may not have flinched simply because I did not know better, but today we do know better about certain matters. We cannot simply use the logic that says since we have erred on issues in the past, therefore we err concerning all other matters in the past and now in the present. And I would boldly say that those in other cultures who hit their wives to discipline them are quite mistaken. Ask the victims how they feel and you shall see. They have not come to know the Truth (capital T) of their error and in due time, hopefully, they will. In the same way that folks thought the world was flat and did not flinch, we eventually came to the Truth that it was round. We are forced to change our views when the contrary is evident. We cannot say the world was flat at one point simply because we thought it was. We were sincerely mistaken. In the moral sphere it is similar. What we once thought was right was not, such as forced slavery. You are misguided if you think individual behavior or cultural behavior is the ultimate test of Truth (Capital T). Besides, I repeat, homosexual activity is not just a question of moral law; it has to contend with reason, logic, natural law, and common sense, none of which favor the homosexual case.

Comment: Do you get some sort of gratification when you show your hate towards gays?
Response: Because I disagree with a man's theory does not mean I hate the man.

Comment: I've heard you speak of God. Here is a hint. Try loving your fellow man as a service to God. That's where it all starts.
Response: That's not where it starts. It begins with loving God first. When that is done, love will naturally overflow to our fellow man. The more we truly love God and His ways, the more we love His people, not the other way around.

Comment: What would you do if your kids turned out gay?
Response: I would love them as my children always, and if they ultimately *choose* that lifestyle they will certainly know my disapproval, and that in no

way do I support it. But, again, they will always know that their dad loves them. I will clearly distinguish between my love for them and my disapproval of their misconduct.

I am tempted to continue, but I believe enough has been said. The bottom line is, the embrace of homosexual unions undermines and weakens the institution of marriage and family, while producing other negative effects. Only opposite sexes constitute a sexual whole. Homosexuality and heterosexuality are fundamentally different and should be treated as such. With the demise of structural prerequisites for a sexual whole, there are no logical arguments that can be used against incest, pedophilia, bestiality, or any other promiscuous behavior. Although these activities are more severe perversions, homosexual activity is more subtle and elusive. But the principles are the same. It is precisely because of the elusive and subtle nature of adult homosexuality that it has been able to progress as it has, in conjunction with a lack thought on the issue, and much indifferentism. There are no rational arguments as to why any sexual union should not be considered marriage. At the pace we are going, we can expect an eventual end to any prerequisites for a legitimate sexual relationship. Self-gratification cannot be the driving force behind our society. We need to control our lower appetites and say no to any immoral cravings we may have.

There are many emotions and flaring passions with this subject, but emotions and feelings seldom govern wisely, as Benjamin Franklin said. All charity and sympathy is due to those who genuinely struggle with this issue. They are carrying a heavy cross, but one cannot support such activity, as a matter of principle, even if it makes an individual feel good. No one is justified doing wrong as a means to happiness.

Many are the things we would love to indulge in and justify, but the tough virtues of righteousness, discipline, and self-control must kick in. That God loves us the way we are is undisputable. But, He loves us too much to leave us where we are.

ABORTION

"Everyone who voted for slavery was free. Everyone who votes for abortion was born. That's how oppression works."

— *Matt Evans*

To be or not to be? Pro-life or pro-choice? That is the question entertained in this chapter, and the last controversy we will strain through our filtering mechanism. I am all about choices, for it is a God-given right that all should have the privilege of choosing his or her own destiny—that is, of course, *within limits*. That is why I shall speak on behalf of those stripped of their innate freedom of choice.

The two sides of the abortion issue are clear. Pro-lifers maintain that an unborn child has human rights regardless of the mother's opinion. They stand firm on their position based on science and moral grounds, and label abortion nothing but a fancy word for killing innocent life. They believe an unborn baby is fully human and that life begins at conception. The pro-abortionists' views are rather contrasting. They maintain that an unborn child cannot be classified as human; for this reason, the unborn cannot be expected to have the same rights. It is a fetus, not a baby. Another premise is that unwanted pregnancy puts women through too much distress and difficulties. In addition, abortion has societal benefits such as population control and keeping unwanted babies from unhealthy homes. The most popular point shared by the majority of pro-abortionist is summed up in this statement: "This is my body and I'll determine what is right for me." Ultimately, not surprisingly, it boils down to the "me" or "I." The gratification and accommodation of self are always at the forefront.

As we have previously discussed, we know personal choices do not make a universal right, so what we must consider then is, are we choosing wisely? One can elect to eat healthily or unhealthily, work out or not, smoke or not, but are we choosing prudently? The same with abortion; is it the prudent choice? Is it a virtue or a vice?

As with any matter in life, we must be ready to reap the consequences of our actions. Unfortunately, we live in a society where personal responsibility holds very little value, if it's even expected at all.

■ ■ ■

Let me be frank and to the point from a moral perspective, especially with Christians who are pro-choice, because even here, Christians differ. The Christian position on abortion is *not* pro-choice, regardless of your pastor's opinion or your personal choice. Truth overrides personal conjecture. The mouthpiece of genuine Christianity is abundantly clear on how God views abortion: it degrades human life, and it is a grave sin. We were created in God's image which gives us intrinsic value (Genesis 1:27). Jeremiah 1:5 reads, "Before I formed you in the womb I knew you, before you were born I set you apart." Psalm 39 states, "For you created my inmost being; you knit me together in my mother's womb."

The catechism of the Church reads, "Human life is sacred, because from its beginning it involves the creative action of God and it remains forever in a special relationship with the creator, who is its sole end. God alone is the Lord of life from its beginning until its end: no one, under any circumstances, can claim for himself the right to destroy an innocent human being" (2258). "Human life must be respected and protected from the moment of conception. From the first moment of his existence, a human being must be recognized as having the rights of a person—among which is the inviolable right of every innocent being to life" (2270). "The inalienable right to life of every innocent human individual is a constitutive element of a civil society and its legislation: The inalienable rights of the person must be recognized and respected by civil society and the political authority. These human rights depend neither on single individuals nor on parents; nor do they represent a concession made by society and the state; they belong to human nature and are inherent in the person by virtue of the creative act from which the person took his origin" (2273).

The Church has always taught that abortion is the killing of innocent life. "This teaching has not changed and remains unchangeable" (2271). An unborn child is certainly innocent, so in essence we are talking about murder. Pro-abortionists prefer the term "abortion" or "terminating pregnancy," since murder is a term that should be used in reference to other human beings. One must wonder: If the baby is not human, is it an alien species? It is interesting that if a pregnant woman survives a car accident with a drunk driver and her unborn child is killed, the driver can be charged with manslaughter, but intentional killing inside a clinic is known as "terminating pregnancy." Quite ironic also is if a woman plans on terminating her pregnancy, it is a "fetus" being killed, but if she intends to go through with the pregnancy, she adoringly calls the fetus "my baby."

From a moral perspective, we know what the Church teaches and we know that we must side with the weak and defenseless, as Christ would have done. That is what a child is in the mother's womb: vulnerable. From a scientific perspective, life begins at the moment of conception. A new being comes into existence. Each baby is a separate and distinct human being, with its own genetic code that decides sex, eye color, body shape, and so forth. Some claim that a baby is not human until some threshold is crossed, such as viability or the capacity to feel pain. "Not a human" is not a scientific argument. It has nothing to do with science, but rather with someone's personal ideology or political inclination. If we are not human in the womb, then we are nothing but a piece of property or a thing. Any reasonable person will have a problem describing a child inside a mother as an object or property. The bottom line is, a baby hippo is a baby hippo from the moment of its conception, a baby human is human—not a tumor or anything else—from its beginning. It does not go from lifeless human matter to life at a pre-arranged moment during pregnancy. We are not talking about a pile of dead cells in the womb; if so, it would be called a miscarriage. The child is very much alive, and growing at an impressive rate. Here are some facts about the "not a human yet" mentality:

- A baby's heart begins to beat eighteen days from conception, and by twenty-one days the heart is pumping blood through a closed circulatory system, independent of the mother.
- At four weeks from conception, a baby's eyes, ears, and respiratory system begin to form. By six weeks, brain waves can be detected.
- By nine weeks from conception, all the structures necessary for pain sensation are functioning.
- Thumb-sucking has been documented at seven weeks from conception, and by eight weeks a baby's heartbeat can be detected by ultrasonic stethoscope.
- Between thirteen and fifteen weeks a baby's taste buds are present and functioning.
- At approximately eight weeks, their unique fingerprints are present.

These facts indicate a human being and nothing else; therefore, the unborn must be afforded the same rights to life and dignity as any other person. Even atheists are becoming pro-life due to what we are discovering through technology. For instance, the executive director of the atheist organization Richard Dawkins Foundation, Elizabeth Cornwell, is quoted as saying, "There's a war on the womb. As a secular pro-lifer, I believe my case is scientifically and philosophically sound. Science concedes that human life begins at fertilization, and it follows that abortion is ageism and discrimination against a member of our own species" (Ingram 148).

Let me punctuate this point with a quote by Dr. Michael Meaney who I had the pleasure of meeting and interviewing. He was one of three candidates for mayor of Corpus Christi, Texas. In a televised debate, the president of the League of Women Voters asked Dr. Meaney, "Why do you feel that you can impose your narrow sectarian beliefs on the entire population of our pluralistic society?" He answered, "The fact that a fetus is alive is not a narrow sectarian belief, but a scientific observation of fetal movement and growth; the fact that a fetus is a new individual is not a religious belief but a scientific observation of a new heartbeat, a new brain wave, new genetics and physical fingerprints permanently unique to that individual; the fact that a fetus is a member of the human species is not a Catholic dogma but a scientific factual observation permanently unique to the human species. Hence defining a 46 chromosome fetus a 'living individual member of the human species' is scientific, forensic and legal—and has many self-evident consequences. That is why I am pro-life, that is why you should be pro-life, that is why everyone should be pro-life."

■ ■ ■

No matter how hard the alternative to murder is, no matter what society allows us to do, and no matter our circumstances, murder is never right. We are not talking about vegetation here. It is a fundamental principle that we do not kill innocent human life. The Supreme Court obviously feels differently, based on the *Roe v. Wade* decision, but this is the same court that has committed grave errors in the past. The Supreme Court is not infallible, but God is and His revelations are clear. We were created in His image, and that is why life is sacred. We all have dignity and worth, even a child in the womb. This lack of reverence for life in our society has unfortunately nurtured a quality of life culture that dismisses personal responsibility. If we want comfort, we should help ourselves by making smart decisions and avoiding unwanted predicaments. If we should find ourselves in a hole, we must own up and select better alternatives. The first and toughest is strapping down and raising the child. It will require endurance, perseverance, and support. No one ever said doing the right thing was easy. That is precisely why many avoid it. There is no question one's life is going to take a complete 180-degree turn by raising a child. Hopefully, our families will be there to help. We might have to let our pride go, humble ourselves, and ask for assistance. Maybe working longer hours is going to be necessary. The partying and certain friends must be dismissed. The hard virtues of righteousness must kick in. That is commendable! We can recover from our mistakes, correctly. Abortion, like suicide, is the easy way out. It is easier to kill than to face the music.

If we are not personally going to fight for the sake of the child, adoption is a far better solution. A person who does not want their dog does not kill it; rather, they give it away to their neighbor, friend, or local pound. There are many couples who can't have a baby of their own and would very much like to adopt one. One can at least make a couple happy by giving them the child they always wanted. Not only does adoption keep the child alive, but it saves the mother's sense of morals. "Abortion kills twice," as Mother Teresa said. "It kills the body of the baby and it kills the conscience of the mother."

■ ■ ■

What if the woman gets raped? This scenario never fails to arise in conversations with pro-choice individuals. Though these cases make up a miniscule percentage of actual abortion cases, we will tackle the issue head on. To approach this question, I must clarify that it is very understandable as to why someone would consider having an abortion, but we must keep in mind that this is about what is right, regardless of heartaches, not what is easier or renders relief. It is easy for one who has not lived through the traumatizing experience of rape to say, "Let the baby live," but all I will suggest is, if one finds themselves in a dilemma, weighing their options, and decision A outweighs decision B, then A is the correct decision, because it is for the *greater good*, even though defying decision B will leave a brutal wake. This is a situation where either choice will take its toll, but I believe having the child wins the dilemma. As difficult as it may sound, and as horrible of a sin as rape is, I believe the right thing to do is to let the baby live. I say that as sensitively and as gently as possible, because I would never want to entertain such a burdensome decision with my wife. My reasoning is simply that we do not fix a wrong with another wrong. Rape is wrong, and murder is wrong.

Let me give an analogy. If a dear family member were murdered, would it be correct to kill one of the murderer's relatives? No. Even in our righteous anger we can err. Killing the murderer's cousin is wrong. No wrong done will bring back our loved one. It would only give us temporary satisfaction. We should let the justice system take its course, not take justice into our own hands. If justice does not catch up in this earthly life, God will vindicate us. "'Vengeance is mine,' says the Lord." *Justice delayed is not justice denied.* There is no question that as believers we face many trials, but even so, above all else, we have been called to faithfulness.

With abortion, a mother who is raped is *always* right because there is no excuse or justification for such action; but if the mother decides to kill the baby, she is putting a wrong on top of the wrong done to her. The child is the innocent bystander, caught in the crossfire of wrongdoing. The better solution is to give the baby up for adoption if the mother cannot handle the situation. Some would argue that "He is just coming into a broken world where he is not going to be loved." Or, "Giving him up for adoption will set him up for abuse and neglect, and the child will eventually become a menace to society." Although I have a hard time thinking of a harsher penalty than death, my question is, how does one know for certain the child will become a sob story? He or she may very well become a menace to society, like any other kid raised in an ordinary home, but it is not for us to speculate. Some of us are dealt a bad hand, but what counts is how we play that hand. Everyone deserves a chance, but a murdered child's chances are zero.

What if the child's destiny was to grow up and be a great politician, doctor, or spokesperson against sexual abuse, rather than a criminal? Why do we assume the child is going to amount to nothing? Who are we to say God can't use them? He might very well grow up to be a productive member of society or he may become a criminal—but as parents we are only called to do our part. Eventually, the child will come to an age where he will be responsible for his choices and actions. God will judge that individual based on his circumstances, variable to the degree at which he or she was responsible. He knows everyone's story.

■ ■ ■

I recognize there are those who couldn't care less about any moral code. It's all about personal choices. But, one has to stand in awe of how abortionists demand the right to individual choice, yet, ironically, they deny another the same right. That is precisely the problem with this abortion issue. It is one thing to have a choice that solely affects the individual, but it is quite another when that choice affects another life. With abortion, our choice tarnishes the rights and dignity of another human. Therefore, we should not turn a blind eye to the matter.

Consider that smoking has become illegal in many public locations because nonsmokers were being affected by secondary smoke. Something had to be done to defend the rights of others who did not want to be exposed to smoke and its hazards. Nonsmokers had the ability to fight and change the law to make it illegal to smoke openly in airports, for example. A child in the womb does not have the privilege of defending himself. If he did, he would fight for life, rather than get a hook through his skull or have his brain sucked through a tube.

Though we are capable of choosing wrong, the law of the land should not give us the right to do what is wrong. That's why it is the government's duty to interject and support a pro-life stance. One of the *core missions* of any government is to protect the defenseless or those who have no voice. If a government fails to protect the sanctity of human life, what good is that government? Abortion should be illegal, and those who participate in it should be dealt with accordingly. At least if one attempts to kill an adult, that adult has a fighting chance. Not the case with a helpless child.

Abortion Comment and Responses

"Children too are a gift from the Lord, the fruit of the womb, a reward."

— Psalm 127:3

Comment: Things are not as simple as you make them. There is a lot of debate as to when life actually begins.
Response: There isn't much debate when you look at scientific findings and facts. We certainly know that life does not begin one month, four months after conception. Even if there were legitimate debate, the prudent thing to do, if uncertain, is to err on the side of safety, just as if you were hunting and not pulling the trigger at any movement behind a bush without knowing for certain what is behind the shrubs. What we know is that it's a biological fact that a baby has a distinct genetic code from conception and that we are not dealing with a pile of dead cells in the womb.

Comment: Abortion can save kids and their parents much sorrow and suffering. No one should have to pay for the rest of their lives for a mistake they committed.
Response: Some scars we carry for the rest of our lives, but that does not mean we cannot recover. You are simply trying to avoid responsibility for your actions. Adding a mistake to another mistake is never the solution to any problem. Being young, going to school, not being financially stable, not being with the ideal partner, etc., are good reasons not to have a baby, but they are not good reasons to kill a baby.

Comment: I am a pro-choice Christian who believes that what a person does with their body is their business. That is something personal a man will never understand.
Response: I do not have to be a woman to understand God's law. Being that you are "Christian" you can appreciate the following Scripture: "Everything is permissible but not everything is beneficial. Do you not

know that your body is the temple of the Holy Spirit, who is in you ...You are not your own, you were bought at a price. Therefore, honor God with your body" (1 Corinthians 6:12, 19-20). We do not honor God by making a womb a source of death when it should be a source of life.

Comment: I am also Christian and don't believe in abortion, but it is not my place to tell anyone what they should choose or push my beliefs on them.
Response: By your own principles, you couldn't even correct someone who sells pornography to high school kids since he does not abide by your Christian views. The fact of the matter is, Christians have an obligation to fight and defend right principles. The faith was not meant for secrecy. Nor have Christians been called to be apathetic. We should not be succumbing to the "wisdom" of this generation; on the contrary, we should be affecting society. When you have done your duty as a Christian, and should abortion still preside, you did your part and it is to be commended, but in no way are we to be silent or indifferent, especially in the political sphere. Follow the examples of the one you call Master, who spoke Truth and stood for what was right, instead of being quiet and indifferent.

Comment: Abortion may be a moral issue, but it is an economic issue also. Raising kids is as expensive as ever before. Imagine the economic toll on parents who are already struggling, with the state of the economy.
Response: I heard a pro-choice politician take the same tone. Economics are not above morality. Politicians don't dare talk about personal responsibility, uprightness in a society that wants self-gratification, not now, but right now. If you do not wish to risk involving another life in this economic climate, take proper measures. Practice some abstinence and restraint. Most people can't even imagine such options. The bottom line is, insufficient take-home pay is a good reason *not* to have a child, but it does not justify killing a child. Truly we live in a society where responsibility has very little value, if it is even expected at all.

Comment: Conservatives claim to be "pro-children" and are the first to neglect the child once born with their anti-children and social policies.

Response: That is not conservative policy. Your statement, by the way, is an oxymoron. Left leaning folks claim to be pro-children, yet they are for killing the child before they even have chance. One cannot be more pro-children than one who protects life.

Also, assuming that it is a fact that conservatives hold an anti-children stance, that incorrect mentality does not justify the incorrect mindset of endorsing the butchery of a child in the womb. It remains wrong independent of your ideas on conservatism.

Comment: Not all subscribe to your religious views, so mind your business and let others do with their bodies as they wish.
Response: It's not just your body—there is another body in the equation which makes it a game-changer. And just because religion has something to say about abortion, it does not mean this is strictly about religion. Science has much to say about it also, and the facts are against you.

Comment: That other body you speak of is not actually independent of the woman. It is still a part of her, not in any way separate, and while it is a part of her only she can decide what to do with it. The baby cannot survive without her. Her body, her choice. No one should be allowed more sway over a woman's body and decisions than the woman herself.
Response: The baby is an independent being, though it depends on the mother for nourishment and development. A day- or week-old baby finds itself in the same predicament. It cannot survive on its own and depends on the parents for nourishment and development, so a parent can decide what to do with them at that point, since it can't survive on its own, right? Live or die, neglect the child whether they want it or not!? That cannot be accepted.

Comment: Abortion must remain legal for the cases where the mother's life may be in jeopardy.
Response: The key word there is "may" because it is not guaranteed that she will perish. But, to avoid a theological dissertation, because this too is a very difficult issue, I will say you fight for both the mother and the child

as best as possible, not just deliberately kill the baby. You bring up what are rare cases in order to justify your "abortion on demand" stance. Folks often have a tendency to bring up unusual or abnormal cases to justify their inclinations, as if it is the norm. Let me share the thoughts of C. Everett Koop who was the surgeon general of the United States and practiced pediatrics for thirty years. His testimony is that during his medical career, with the medical advances in understanding and technology, he was not aware of a single case in his own practice or his colleagues' practices where a choice had to be made between the life of the mother and the child. That argument is a "straw man." It's a very emotional argument based on a circumstance that just doesn't happen (Ingram 156).

Comment: Abortion is ugly, and personally I believe it to be the worst of all available choices. I would counsel women against it, but I would not deny them the choice. I don't see the good of making abortion illegal though. Banning anything does not end it. Look at drugs or guns. We already have crowded prisons, and they will get worse in the name of moral high ground. Let's say we ban abortion. How would you prosecute and punish? How do you force someone to care for themselves while carrying an unwanted child? You will also have women seeking illegal abortions through underground butchers causing their fatality. This is an issue where the moral stance is simple, yet the reality is much more complicated.
Response: There are many things that are illegal that people do anyway, but the fact that they are illegal makes it a deterrent. In the same way, making abortion illegal will not completely stop abortions, but it is a step in the right direction. Now using a back alley butcher is not the answer anyone wishes, but statistics are against when it comes to fatalities. More women have died from legal abortions than have from illegal abortions, so let's not skew the facts. As far as consequences or punishment, there is a due process for that, but saturated jail cells should not be our concern. You are thinking about practicality, not what is right. Would you propose legalizing multiple crimes to make more space for inmates, since accommodations or crowded jails appear to be your concern? I suggest we build more prisons according to need. The solution to the problem is not legalizing

abortion or laxity in morals. Another wrong never is. If we made it illegal for doctors to perform such practices or revoked their licenses for doing so, this one step would do leaps of good.

You mention, "How do you force someone to care for themselves while carrying an unwanted child?" That goes back to the lack of responsibilities, morals, and virtues we have as a society. If you can't have a child because you can't take care of yourself—here is a difficult concept to accept—don't have a child. That is hard for the irresponsible to hear, but I understand we have a tendency to cater to the irresponsible. Also, let me mention that if we focused more on strengthening family, rather than redefining it, this alone will do tons of good in alleviating the problem. Family is where it all begins.

This is another lengthy subject, but certainly worthy of review, since it is often in the spotlight. There are several conclusions that become evident. One is that this abortion issue does not pass the screening process laid out in this book. Secondly, we can confidently say that the quickest way to "get off the hook" is to deny responsibility in order to avoid an inconvenience. Thirdly, the killing of an innocent is always wrong. And it is my position that abortion kills innocent life; for this reason, abortion is always wrong, regardless of circumstances. Life begins at conception. At no point in pregnancy is the child "lifeless" or not human. No one, especially Christians, should ever condone this culture of death. "Human life must be respected and protected absolutely from the moment of conception. From the first moment of his existence, a human being must be recognized as having the rights of a person—among which is the inviolable right of every innocent being to life" *(Catechism of the Catholic Church, 2270).*

THE CHRISTIAN CHALLENGE

"A great civilization is not conquered from without until it has destroyed itself within."

— W. Durant

"He who passively accepts evil is as much involved in it as he who helps to perpetrate it. He who accepts evil without protesting against it is really cooperating with it."

— Martin Luther King, Jr

There is an old saying in the Dominican Republic concerning the slaughter of a cow, which states, "Whoever holds the cow down is just as guilty as the one who pulls the trigger." In other words, if one condones an action, that individual is as responsible as those who committed the actual act. If a person, for instance, aids a criminal in his plot, they are going to share in the demise when justice catches up. One cannot claim innocence, knowing they supplied a criminal the means to commit a crime. That person will accompany the other culprit to jail for aiding and abetting. This same principle applies if it's a virtuous act;

everyone involved in a noble deed gets praised—the whole team reaps the benefit.

I bring this up because too many Christians are indirectly hurting their own cause by helping folks, such as politicians, who are against principles of their faith. It is imperative that believers stay knowledgeable of current events. Information is power, and we can't continue to hide behind ignorance. Do not give people the means or positions of authority to go against the teachings of the faith. We must watch who we support monetarily, politically, and socially. As believers, we must stop being bystanders! We must act and create, and be messengers for the faith wherever we go, to distinguish ourselves from the crowd, not blend into it. We must be doers of the word, not just listeners.

Christian citizens have an obligation to expose the wicked motives of politicians who hide behind sugar-coated agendas. We can't uncouple what we do from what we claim to believe. If we do, we are plain hypocrites. If we consciously know that someone is acting against the principles of our faith, it is our duty not to support them. I am not here endorsing any political party or politician, but that *we must do everything in light of Christian truth, not political inclination or ideology.* By supporting those who act contrary to the faith, though we are not directly pulling the trigger, we are indirectly holding down the cow, because our vote is our voice. Secular folks do not support Christian ideals, so why should we support theirs? It is true that "People are going to do what they are going to do" or "Where there is a will there is a way," but let's not be a part of that way.

■ ■ ■

Right principles are the same yesterday, today, and tomorrow—they don't expire. Do not conform to the ways of this world. Many take refuge in Romans 3:23 to justify holding down the cow. It states, "We are all sinners and fall short of the glory of God." We are sinners; however, we must not use that as an excuse to knowingly support those who err. We cannot use the logic that says that since we are all sinners, let's all sin anyway. Although we fall short, it does not exempt us from our duty to do what is right. We forget our own principles as believers. We must do what is right because it's the right thing to do, regardless of what the secular world endorses.

As believers, we need to put God first and trust in Him always. We need to seek first the kingdom and his righteousness, and all things will be given to us (Matthew 6:33). Not some things, but all things. We live by faith, not by sight. "In God we trust," not a man in a political office.

Christians everywhere need to wake up and smell the coffee. The faith is being attacked on all fronts by atheists, secularists, and many others. In turn, what most Christians are doing is turning their cheeks to the criticism and the attacks, posturing an attitude of indifference, leading to a callous mentality of disastrous consequences.

Our country is slowly turning its back on the very values, virtues, and principles that laid the bedrock of our Christian nation. Today our foundations are being dismantled before our very eyes. Anything suggesting the existence of a Christian God must be purged from the public arena. In essence, Christianity needs to be a closed-door practice, if it even needs to be practiced at all. We have a laziness of spirit. One truth undeniably portrayed throughout history is that all great nations or empires have fallen, and the United States will be no different if we continue on our current path. Truly the only thing we learn from history is that we learn nothing from it! It is a shame that we find ourselves in such a predicament, considering how young we are as a country, but while we still breathe there is hope. That very hope lies in the arousal of the silent Christian majority.

Christians can mainly be classified into three categories, as president of B.O.C. Ministry Gerardo Hernandez explains: "There are those Christians who make things happen. Those who watch things happen. Then you have those who wonder what happened." The point being, very few are making anything happen. We need to rejuvenate our passion. If we really believe in God, we must let it show. We cannot be seeking God's blessings while being afraid of letting Him shine through us. We must stop being spectators in life. We must get off the sidelines, grab some rope, and do some tugging. Christ hit it on the head when He said the harvest is plentiful, but the workers are few. We have a situation where the same

10 percent do all the work while the other 90 percent watch or succumb to the influences of this generation. "It's OK so long as it does not affect me," or "I won't bother anyone so long as no one bothers me"; this is the kind of mentality we harbor, but it will probably be too late when the problem reaches our doorstep. Societal issues are like cancer. If the illness is not tended to in its early stages, it will quickly spread, with disastrous consequences. Action must be taken swiftly to tackle the problem at the source.

We are allowing this spiritual cancer to spread slowly, and it will eventually lead to our demise, like the proverbial frog in a pot of warm water that eventually boils to death. This is why issues such as the legalization of homosexual marriages, abortion, stem cell research, cloning, promotion of pornograghy, etc., are no surprise these days. As harmless as some may think these matters are, they are only opening up the door for deeper infiltration.

Stand up for what is right. Stand up for what is true. There is nothing nobler for a person to do. It is not about being intolerant or judgmental. Too many anti-Christians take refuge in such words to push their agendas, making the naïve opposition think they really are about bigotry. Bigotry is a word that can go a long way, if exploited correctly. Treating others with dignity and respect does not mean we should support their theories, nor should charity keep one from telling the truth.

There is a time for everything under heaven. This is *not* the time to turn the other cheek for the sake of political correctness. Many of us believers are too comfortable being spineless, seeking safe haven through conformity, but we are called to be the light and salt of the world. This is the time to hold the line. We must live what we believe with more tenacity and courage, both in the private and public sectors—but only the *right way*! The substance of the faith is there, but it has to be transfused correctly with love and charity. In walking uprightly, one can expose the wretchedness of others.

Let me further clarify: there is a wrong way to be right and a right way to be right. A person can be right and yet, due to their conduct, so wrong. Anger is not necessarily bad, either. There exists the notion of righteous anger, and many of us should be rightfully angry. What can be wrong is how we use our anger. We should not let anger lead us into sin; instead, we should harvest that energy to make great deeds happen. Just as if someone is angry about the crimes in our neighborhoods, the quality of our schools, or the destruction of our environment, they lobby and protest to make vital changes. Anger has led to many righteous and noble deeds.

■ ■ ■

Lastly, remember we are called to spread the good news, Christians. This evangelization is also known as the Great Commission, not the Great Suggestion. We are *commanded* to go and make disciples of all nations with gentleness and respect, not coercion and self-righteous, judgmental behavior. We have enough of those kinds of Christians. We need more courageous believers who are active witnesses to the faith. This does not mean one has to go out and start preaching in the middle of Central Park. Many of us are not called to such duties, but we can certainly minister to those around us at home or work. That's where it all begins, in planting seeds. Let God deal with the rest, for He is the one who alters human hearts. For those who are called to pastoral or leadership duties, do it boldly, and with love. Tailor the message but never compromise truth. Sometimes to love someone is to not be kind. Ultimately, it is how we live our faith that will transform our culture, values and morals and infiltrate all arenas in our society including government policies. By our fruits they will know us. To do this we must align ourselves with the Gospel, and again, not a political party.

I must also mention the genius of the enemy. What he can't destroy he will divide, and that's exactly what he has done with Christianity. We have countless denominations bickering at each other instead of working together to attain common goals. That is one reason Christianity has lost so much steam in the United States. While Christians are quarreling with each other, the enemy is quietly gaining ground, like a lion stalking its prey. The early Church was potent precisely because all were of one accord. There is power in unity. Today, we have complete disarray within the house of the Lord, though we serve a God of order. "Order is heaven's first law," as poet Alexander Pope once wrote. Though I acknowledge that the problem of church denominations must be solved, surely our energies can be used more efficiently. There are critical issues in this world that need the attention of true Christians. Wake up! A united team goes much further than a divided one. A divided house will eventually fall.

MY FINAL VERDICT

"The truth always turns out to be simpler than you thought."

— *Richard Feynman*

"The truth is like a lion. You don't have to defend it. Let it loose. It will defend itself."

— *St. Augustine*

The material presented contains some of the most common and passionate concerns I have tended to in the philosophical and moral domain. Much has been covered, and, grudgingly, much has been excluded. That is why it is of vital importance to pursue personal study. We are not born knowing; knowledge is acquired. Hopefully the information presented has whet your mental appetites and prompted further inquiry into the countless whys of life.

"*Why*"—a simple yet powerful word. It seems the more *whys* that get answered, the more that surface. Ultimately all *whys* lead to God. Which makes sense, since why anything exists at all is because of Him. This explains the difficulty in taking a stance on any issue without referring to the author of all. That is why we first made a case for God. Without Him, we would be making ourselves the source of authority as to why anything is or ought to be, and that cannot be accepted in a world with such diverse opinions. To find Truth, we must go to the source of Truth. Therefore, God must be part of the conversation. And when speaking of God, religion is not far behind.

Although there are many difficulties encountered in answering so many questions, we must concentrate on what we know for certain, and accept the rest on reason and authority. We are not God; we cannot think at His level. So instead of trying to understand all, let us cling to the one who does understand all. This does not mean we should cease to acquire understanding, but we can at least hold on to and defend what we know, and expect better understanding in due time. The bottom line is, we cannot straddle the fence our whole lives. There comes a time when a decision must be made; a *final verdict*. No one wants a half-committed person on their team. "Take a position and hold your ground," as Ulysses S. Grant once said, even in this delicate and sentimental society. As the sayings goes, *He who defends everything defends nothing. And He who does not stand for anything falls for anything.*

Not only should we hold our ground, we should do so while ready to give a sound and logical explanation for our standpoint, rather than standing on credulity. Unfortunately, we are in an age where the search for truth has become a pursuit of self-gratification. There is an accommodating spirituality of self-service known as "Me" or "I." It's all about whatever feels "right for me" or "convenient for me." We live in a generation where no one should dare claim one group is right while another is wrong. And by all means, don't dare sway anyone else's mind! But we cannot admit for a second that all ideas possess equal value with the obvious inclination for error that resides in man.

■ ■ ■

Hopefully I have expressed my verdict clearly and why I believe it to be the most reasonable. In conveying these views, I unfolded what I think to be the most accurate filtering mechanism by examining God, religion, Christ, and His Church. I screened two hotly debated topics through the process to see what the end results would yield. What else is there? What other method is more accurate when dealing with the immaterial? Our mere opinion? Though I understand that some accept this premise, others say it's just "the universe and me," or "the Bible and me," or your own personal god. No, none of these can be. We have already examined the problems deriving from such mentalities. If it is up to the self, then anything goes, and we know for sure that anything does not go. Truth is independent of us. Our mission is to find out what it is. I understand that others think quite differently than me, but the one who is correct is he who is embedded in reason. Now, I hope the reader will make a decision or verdict after contemplation, instead of dismissing the matter altogether.

Let us review my verdict and what is at stake, beginning with the existence of God—for me, it takes more faith to not believe than to do so. I don't think the overwhelming majority of humanity that has ever walked the earth has lived a lie. Though we have only highlighted various classical arguments, hopefully it has been demonstrated that reason alone is powerful enough to make a solid case for God's existence. Material evidence does not cover the totality of reality. There is experiential knowledge and there is knowledge based on reason and authority. Through this second form of evidence, one can conclude a destiny beyond the grave.

Our finite mental capacity cannot be the end-all. To reject God because we can't understand each and every question to our satisfaction is to say the human mind is the ultimate test of truth. That is absurd. I know the difficulties atheists may have reconciling this world with an all-powerful loving entity, but experience has taught me that most men reject God not because of a lack of evidence, but because God interferes with their passions. They simply don't want Him to exist.

All men have the capacity to know God, but most nonbelievers reflect a disposition of one who couldn't care less about the matter while entertaining false ideas of God. Others in their genuine pursuit attempt to assess the issue from an intellectual standpoint only, failing to ask for God's help, as if smarts were the only way to know God. That cannot be the case, or else the more intelligent would have a better chance than the less intelligent.

Regardless, it stands to reason that if there is a God, we must entertain the notions of universal standards and Truths. Many groups claim to possess them. To decipher this issue we ventured into the world of religion.

■ ■ ■

When speaking of God, it is impossible to avoid the subject of religion, for this is how we relate to Him and honor Him. Not because He needs religion, but because we need Him. With so many claiming to illuminate *the right path*, we inspected a few of the most popular religions, and what immediately surfaced is how divergent they are in their teachings. Although similarities are found in the mere fact that they are religions, what must be grasped is that the man in search of truth does not concentrate on what's alike, but on what differs. When he does so, he will see that they are irreconcilable; reason and logic begin breaking down. This is why each religion must be judged on its own merits, to see which can withstand the most scrutiny.

My verdict is clear as far as Christianity being *the path*. Christianity says that we have sinned against God and need a savior to reconcile us to Him. That savior cannot be another mere human being who also needs to be saved. Following rules, laws, meditation, and spiritual endeavors is nice, but does not suffice, because no one has followed every rule of purity or holiness. We all fall short, and due to this condition, nothing we do can restore us to our rightful place with God; therefore, the sacrifice of Christ was necessary because of the dignity of the one we have offended (God). And since it was God we offended, and no mere human, only God Himself (Christ both divine and human) can reconcile us to our rightful place with Him.

Ultimately, what a careful study of comparative religion shows is that Christianity surpasses other outlooks in its teachings, historical foundation, authority, reasonableness, and the origin and conditions of man and his destiny. Again, others think differently, but I dare say this is *mostly* due to factors such as a lack of information or understanding, geopolitical considerations, pride, certain loyalties, indifference, peer pressures, and so forth, and not because they have carefully studied the facts about the faith. Also, I repeat, just because you think your religion is correct does not prove that it is correct, but only that you think it is right. He who is correct is the one who has reason behind him.

The bottom line is, numerous "prophets" have surfaced throughout history, and many teachings have derived from wise teachers, but in the end, all of these men find themselves six feet under. Christ, through His virgin birth and resurrection, is leagues ahead of any man who has walked this earth. Powerful words such as "I am the way and the truth and the life" cannot be ignored. "I am the bread of life" (John 6:48); Christ said, "I am the good shepherd" (John 10:11); "I am the light of the World" (John 8:12); "I am the true vine [path]" (John 15:1); "I am the resurrection and the life" (John 11:25); "I am the Alpha and the Omega" (Revelation 22:13). If He is not who He claims, He should rightfully be ignored. He is a lunatic and a liar, not a good man or a teacher or anything else. The most important question we will ever ask ourselves is, who is Jesus Christ? The answer to that question will affect our eternal destiny. As C.S. Lewis writes, "Christianity is a statement which if false is of no importance, and, if true, of infinite importance. The one thing it cannot be is moderately important."

Though the exclusivity of the Christian faith does not sit well with many, Christians are to always remember the humility of Christ. If His message is not dressed with love, all one becomes is an irksome messenger. Truth is to be proposed, not imposed. It is a balancing act that requires the steadiness of threading a needle.

■ ■ ■

Now, historically, Christ lived, claimed to be God, and established a permanent church to teach all nations. This brings about the next step in the filtering methodology as we focus our lenses deeper. Christ, truth Himself, left provisions behind. Like the multitudes of religions around the world claiming to possess the truth about God, many Christian sects claim to possess the full teachings, merits, and authority of Christ. But only one can take credit for such honor historically, reasonably, logically, and scripturally. That church can only be the Catholic Church, which fulfills all credentials necessary. All others do not hold proper prerequisites and are many centuries late in coming to the Christendom scene.

None of these churches, whether Eastern or Protestant, have any divine authority for their existence, but rather can be attributed to the conflicts and distortions of men. Their very nature is to divide, not unite. They can't even agree amongst themselves on what is genuine Christian teaching. At our current rate, we will soon have as many Christian sects as we have Christians.

A colleague once uttered, wisely, "I don't believe in any church I am older than." Yet tomorrow there will be another church claiming to be "the one," teaching the doctrines of Christ as He Himself intended, which will only add to the chaos. Even in His days, the great apostle Paul faced issues with church division. He writes, "I appeal to you, brothers, in the name of our Lord Jesus Christ, that all of you agree with one another so there may be no division among you and that you may be perfectly united in mind and thought" (1 Corinthians 1:10).

It is an interesting phenomenon, debating Christians. Too many simply don't have their facts straight or fail to interpret them correctly. Many folks naïvely believe the Church is easily refuted, as if this two-thousand-year-old institution has no response to distorted views concerning Christian teachings. She is treated like an amateur, but two millennia of history and countless volumes of writings from some of the most brilliant minds in history say otherwise. Though tempted to venture into specific church teachings such as confession, saints, relics, the Eucharist, and popes, among others, I covered matters in a general scope with an arrow pointing in the right direction. I challenge non-Catholic Christians to *honestly study* the pertinent material without bias. If so, they will find the Catholic claim impressive, justifiable, and most difficult to deny. Truth-seekers cannot come to the table with their minds made up. That violates reason to the second degree. Those who don't investigate at all violate reason to the third degree. If investigation is undertaken with sincerity, God's grace will see that person through this sectarian problem.

Many external factors might collaborate to keep a man from becoming Catholic, but not reason. Thinking compels a man to become Catholic. History is so evident. God first sent the prophets to teach His people, followed by His begotten son. Christ then sent His Church to continue His work on earth, and that church still stands today. The faith has not been left to become a matter of individual opinion. We can't just see only the evidence that supports our theories while being blinded to everything that goes against our theories.

To be absolutely clear, I don't pretend to defend the behavior of all 1.3 billion Catholics today or the hundreds of millions that have come before, nor for a minute would I defend the misconduct or corruption of anyone, Catholic or otherwise. There is no doubt there have been repugnant Catholics who have embarrassed and tarnished the Church. In 1994, Pope John Paul II called for the acknowledgment of the dark side of the Church's history, but he does not apologize for what it teaches. Some Catholics have and are indeed an embarrassment to the faith and have failed to walk the talk. But failure to walk the talk does not necessarily mean failure in doctrine. A bad teacher can certainly teach truth in spite of being a poor teacher. Every genuine Catholic is deeply saddened and made indignant by those responsible for scandals, but one cannot condemn a whole army for the unworthiness of a small minority. Catholics can fail (we are not deprived of our free will), but the Church cannot. The potential for evil in man will forever be present no matter what walk of life, as Ecclesiastes 7:29 states: "God made mankind upright, but men have gone in search of many schemes." Matthew 18:7 states, "Woe to the world because of the things that cause people to sin! Such things must come, but woe to the man through whom they come!"

Despite human failures, the divine continues to work throughout the Church. This divine element is the reason she has stood the test of time against enemies both within and without. It is a shame that those ignorant of the Church continue to label as evil the one great stronghold of Christianity in the world, a church battling every day to spread the Gospel around the secular world. She works tirelessly to keep God in our schools, and tends to the needy with all sorts of charity work. She defends the sanctity of marriage and stands for the unborn. She is everywhere, intervening and fulfilling her commission. Tens of thousands of priests and nuns around the world give up family and certain comforts, and earn pennies for the sake of the faith. Some are even persecuted and killed, while some of her Christian brethren lounge back, call her evil, and squawk "Jesus" but do little to nothing for the name. But the Church will not and cannot sway from her entrusted task of teaching and preserving the Christian faith, whether popular or not. That is the sole purpose of her existence. In retrospect, persecution is not a surprise, for Christ predicted that such would befall His church.

■ ■ ■

Since we have spoken of God, religion, Christ, and His Church, it is only appropriate to tackle some prominent social issues flaring today. It is only fitting to do so in this kind of book. When it comes to delicate issues, we all, of course, have our takes on what ought to be or not; surprisingly, many of us believe that all laws or rules should conform to our own ideas. Being in error is something we can't even imagine. As stated, universal laws or standards point us to a higher realm, that is, to a higher authority than self or society. Homosexual activity and abortion not only violate God's law, but they must also answer to science, logic, natural law, reason, and common sense. Enough has been said on these issues. A person can certainly choose to exercise these practices, but their personal endorsements of these practices have no bearing on the question of whether the actions themselves are virtuous or not.

Truth, we must admit, occasionally has a ring we don't want to hear, since it may require drastic change. The solution then is to plug our ears, to choose to stay ignorant in order to avoid the responsibilities that come with knowledge. But ignorance is one thing; willful ignorance is quite another. Choosing to remain ignorant of a certain clause in a business contract does not relieve one of their contractual obligations.

I hope the material found in these pages has proven beneficial to readers and provided insight on the powerful claims of reality. If one will walk away pondering and thirsting for more, then my mission is accomplished. Though many questions have been answered, surely others will persist, but don't believe that there aren't solid responses to these lingering questions. Throughout the ages, the same questions have been asked and pondered by men across the globe; they are nothing new. We do not have to reinvent the wheel, but simply investigate.

What is your verdict, and *why?* My filtering methodology shows where I stand. It is abundantly more reasonable to believe in God. If He exists, we then live by virtue of His standards and Truths. His will is known through revelations, via His religion. That religion is Christianity, through His Church. Ultimately, the works, veracity, authority, and qualifications of Christ are the source of what I believe. He is our only hope. And what I believe to be true is brilliantly summed up in the Nicene Creed:

> I believe in one God,
> the Father almighty,
> maker of heaven and earth,
> of all things visible and invisible.
> I believe in one Lord Jesus Christ,
> the Only Begotten Son of God,
> born of the Father before all ages.
> God from God, Light from Light,
> true God from true God,
> begotten, not made, consubstantial with the Father;
> through him all things were made.
> For us men and for our salvation
> he came down from heaven,
> and by the Holy Spirit was incarnate of the Virgin Mary,
> and became man.
> For our sake he was crucified under Pontius Pilate,
> he suffered death and was buried,

and rose again on the third day
in accordance with the Scriptures.
He ascended into heaven
and is seated at the right hand of the Father.
He will come again in glory
to judge the living and the dead
and his kingdom will have no end.
I believe in the Holy Spirit, the Lord, the giver of life,
who proceeds from the Father and the Son,
who with the Father and the Son is adored and glorified,
who has spoken through the prophets.
I believe in one, holy, Catholic and Apostolic Church.
I confess one Baptism for the forgiveness of sins
and I look forward to the resurrection of the dead
and the life of the world to come. Amen.

What is your verdict and why? Don't take my word for it—put emotions aside, investigate sincerely, reflect, and ponder. Socrates said the unexamined life is not worth living. Are you leading an unexamined life?

"Everyone who belongs to the truth listens to my voice."

— Jesus of Nazareth (John 18:37)

WORKS CITED AND FURTHER READING

Abdel-Haleem, Muhammed. *The Qur'an*. Oxford, England: Oxford University Press, 2004. Print.

Ali-Karamali, Sumbul. *The Muslim Next Door*. Ashland, Oregon: White Cloud Press, 2008. Print.

All about Science.com (2002-2015). Second Law of Thermodynamics. Retrieved Aug 2, 2013

Beebe, J. The Design Argument for the Existence of God. (2002) Retrieved September 4, 2014. http://www.acsu.buffalo.edu/~jbeebe2/design.htm

Bhutto, Benazir. *Reconciliation: Islam, Democracy, and the West*. New York, New York: Harpers Collins, 2008. Print.

Christiantiy.net.au. Why is Hell Eternal? Retrieved Sep 22, 2014

Comfort, Ray. *How to Know God Exists*. Alachua, Florida: Bridge-Logos, 2008. Print.

Catholic Church. Catechism of the Catholic Church. 2nd ed. Vatican: Libreria Editrice Vaticana, 2012. Print.

Dawkins, Richard. *The God Delusion.* Boston, Massachusetts: Mariner Books. 2006. Print.

D'Souza, Dinesh. *What's So Great About Christianity?* Washington, D.C.: Regnery Publishing, Inc., 2007. Print.

Dutko, Bob. Toptenproofs.com (2015). Scientific Evidence of God. Retrieved Sep 4, 2013

Existence-of-God.com. The Moral Argument. Retrieved Nov 14, 2012

Gracyk, Theodore. St. Thomas Aquinas—Summa Theologicae. Retrieved Sep 4, 2014.

Graham, Henry G. *Where We Got The Bible.* El Cajon, California: Catholic Answers, Inc., 1997. Print.

Halverson, Dean C. *The Compact Guide to World Religions.* Minneapolis, Minnesota: Bethany House Publishers, 1996. Print.

Houdman, Micheal. GotQuestions.org. What is Moral Relativism? (2002-20015). Retrieved Sep 10, 2012.

Houdman, Michael. GotQuestions.org. Can A Person Be Born Gay? (2002-20015). Retrieved Nov 1, 2013

Ingram, Chip. *Culture Shock.* Grand Rapids, MI. Baker Books, 2014. Print.

Johnson, Kevin. *Why Do Catholics Do That?* New York, New York: Ballantine Books, 1994. Print.

Kant, Immanuel. *Critique of Pure Reason*. Amherst, New York: Prometheus Books, 1990. Print.

Kreeft, Peter and Tacelli, Ronald. *Handbook of Christian Apologetics*. Downers Grove, Illinois: Intervarsity Press, 1994. Print.

Kreeft, Peter. *Your Questions, God's Answers*. San Francisco, California: Ignatius Press, 1994. Print.

Lutzer, Erwin W. *Christ Among Other Gods*. Chicago, Illinois: Moody Press, 1994. Print.

New American Bible. New Jersey. Catholic Book Publishing Corp. 1970 Print

New International Bible. Wheaton Illinois. Tyndale House Publishers, Inc.1997. Print.

Olson, Carl (1996-2015) Are the Gospels Myth? Retrieved Sep 15, 2012

Pro-Life Action League (2015). Prolifeaction.org/. Retrieved Jan 15, 2012

ReligionFacts.com (2015) Buddhism. Retrieved Mar 12, 2014

ReligionFacts.com (2015). Hinduism. Retrieved Mar 12, 2014

Rooney, Anne. *The Story of Philosophy*. London, U.K.: Arcturus Publishing, 2013. Print.

Rumble, Leslie and Carty, Charles. *Radio Replies, Vol. 1*. Rockford, Illinois: Tan Books and Publishers, Inc., 1979. Print.

Rumble, Leslie and Carty, Charles. *Radio Replies, Vol. 2*. Rockford, Illinois: Tan Books and Publishers, Inc., 1979. Print.

Rumble, Leslie and Carty, Charles. *Radio Replies, Vol. 3*. Rockford, Illinois: Tan Books and Publishers, Inc., 1979. Print.

Strobel, Lee. *The Case for Faith*. Grand Rapids, Michigan: Zondervan Publishing House, 2000. Print.

St. Thomas More Chapter of Catholics United for the Faith May (2001). Who Started Your Church? (http://www.mncuf.org/origins.htm). Retrieved Oct 2, 2012